HARVARD STUDIES
IN COMPARATIVE LITERATURE

VOLUME XII

HARVARD STUDIES IN COMPARATIVE LITERATURE
VOLUME XII

ENGLISH LITERATURE AND CULTURE IN RUSSIA
(1553–1840)

BY

ERNEST J. SIMMONS

1964
OCTAGON BOOKS, INC.
NEW YORK

Reprinted 1964
by special arrangement with Ernest Joseph Simmons

OCTAGON BOOKS, INC.
175 FIFTH AVENUE
NEW YORK, N. Y. 10010

LIBRARY OF CONGRESS CATALOG CARD NUMBER: 64-24841

Printed in U.S.A. by
NOBLE OFFSET PRINTERS, INC.
NEW YORK 3, N. Y.

TO

MY MOTHER

PREFACE

THE part that France and Germany have played in the history of Russian culture has been investigated with some thoroughness, but comparatively little attention has been payed to the corresponding rôle of England. Although Russian scholars have long recognized the importance of England in the development of their country's civilization, no comprehensive study of the subject has been made. In the present work, therefore, I have attempted to trace the history of English literature and culture in Russia from 1553 to 1840. The results of the study indicate that England's influence in Russia during this period was of great consequence; and something is added, I hope, to the general knowledge of the far-flung dissemination of English literature and culture.

In the bibliographies at the end of each chapter I have made no attempt to be definitive; the subject is altogether too vast for this. For practical purposes I have confined myself to selective bibliographies of the sources and studies chiefly used, and for the same reason I have arranged all the items chronologically.

Occasionally I have borrowed from published articles of my own on various phases of the subject. In every case acknowledgments are made in the notes.

The kindness of the staffs of the Lenin Public Library, the Museum of Books, and the Historical Museum of Moscow, and of the Widener Library of Harvard University in rendering me every service desired has been much appreciated. In the matter of obtaining material, often impossible to secure in this country, I am indebted to my Moscow friends, Professor B. I. Yarkho, T. M. Levit, and Madam I. M. Brusova. My colleagues at Harvard University, Professors S. H. Cross and M. M. Karpovich, and Professor G. Z. Patrick of the University of California have been kind enough to read the manuscript, and I am much obligated to them for helpful suggestions and corrections.

Professor G. L. Kittredge has given me invaluable assistance in the preparation of the manuscript and in the proofreading. For his kindness, encouragement, and painstaking care I am profoundly grateful.

E. J. S.

LEVERETT HOUSE
HARVARD UNIVERSITY
November, 1934

CONTENTS

TRANSLITERATION

[There is no universally accepted method of transliterating the letters of the Russian alphabet into English. The present system is based on that employed by the Library of Congress, with a few changes which seem to make for simplicity in English orthography without essentially violating the phonetic value of the Russian letters.]

а	a		с	s
б	b		т	t
в	v		у	u
г	g		ф	f
д	d		х	kh
е	e		ц	ts
ж	zh		ч	ch
з	z		ш	sh
и	i		щ	shch
і	i		ъ	(omitted)
й	i (omitted when combined with i or й)		ы	y
к	k		ь	(omitted)
л	l		ѣ	e
м	m		э	e
н	n		ю	iu
о	o		я	ya
п	p		ѳ	th
р	r			

ENGLISH LITERATURE AND CULTURE IN RUSSIA
(1553–1840)

CHAPTER I

EARLY CONTACTS. THE ANGLOMANIA OF IVAN THE TERRIBLE (1553–1584)

IN COMPLETE defiance of historical forces the Pan-Slavists of the middle of the nineteenth century raised the cry: "Back to Russian nationality, orthodoxy, and autocracy!" But history is no respecter of nationalities and before its forward progress nations must surrender their political, economic, and cultural isolation. Russia, perhaps more than any other great power of Europe, was for centuries wide open to the pervasive influence of her many neighbors. Various political and economic factors, often unique in their nature, militated against the development of a purely Russian nationalism and culture.

However, when foreign influence on a backward country reaches the extreme of aggrandizement it invariably stimulates a period of national consciousness. And throughout the whole history of Russia there were periodic awakenings, sudden reversions to the national *idea* and culture during which Russia struggled against the engulfing waves of foreign ascendency. Naturally it was the early centuries of the country's existence, those least contaminated by outside influences, that the Slavophiles turned to for examples of undefiled Russian nationalism. But at best this was a benighted nationalism, fitfully illuminated by the temporary brilliance of Kiev in the eleventh and twelfth centuries. And even the indigenous character of the Kiev Period is much in question, for Byzantine Greek and Scandinavian influences undoubtedly played a large part in the cultural growth. After the fall of Kiev the encircling gloom brought on by the Tatar invasions, the internecine struggles among the ruling princes, and the non-intellectual character of Greek Orthodoxy deepened into a Cimmerian blackness from the thirteenth through the fifteenth century. The commercial relations of Pskov and Novgorod with the Hanseatic League and with independent German and Swedish traders were the only important contacts with the West. What nationalism existed during this whole period was of a primitive and negative kind. In the reign of Ivan the Terrible (1533–84), however, Russia opened her windows on Europe, and one of the countries that found most favor in his eyes was England.

Ivan possessed those strange qualities of mind which when found in rulers are described as "genius" and in ordinary mortals as "psychopathic." More than any Russian sovereign who preceded him he understood his country's backwardness and desired to remedy it. On the other hand, a fatal reactionary streak in his nature and a pathological fear of enemies, native and foreign, vitiated his best efforts. The country he ruled was centuries behind Western Europe. Its political and economic structure resembled that of mediaeval feudalism, and its culture was literally *nil*. Apart from an insignificant collection of religious books and tracts, there was virtually no printed literature; and judicial practise, drawn from the civil sources of Greek legislation, often amounted merely to trial by combat or the casting of lots on the theory of divine intervention. Symbolizing his dissatisfaction with everything Russian by proudly proclaiming himself of Teutonic origin, Ivan turned to the West for enlightenment and aid. It was a practical kind of aid he sought, European technical knowledge, artisans, physicians, and the advantages of foreign-made products and commerce. He was naturally enough, then, in a very receptive mood when he learned that an English ship had anchored off his northern coast and that its commander craved an audience with the tsar of all the Russias.

The trade war that raged among the more advanced nations of Western Europe in the sixteenth century obliged England to keep an eye open for prospective new markets for her products. The spirit of competition was keen and the famed zeal of Elizabethan voyagers was actuated in no small degree by the necessity of discovering fresh outlets for trade. With this as the main motive a number of London merchants in 1552 discussed plans for a voyage to the northeast, having as their ultimate objective a new trade route to Cathay. They employed as their scientific director the well-known navigator Sebastian Cabot. The result was the formation in the following year of a company, the Merchant-Adventurers for the Discoverie of New Trades (generally known after its reorganization by the short titles, the Russian Company or the Muscovy Company). Besides the merchants, some eminent members of the nobility were interested in the venture, among them the Marquis of Winton and the Earls of Arundel, Bedford, Pembroke, and Leicester. On May 23, 1553, three ships of the company set sail from Harwich on a voyage to the East by the little-known northern route, the *Bona Esperanza* under Sir Hugh Willoughby, the *Bona Confidentia* under Cornelius Durforth, and the *Bona Fortuna* under Richard Chancellor.

Disaster overtook the ships of Willoughby and Durforth, but on August 24, 1553, Chancellor's *Bona Fortuna* cast anchor in the Bay of Kholmogory at the mouth of the Dvina, hard by the Monastery of St. Nicholas. This was England's first direct contact with Russia, a country which up to this time had existed vaguely in the English popular imagination as a land of cruel barbarians, weird monsters, and astounding miracles.

Ivan, fresh from the important conquest of Kazan and with his mind filled with dreams of Russian expansion, was informed of the strangers who had landed on his northern coast. He at once invited them to appear at court, but Chancellor was already on the way and arrived at Moscow in November. His kind reception and the friendly reply to his letter of introduction indicate that the tsar was quick to seize upon the possibilities of commercial and diplomatic relations with England. And Chancellor, on his part, observed closely the benefits that might accrue to his country from trade with Russia.

Chancellor's favorable report on his return home certainly encouraged the company to consider the feasibility of establishing a formal trade agreement. A charter was obtained from Queen Mary in 1555, and Chancellor was sent back to Russia with two special agents of the company, Richard Grey and George Killingworth. Their instructions are convincing proof of the thoroughness of English commercial enterprise, even at this early date. Indeed, the tale of the long line of capable merchants and intrepid explorers sent by the company to Russia in the sixteenth century, and often across the whole of that vast country to the East, forms another glorious chapter in the growth of England's colonial empire and world trade.   Grey and Killingworth were required to study minutely the character and habits of the Russians, their taxes, coinage, and weights and measures. They were likewise directed to see that their companions obeyed the laws of the country, and to note the kind of merchandise that would be likely to find a good Russian market. Finally, they were instructed to keep an eye open for a possible trade route to the East.

Ivan welcomed the offer of trade and in 1556 granted the company a charter containing generous privileges, — all merchandise tax-free, special jurisdiction for Englishmen living in Russia, and the right of settling legal difficulties among themselves. Later these privileges were amplified until for a time the English had a virtual monopoly of foreign commerce. Despite this auspicious beginning, England's commercial relations with Russia throughout the remaining years of Ivan's reign were put to many severe tests.

At first the Muscovy Company prospered and enormous profits were made. The vast prospect of gain opened by the company's monopoly attracted much outside capital. We find the Earl of Leicester, for example, writing enthusiastically in 1574 to the Earl of Shrewsbury:

For our voyage, my Lord, we are now at a point for eleven ships which will be set forth by the company of Muscovy; and I am sorry your Lordship is no adventurer; for, surely, my Lord, I am fully persuaded it will fall out the best voyage that ever was made out of this realm, Drake or any; but I thank your Lordship that

you do adventure this you do for company of me. I assure you if
I had had £10,000 in my purse I would have adventured it every
penny myself.[1]

The chief export to Russia was cloth, but the traders likewise brought into the country sugar, paper, copper, drugs,
and quantities of raw and manufactured war supplies. More
significant than English exports, however, were the artisans,
engineers, architects, physicians, and apothecaries sent over
on Ivan's request and at the company's own instance. The
tsar granted the company large landholdings for dwellings
and warehouses. The Englishmen were even given permission to manufacture rope in Russia and to work iron mines,
Ivan insisting only that the English artisans instruct the
Russians in their crafts.

But the course of the merchants in Russia did not always
run smoothly. They had to contend with illegal foreign competition, unauthorized English traders, and the occasional
malfeasance of their own members. The chief difficulty, however, was the fluctuating favor of the unstable Ivan. To be
sure, there was more method than madness in his swift rever-
sals of policy, which were often dictated by the unsatisfactory
way in which his diplomatic overtures were handled in England. Soon after the inception of trade relations Ivan began
to manifest an interest in England which historians have described as an "Anglomania." It seems clear that the idea
early took shape in his cunning mind that England could provide him with benefits other than merchandise, war supplies,
and the services of skilled workmen. And from this point
until his death he continued a persistent policy of bartering

privileges to the English merchants for certain favors from the English court.

He opened formal diplomatic relations by sending an ambassador, Osip Grigorevich Nepeya, who after many vicissitudes arrived in England in 1557. The ambassador was well received with a lavish display of attention by the Lord Mayor of London and a company of merchants. In an audience with Queen Mary he obtained a reciprocity of commercial privileges and the additional favor of engaging Englishmen for the tsar's service. No less a person than Roger Ascham, the Latin Secretary, drew up the royal answer to Nepeya's message. But the ambassador was untutored in the finer matters of diplomacy and it was thought advisable to send back with him to Russia Anthony Jenkinson, who was commissioned to clear up all points of dissension, and particularly to search out a trading route to the East. In all her relations with Russia during this period, England never lost sight of the possibility of an overland route to the fabled Cathay. A doctor, an apothecary, and several artisans were sent with the ambassadors at the tsar's request, as well as a large cargo of war materials.

Jenkinson landed in Russia in 1557 and made such an excellent impression on Ivan that in the future he preferred to have diplomatic dealings with him rather than with any other Englishman. Jenkinson was a splendid type of the English voyager, courageous in travel, skilled in diplomacy, and ever mindful of the best interests of his country. In the course of the next ten years he made several trips to Russia in the employment of the Muscovy Company and also in the capacity of a court messenger. Likewise, with Ivan's encouragement and direct aid, he journeyed eastward as far as Bokhara in an effort to establish commercial relations between that region and England. And he managed to obtain from the tsar a new charter confirming the old monopolies of the Muscovy Company and adding new ones of considerable value, including free passage for all merchandise sent to Bokhara and Samarkand.

The extreme generosity of the privileges might be taken as an indication that Ivan had a special cause of his own to plead. Such was actually the case, for about this time the tsar had conceived the idea of an alliance with England. Always in imminent danger from the Poles and Swedes, and fearing internal dissension in Russia, he clearly recognized the value of England's wealth and fleet. The initial overtures are not precisely known. All that we can gather is that when Jenkinson returned to England in 1567 he bore a secret message from Ivan to Elizabeth, the contents of which were never divulged in the diplomatic records. From subsequent correspondence, however, it appears that Ivan proposed an offensive and defensive alliance. Furthermore, he added a strange request, that in case his safety was threatened by his own subjects he should be accorded an asylum in England. And curiously enough, more as a matter of self-pride than diplomatic etiquette, he demanded that Elizabeth request the same favor from him, — a refuge in the Kremlin if her life were ever endangered by rebellious subjects.

Elizabeth must have been somewhat puzzled by the proposals of the quixotic tsar and she delayed her reply for many months. She realized that Russia, so far removed from the center of things in Western Europe in those days of slow communication, could be of little assistance against England's enemies, and there was certainly nothing to be gained from embroiling herself with Russia's foes. Time and history would one day change this attitude, but in the sixteenth century Russia, politically, signified nothing to England. Elizabeth regarded the country merely as a field for profitable commercial enterprise. Accordingly, when she heard that Ivan, apparently vexed at her delay, was making life miserable for the English merchants, she hastened in 1568 to send an ambassador, the efficient diplomat Thomas Randolph, with instructions to reëstablish order in commercial affairs, and to avoid, so far as possible, any discussion of the tsar's secret proposals.

Randolph fared badly at first and was made to feel the force of Ivan's displeasure. For months he was virtually kept a prisoner in his quarters, and when the tsar finally consented to see him he was received with marked discourtesy. What occurred at this meeting has not been authentically recorded, but Randolph appears to have handled the situation with tact. Ivan was angry because Jenkinson had failed to return immediately with an answer to his secret proposals, and he was annoyed with Elizabeth for concerning herself with commercial matters to the exclusion of the real business of princes. We do not know how Randolph treated the question of alliance, but he did assure the tsar that he would be received in England with all hospitality should he desire to leave Russia. At any rate Ivan's attitude suddenly changed and he invited the ambassador to the palace again, insisting now upon the greatest secrecy. Randolph was obliged to go at midnight and to wear a disguise. What weighty matters were discussed at this nocturnal audience have remained a mystery. Conditions in the tsar's realm at this time were in a chaotic state and he may have wished private information on the possibility of a refuge in England; or, as later developments suggest, he may have been dallying with another scheme that would bring him into even closer relations with England than an offensive and defensive alliance.

Randolph's assurances must have been decidedly satisfactory, for the immediate result of the parleys was a restoration of all the former privileges of the Muscovy Company. And, again with suspicious generosity, Ivan conferred extra privileges, — the full right to trade with Persia through his domains, to mine iron and to coin money in Russia, and authority to drive out of the White Sea the merchant ships of competing nations. The occasion marked the height of royal favor to the company and English trade prospered more than ever.

As an interesting literary sidelight on this embassy it is worth noting that George Turberville, the poet, accompanied Randolph as his secretary. Turberville employed his leisure hours in Russia, which seem to have been many, in writing occasional poetry and verse epistles to his friends in England. These efforts were published, along with his *Tragical Tales*, in 1587, and they contain much curious information about Russian living conditions at this early period. He complains in none too polished verse of the hardships one must endure in this cold, inhospitable land, "where the bedding is not good, the bolsters are but bad." And in a moment of acute homesickness he was not above heaping on the Russians this final opprobrium:

Wilde Irish are as civil as the Russies in their kinde,
Hard choice which is the best of both, each bloody, rude, and blinde! [2]

In short, the poet could find little to praise. Yet one must admire, in some instances, his keen observations on the customs and manners of the natives.

When Randolph and Turberville returned home they left the affairs of the English merchants in a flourishing condition, their future apparently well assured by the unusually expansive good will of the tsar. But Ivan was eager to secure the performance of the promises with which Randolph had flattered him. Accordingly, when Randolph landed in England in 1569, he was accompanied by Andrei Grigorevich Savin, the tsar's ambassador, who was instructed to obtain specific terms from Elizabeth. The astute queen treated him to her special brand of diplomatic procrastination. Perhaps a little misguided by Randolph's easy success, she did not see any real necessity for acceding to Ivan's demand for a political alliance disadvantageous to England. Thus, after ten months of shilly-shallying, Savin returned to Russia, bringing to his impatient master merely the greetings of Elizabeth, protestations of her everlasting friendship, and a repetition of her willingness to receive the tsar as her guest.

The queen soon learned, however, that she had underestimated the quality of the terrible Ivan. His retort was quick, bitterly sarcastic, but not without dignity, and it was accompanied by reprisals swift and devastating. Because she offered him alms instead of an alliance with the tsar of all the

Russias, he dismissed her in his letter with a truly regal rebuke:

And wee had thought that you had been richer over your lande and had sought honor to yourself and profitt to your countrie, and therefor wee did pretend those weightie affairs between you and us; but now we perceive that there be other men that doe rule, and not men but bowers and merchaunts the which seeke not the wealth and honor of our maiesties, but they seeke there owne profitt of merchauntdize: and you flowe in your maydenlie estate like a maide.[3]

Such a lack of *politesse* in royal correspondence was no doubt a new experience for Elizabeth, and the censorious tone of the letter may have been a welcome relief from the fulsome compliments of cloying sonnets and epistles dedicatory. Under other circumstances Elizabeth might have been simply amused at this unique verbal castigation by a Russian tsar, but since it was attended by the news that Ivan had once again deprived the Muscovy Company of its privileges, confiscated its merchandise, and prohibited trading, she was naturally alarmed. The English were faced with the immediate danger of losing their prized Eastern markets to Portuguese and Venetian competitors, and Elizabeth hastened to send Richard Best and the favored Jenkinson to win back the patronage of Ivan.

They landed in Russia in 1571 and Jenkinson proceeded to Moscow, despite the fact that he was informed that Ivan, who blamed him personally for the original miscarriage of his secret proposals, had threatened to cut off his head. Jenkinson bravely faced the autocrat, his safety somewhat guaranteed by a conciliatory letter from Elizabeth. Wisely ignoring the tsar's rebuke, she stated her position with queenly dignity.

Reiterating her offer to receive him in England, she explained, however, that there was no reason why she herself should seek refuge in a foreign land. Furthermore, she intimated that such a request would be tantamount to an insult to her loyal subjects and would only result in placing her in an awkward position. Finally, she insisted on her friendliness for Ivan and her desire to show him convincing proof of it if only he would restore the English merchants into his good graces. But Elizabeth still cautiously evaded the tsar's fond project of an alliance. Her tactics in this respect strongly remind one of the diplomatic shuffling of Russia's great queen some two hundred years later. Catherine II, in her turn, cleverly played with England's hopes for an alliance which she thought not altogether for the best interests of Russia.

Ivan at first appeared to be content with Elizabeth's veiled promises and assurance of friendship, but when Jenkinson left Russia for the last time, in 1572, the troubled affairs of the English merchants were not materially altered. Employees of the Muscovy Company had caused various disturbances on Russian soil, and the tsar charged some of them with treasonable relations with his enemy, the king of Poland. A new English envoy, Daniel Sylvester, made several trips between 1573 and 1575 in an effort to regain Ivan's favor for the harassed merchants. He was instructed to offer more liberal promises to the tsar, and it is possible, though the fact has never been determined, that he was permitted to discuss terms of an alliance. The mystery surrounding this, as well as other diplomatic dealings, is largely accounted for by Ivan's strange demand that all correspondence between him and Elizabeth on such matters should be of a strictly personal

nature. He would not admit the medium of regular diplomatic channels in what he believed to be his own private
affair with the queen, and Elizabeth's occasional violation of
this unusual secrecy drew upon her the anger of the tsar.

In his last mission, in 1575, Sylvester was told that unless
Ivan obtained complete satisfaction (apparently in the
matter of the alliance), he would hand over the commercial
privileges to England's competitors. On his return Sylvester
was killed by lightning at Kholmogory and his papers were
burned. Whether Ivan's terms in this instance reached
Elizabeth is not known, for diplomatic relations between
the two countries lapsed for several years.

When relations were resumed Ivan's Anglomania had
taken a new turn. The tradition that the tsar intended to
offer himself in marriage to Elizabeth, or that he actually
made a proposal, will perhaps always remain a matter of pure
conjecture. The notion is said to have been suggested to him
by Elysius Bomel,[4] a pseudo-scientist and dabbler in astrology, who procured his release from an English prison in order
to take service with the tsar. Bomel gained an evil reputation
in Russia, was discredited, and finally put to death. At the
height of his favor he is reported to have urged Ivan to make
a match with the queen, drawing an alluring picture of
Elizabeth's feminine charms. But there is no valid documentary evidence to substantiate the tradition of this intended
marriage, and the best Russian authority flatly denies it.[5]

It is not that the egocentric Ivan would have hesitated to
aim so high. As a self-proclaimed descendant of the Caesars
he was perfectly capable of considering a matrimonial offer to
Elizabeth as little short of condescension on his part. Despite

his many failings, however, Ivan was essentially a practical ruler, and he would certainly have recognized the impossibility of such a match. Although he eschewed the queen, he did decide that to marry into English nobility would consolidate his relations with that country.

In 1580 Jeremy Horsey, an agent of the Muscovy Company, was commissioned by the tsar to request Elizabeth to send him a large supply of military stores, which he badly needed in his war with Poland. Horsey was also entrusted with certain secret instructions, and we may fairly suppose, from the events that soon followed, that they had reference to Ivan's desire to marry an Englishwoman.

Horsey returned in the spring of 1581, bringing with him thirteen ships laden with war supplies, physicians, and apothecaries. Ivan had great faith in foreign doctors, although his own subjects could hardly have been persuaded under torture to accept treatment from them. Among these medical men was James Roberts, a man whom Elizabeth valued highly, and who was intended as the tsar's personal physician. All the facts seem to indicate that Roberts was instructed to furnish information to Ivan about his matrimonial project. For in the course of the same year Feodor Ivanovich Pisemski was sent to Elizabeth to discuss once again the question of a political alliance and the possibilities of a marriage between Ivan and Mary Hastings, the daughter of the Earl of Huntingdon and a relative of the queen. The tsar had a weakness for feminine beauty and Pisemski was strictly enjoined to obtain precise information about the height, figure, and complexion of the intended bride, and if possible, a portrait of her. Since Ivan already had a wife, his seventh to be exact, the ambassador was ordered to say, if any objections were raised on this score, that his sovereign would put aside his present wife, and that any children by his English bride would receive every recognition, except a claim on the throne.

In so far as it is possible to understand the tsar's devious intentions at this point, it may be plausibly conjectured that he felt that such a marriage would further his chances of obtaining the long-desired offensive and defensive alliance. The warlike Batory of Poland was causing him no end of uneasiness, and an alliance would guarantee Russia much-needed aid from England. Furthermore, the internal dissension was most formidable at this time, and Ivan perhaps believed that he should be more acceptable in England with an English wife; for Roberts, who accompanied Pisemski on the mission, was charged with informing Elizabeth that the tsar might soon be forced to take up his abode in her country.

Pisemski arrived in September, 1582, but Elizabeth put him off on one pretext or another for several months while she treated with the Poles, who at that time were just as eager as Ivan to gain the favor of England. In January of the following year the ambassador was granted a secret audience and at once broached the question of the marriage. Elizabeth's real reactions to the project are not easy to ascertain. For a time she certainly beguiled Pisemski with some hope of success. Thus she expressed concern about the conditions of the marriage and the future prospects of any daughters born to Mary Hastings. Pisemski proudly assured her that Russian rulers always married their daughters to leading European potentates. On his insistence Elizabeth even provided an opportunity for him to view Mary Hastings as she walked with her attendants in the garden. And Pisemski dutifully itemized in his report to Ivan the several charms of the bride-to-be. But when the ambassador declared himself most favorably impressed with the lady, his enthusiasm appears to have brought about a change in Elizabeth's tactics. She began to insinuate that Mary Hastings scarcely possessed the qualifications and beauty to satisfy such a connoisseur as his sovereign. And, apparently, eager to get his mind off the marriage question, she reverted to the alliance, and actually agreed to furnish armed assistance against the enemies of Ivan. But this was to be contingent upon a monopoly for England of all Russia's import trade. The ambassador was baffled by the English demands and counter-proposals, for which his instructions were quite inadequate, and Elizabeth finally gained the point which she had undoubtedly been working for. Pisemski was to return to Russia with her own envoy, Jeremy Bowes, who would be vested with the necessary power to treat with the tsar on all questions in dispute. Accordingly, in the same year (1583), Bowes and the disappointed Pisemski set sail, carrying a portrait of Mary Hastings, which was the only tangible result of the whole marriage proposal. A wiser diplomat than Pisemski would have perceived that Elizabeth had no desire for anything more intimate than a trade agreement, and that she had intended from the very beginning, at least so far as Mary Hastings was concerned, that all the tsar's matrimonial plans should come to nought.

The account left by Bowes of his negotiations with Ivan during the first two months of 1584 is at wide variance with the records of the proceedings in the Russian chancery. Bowes appears to have behaved in an officious manner, and furthermore he adopted the dangerous attitude of condescension towards the Russians. Although the tsar admired his devotion and courage, on one occasion Bowes angered him so that he threatened to have him thrown out of the palace. In his report Bowes represents himself as on the road to success, but the Russian records provide a very different picture. Ivan seems suddenly to have recognized the great value of the unusual commercial privileges he had granted England, and he now demanded a substantial return. He requested the intercession of England in his attempt to force the Poles to return some captured territory; he insisted that the French and Dutch should have the same trading rights as the English in certain Russian ports; and he demanded the punishment of offending Englishmen employed by the Muscovy Company. Finally, he complained that the company was shipping useless merchandise into Russia and that its prices were excessive.

In a secret audience Ivan returned to the marriage question, and Bowes admitted that Elizabeth did not favor his proposed union with Mary Hastings. In lieu of this Bowes offered to draw up a list of eligible English ladies, but later, when the tsar called for the list, Bowes denied ever having made the statement and pleaded the necessity of further instructions. On the whole, relations between Ivan and Bowes were becoming strained when the tsar suddenly fell ill and died.

Several months later, after suffering many indignities, for he had got himself cordially hated by Ivan's ministers, Bowes was sent home with a perfunctory letter to the queen, containing no mention of an alliance and no confirmation of com-

mercial privileges. Thus the first period of England's relations with Russia came to an end, and the thriving trade she
had built up was gradually undermined by the merchants of
other countries.

These first thirty years of Anglo-Russian relations were
not without their significance in the early history of Russia.
England's gain was primarily a commercial one, but Russia
received benefits which essentially extended her cultural
horizon. There was, to be sure, no influence of a literary nature. Despite the close contact between the two countries,
the glorious Elizabethan Age of literature went entirely unheeded. For this kind of cultural seed Russian soil was un-
fertile. The time was not ripe and more than another century
was to pass before English authors attracted any attention in
Russia. But that phase of culture which is connected with
material advancement in the handicrafts and with improved
standards of living was unquestionably influenced by the
Englishmen who went to Russia in the latter half of the sixteenth century.

As has already been pointed out, Ivan himself was fully
aware of the advantage to his country of this kind of influence, and he gave every encouragement to the importation of
English artisans, engineers, architects, and physicians, according them special privileges and requiring that they teach
their skill to the natives. Other nations followed the initiative
of England in this respect, and for the first time in its history
Russia adopted an open-door policy to foreigners trained in
the arts and trades. Settling in the country they provided a
valuable example to the backward Russians of improved
methods of work and civilized conditions of life.

Later, Western influence often brought in its train customs and manners that the young country did not need. But at this stage in her political expansion and social growth Russia had everything to gain and nothing to lose from such contacts. The very merchandise that England shipped in quantities enabled Ivan to stand on a more equal footing with his enemies. The protests of the enemy nations bear eloquent testimony to the significance of this type of English aid. Denmark, Sweden, and Poland remonstrated with Elizabeth, and the complaining letters of the Polish king, Sigismund II, to the queen bring out in some detail the importance of Russia's debt to England. In one letter he protests that Russia not only obtains the necessities of war from England but that Englishmen disseminate among his Russian enemies useful information on all manner of technical production. And he concludes another letter to Elizabeth with the following significant sentence:

The Moscovite, enemy to all liberty under the heavens, dayly to grow mightier by the increase of such [English] things as be brought to the Narve, while not only wares but also weapons heretofore unknowen to him, and artificers and arts be brought unto him: by meane whereof he maketh himselfe strong to vanquish all others. . . . We seemed hitherto to vanquish him onely in this, that he was rude of arts, and ignorant of policies. If so be that this navigation to the Narve continue, what shall be unknowen to him?[6]

Poland, indeed, had much to fear, but Elizabeth did not halt her merchants, and from this period we may date the serious beginning of the Westernization of Russian arms.

Historians of the old school dismissed Ivan's Anglomania as merely another obsession of his distorted nature. But modern investigators have come to recognize in him a genius for statecraft which was at fault mainly in the methods he employed to execute his policies. Certainly he showed vision in understanding and acting upon his country's urgent need of contact with the West. For it is now clear to us that Russia's only hope of development in this backward period of her existence lay in her willingness and ability to assimilate the best features of Western European civilization. Ivan initiated a movement that was to continue to Russia's advantage, with few interruptions, for the next two hundred years.

His turning especially towards England is not to be attributed wholly to the accident of Chancellor's arrival off the northern coast. England could provide him with all the manufactured goods his people needed, and he obviously saw in this great nation, with its secure position in world affairs, its wealth, and its powerful fleet, a potential bulwark against his many enemies. It is to Ivan's credit as a statesman that he persistently sought the friendship of England and a protecting political and personal alliance. Only in the methods he used to achieve this end does he deserve censure. For the most part he admired the Englishmen he came in contact with, the capable ambassadors, brave explorers, and efficient merchants, and his enthusiasm is amply attested by his determination to reside in England if he had to flee his own country. It is little wonder that one of his unsympathetic ministers, on the occasion of Ivan's death, announced the news scornfully to Bowes: "Your English tsar is dead!"

BIBLIOGRAPHY

SOURCES

R. Hakluyt, *The Principal Navigations, Voyages, Traffiques and Discoveries of the English Nation*, London, 1600. (See the London edition of 1927, vols. I–II.)

E. Bond, *Russia at the Close of the Sixteenth Century*, London, 1856. (Contains Dr. Giles Fletcher's *Of the Russe Common Wealth*, and *The Travels of Sir Jerome Horsey*.)

Iu. Tolstoi, *Pervyya sorok let snoshenii mezhdu Rossieiu i Anglieiu, 1553–1593*, St. Petersburg, 1875.

K. Bestuzhev-Riumin, editor, *Pamyatniki diplomaticheskikh snoshenii moskovskago gosudarstva s Anglieiu, 1581–1604* (*Sbornik imperatorskago russkago istoricheskago obshchestva*, St. Petersburg, 1883, vol. XXXVIII).

INVESTIGATIONS

J. Hamel, *England and Russia*, translated by J. S. Leigh, London, 1854. *Anglichane v Rossii v XVI i XVII stoletiyakh*, St. Petersburg, 1865.

A. Brückner, *Geschichte Russlands bis zum Ende des 18-ten Jahrhunderts*, Gotha, 1896, 2 vols. (See vol. 1.)

K. Waliszewski, *Ivan the Terrible*, Philadelphia, 1904.

I. Lubimenko, "Angliskaya torgovaya kompaniya v Rossii v XVI veke" (*Istoricheskoe obozrenie*, 1911, XVI, 1–23).
"Les marchands Anglais en Russie au XVI⁰ siècle" (*Revue Historique*, 1912, CIX, 1–26).
Istoriya torgovykh snoshenii Rossii s Angeliei, St. Petersburg, 1912.

A. Gerson, *The Organization of the Early History of the Muscovy Company*, New York, 1912.

I. Lubimenko, "The Correspondence of Queen Elizabeth with the Russian Czars" (*American Historical Review*, 1914, No. 3, pp. 525–542).

CHAPTER II

RUSSIA AND ENGLAND FROM BORIS GODUNOV TO PETER THE GREAT (1584–1682)

IVAN'S pro-English sympathies were resented by certain ministers and nobles close to the throne. With good reason they suspected their sovereign's ulterior motives, and in some few cases they had fallen foul of the English merchants and ambassadors. On the death of the tsar these disaffected persons sought to influence the new ruler, Fedor Ivanovich, against England. But the Muscovy Company had risked too much to submit without a struggle to this new hostility. Large sums of money had been invested and many English lives lost in carrying on the trade, and there still remained the hope of further profits. Also the Crown was intimately connected with the business, both commercially and politically. Elizabeth was unwilling that competing nations should reap the benefits of the pioneering efforts of her merchants and she stood solidly behind the interests of the company. Fortunately for the English at this juncture Boris Godunov, who soon became regent (1587) and later tsar, was allied to their cause.

Godunov was an able statesman and in the matter of foreign relations he pursued the enlightened policy of Ivan, always seeking to bring his backward country into contact with the civilizing influence of the West. Unlike Ivan, however, he was not disposed to favor the English to the exclusion of other foreigners. He was fully aware of the fact that commercially Russia was gaining little from the English trade monopoly, and his real efforts were directed towards opening the door to the merchants of all countries in order to stimulate a degree of competition profitable to Russia. But this policy did not prevent him from appearing as the friend of the English or from pleading their cause at the Russian court. During the next twenty years, while he remained in power, the many good offices Godunov performed for the English entirely justify the title of "their lord protector" which they accorded him.

In the first four years after the accession of Ivan's son there was a frequent exchange of letters between the two countries. Fedor had complaints and demands to make. He complained of the insolence of Bowes and of the conduct of some of the merchants; and he demanded the right of free trade with England and the abrogation of the exclusive commercial privileges of the Muscovy Company. Elizabeth, on her part, adopted a more yielding and straightforward diplomatic policy with the new régime. She no longer had to contend with the cunning Ivan and his personal and often compromising requests. The queen apologized for Bowes and freely accorded Russia the right to trade with England (she had little to fear from this direction, for as yet the Russians had no merchant marine). But she still hoped to maintain the company's monopoly.

The messenger employed by both countries for these and subsequent negotiations was Jerome Horsey. He was an extremely capable and resourceful person who had spent a number of years in Russia in the service of the Muscovy Company. Horsey knew the language, the customs of the people,

and the devious ways of court intrigue. Unfortunately he was
not averse to exploiting his knowledge in questionable practises, a fact which ultimately strained diplomatic relations
between England and Russia. As we have already observed,
he managed to gain the good will of Ivan, and on the death of
that ruler he assiduously cultivated the favor of Boris Godunov. The latter even went so far as to employ Horsey in
several personal commissions of a rather unsavory nature.

With such a clever spokesman of the English cause at the
Russian court the affairs of the Muscovy Company took a
turn for the better. The advantage of Horsey's intimate
knowledge of Russian methods soon manifested itself. Besides writing to the tsar, Elizabeth now addressed flattering
letters to the powerful Godunov, who in turn softened or
blocked the hostility of the anti-English ministers and nobles.
The queen also plied the tsar, the tsarina, and Godunov with
rich presents. Horsey tells us with what enthusiasm they received English gifts of "lyons, bulls, doggs, guilt-halberds,
pistolls, peces, armor, wynes, store of druggs of all sorts,
organes, virgenalls, musicions, scarletts, perrell chaines, plate
of curious makinge and of other costly things of great value."[1]

These more practical methods of achieving the company's
ends finally prevailed against all opposition, and in 1587 a
new charter was granted, containing more extensive privileges than had ever been enjoyed by the English merchants.
Horsey returned to England in triumph with the new charter
and many presents for the queen. Elizabeth received him
with marked favor and he tells us how she perused the Russian statement of the privileges with much curiosity, noting
the similarity of some of the letters to those in the Greek al-

phabet. "I could quicklie lern it," remarked the scholarly
queen. And she "preyed my lord of Essex to lern the famoust
and most copius language in the world." [2] Essex took much
delight in the language, Horsey informs us, but he wisely re-
frained from making a study of it.

Despite the fact that virtually all the demands of the Muscovy Company had now been granted, Elizabeth thought it
necessary to send Dr. Giles Fletcher, with full ambassadorial
powers, to obtain a confirmation of the privileges and to
straighten out the tangle into which the affairs of the company had lapsed since the death of Ivan. He belonged to a
remarkable literary family, being the uncle of John Fletcher
the dramatist, and the father of Phineas and Giles Fletcher,
the authors of *The Purple Island* and *Christ's Victory and
Triumph*, justly famous poems in the Spenserian tradition.
The ambassador was himself a poet of ability, and his sonnet
cycle, *Licia* (1593), was much esteemed in Elizabethan times.
From his Russian experiences he gathered material for a
book, *Of the Russe Common Wealth*, published in 1591. It is
an authoritative account of the country at this period, but
the writer's outspoken criticism resulted in the suppression of
the book at the instance of the Muscovy Company, which
feared the effect it might have on their commercial relations
with Russia.

Fletcher arrived at Moscow in 1588, but in the interim a
serious situation had developed which threatened to ruin all
that had been accomplished. Horsey's double-dealing in the
affairs of the company had been discovered, and although he
was ordered to remain in England, he escaped secretly to
Russia. He was guilty, among other things, of private trad-

ing and of diverting the company's funds to his own use. As it happened, his shady operations touched closely the chancellor, Shchelkalov, an inveterate enemy of the English merchants, and one whom Horsey had particularly antagonized. Shchelkalov was quick to use the occasion to discredit the whole Muscovy Company. Furthermore, the merchants had refused to move their trade from Narva, which had fallen into the hands of the Swedes, to the Russian port of St. Nicholas on the White Sea. Perhaps something of the changed disposition may also be attributed to the fact that an alliance had been proposed between the tsar and the king of Spain. The Armada was then preparing to descend upon England, and the Russians can hardly be blamed for expecting a sweeping Spanish victory. And to top the whole matter, Elizabeth had unwittingly offended Godunov by transmitting letters to him which coupled his name with that of the chancellor. Godunov made it clear that his princely dignity was outraged by such procedure. These objections and complaints, along with others of less significance, now confronted Fletcher, who had anticipated a most favorable reception after Horsey's recent successful negotiations.

As might be expected, however, he was received coldly and treated with studied neglect, if not, as he later declared and the Russians denied, with downright indignities. Nor was his task made easier by the fact that the conduct of the negotiations was placed in the hands of the hostile Shchelkalov.

But Fletcher's patience and diplomatic skill eventually brought about a victory for the English cause. The injured feelings of Godunov were assuaged, and the news of England's great triumph over the Spanish Armada undoubtedly had something to do with the restoration of Russian favor. Fresh letters from England threw light on Horsey's corrupt dealings which had compromised the Muscovy Company, and Shchelkalov's complicity therein was clearly indicated. Elizabeth demanded that the culpable Horsey be sent back with Fletcher, and her request that the company's affairs should be removed from the jurisdiction of the chancellor was complied with. The final outcome of the negotiations was a confirmation of the privileges in the charter obtained by Horsey, and several others of considerable importance were added.

After this there was little serious cause for complaint on either side. Some further difficulties arose over Horsey and the charges of Fletcher that he had been treated with scant ceremony at the Russian court. But a mutual conciliatory spirit soon righted these matters. Gradually Elizabeth became convinced of the impossibility of maintaining the strict trading monopoly of the Muscovy Company. This feature, obviously harmful to the cause of Russia's growing interest in foreign relations in general, had been at the root of most of the controversy between the two countries. Eventually the queen lessened her demands in this direction. The correspondence on both sides became very friendly and Elizabeth rarely missed an opportunity of complimenting Godunov on his noble lineage and great wisdom. By 1593 practically all friction in commercial relations between Russia and England had disappeared. Boris Godunov, while he lived, was highly valued by the English merchants as their friend and protector.

Like Ivan's, however, Godunov's interest in England went deeper than the matter of commercial relations, but the way in

which he manifested it was more eclectic and less personal
than that of his great predecessor. It is true that Horsey in
his *Travels* asserts that Godunov likewise contemplated seeking a refuge in England in case he were forced to flee from
Russia,[3] but in the absence of any other authority for this
statement one hesitates to trust Horsey. After he became
tsar, Godunov did entertain the hope of a matrimonial alliance between his children and members of the English royal
house, but nothing came of this ambitious project.

In his eagerness to bring the light of knowledge to Russia,
Godunov's aspirations transcended those of the purposeful
but often reactionary Ivan. During his reign all foreigners
living in Moscow enjoyed unusual freedom and privileges. He
even conceived the idea of founding a university, and as a
step in this direction he sought the services, though unsuccessfully, of the famous English mathematician, John Dee, as
well as other foreign scholars. But it was many years after his
death before a Russian university was established. Nevertheless, he did execute a scheme for sending the sons of nobles
abroad, with the general purpose of using them as teachers on
their return. In 1601–02 eighteen Russian youths were sent
to Western European countries, four of them going to England. They made a beginning, at least, in learning the language and in acquiring a formal education in the English
schools. But for ten years little was heard of them, and meanwhile Boris Godunov had died and many changes had taken
place in Russia. In the reign of the first Romanov, Michael
Fedorovich, the government suddenly remembered about its
travelling scholars and inquiries were made at the court of
James I in 1613. Of the youths allotted to England the gov-

ernment could find trace of only one and he, curiously
enough, was earning his livelihood as a minister of the English Church. As a matter of fact, of the whole eighteen students, only one returned. Apparently these youths had
succumbed to the more attractive culture and better living
conditions of the West. Thus Godunov's attempt to train
Russian teachers abroad ended in failure. Peter the Great
was to try a similar scheme with more success.

In the Russian ambassadorial reports of this period it is not
unusual to find detailed accounts of English life that have
considerable historical worth. Such documents must have
provided a mine of information for those authorities at the
Russian court who were beginning to show an interest in
everything foreign. Grigori Ivanovich Mikulin, for example,
who was sent to London as ambassador in 1600, wrote a full
report of his stay there, giving his enthusiastic impressions of
the city, its festivities, church services, court affairs, and the
customs and manners of the people. Mikulin's descriptions of
the queen and several of her statesmen have the freshness of
the contemporary reporter, and it is certainly a loss that the
great literary figures who walked the streets of London then,
and of whom we know so little, did not fall within the scope
of his curiosity. He tells with some detail of a procession in
the city led by Elizabeth and her courtiers, and he notes how
the queen would occasionally turn to the admiring towns-
people lining both sides of the street to ask them "about
their health and if anyone had done ill to them." [4] Mikulin
likewise gives a fairly circumstantial narrative of the trial of
Essex and the state of popular feeling over the event. After

the execution, he writes, "there was great lamentation and weeping over him among all the people of London." [5]

The road from England to Russia was now a much-travelled thoroughfare and the relations between the two countries were more vitalized than in the time of Ivan the Terrible. After he became tsar, Godunov followed Ivan's policy of attracting all manner of foreign artisans and learned men to Russia, but in this he had a definite educational purpose in mind. If she were to take a place among the advanced nations of Europe, Russia had centuries of accumulated reactionary tradition and cultural backwardness to overcome. Godunov well understood the efficacy of example and he cast his net far and wide for foreign models. In this respect he laid England under heavy contribution. He had a high opinion of the accomplishment of English physicians, and a number of doctors and apothecaries were invited to practise in Russia. When his sister, Irina Fedorovna, was ill, he requested of Elizabeth the services of a midwife and a doctor. His partiality for foreigners, as in the case of Ivan, often drew upon him the suspicion and enmity of his countrymen. In the Russian mind, for example, sickness was still considered pretty much a visitation of God, and prayer was prescribed as the best remedy. Hence the native attitude towards doctors was equivocal, if not absolutely antagonistic. There exists an amusing report of an examination to which an English physician, Timothy Willis, was subjected by one of the "learned" secretaries of the court. Since the doctor had been forced to leave all his books behind, the secretary was unable to understand how he could prescribe remedies. The doctor explained that he carried his medical books in his head, and that he could diagnose illness by making tests of the bodily fluids. However, the secretary remained quite unconvinced and expressed his displeasure to the tsar.[6]

But Godunov did not allow the native hostility to curb his ardent desire to improve the country. It is said that he enjoyed spending long days at his home in the society of English physicians, and it is logical to suppose that his receptive mind was a good deal influenced by such company. In all his relations with foreigners he never lost sight of the practical purpose of bettering the material and cultural conditions of his realm. The Westernization that Ivan had begun was continued and intensified by Boris Godunov.

After his death in 1605, Russia went through a period of political strife and warfare which has been appropriately called the "Times of Trouble." A pervading discontent among all classes of the population, coupled with a palace struggle for the crown, resulted in years of bloodshed and devastation. With the accession of Michael Fedorovich Romanov (1613–45), something like order was reëstablished. Although the Times of Trouble interrupted the refining influence of the West, the period also brought into existence a new political and social development which was to be more favorably disposed towards economic and cultural contacts with European countries. In the wars with the Poles it had become increasingly evident that Russia badly needed armies equipped and trained after the European fashion. In the reign of Michael foreign military officers were engaged on a large scale to instruct the Russians, and foreign artisans were employed to build arsenals and foundries. The tsar once again encouraged foreign commerce, now opening the country to various nations, though the English still maintained an advantage in the matter of privileges. The tsar negotiated a loan from England and solicited her aid in making his peace with Sweden. France likewise made a special bid for commercial privileges, and the royal families of Europe began to look with more favor upon marriage alliances with the ruling house of Russia.

There is an interesting story connected with Michael's request for a loan. The embassy sent over in 1618 by James I, under Sir Dudley Digges, to discuss the terms, included among its members John Tradescant, who later became gardener to Charles I. Tradescant made the journey in order to study the native plant and animal life, and his subsequent report contains the earliest extant account of Russian plants.[7] In the same company, serving as chaplain, was a learned Oxford scholar, Richard James. After having been received by the tsar, the embassy returned home by the overland route, leaving James behind with a few members, who remained in the frozen Archangel region until 1620. James spent part of his time collecting Russian popular poetry, which was carefully written out for him. He later deposited in the Bodleian Library a manuscript containing six Great Russian historical and lyric-epic songs, excellently inscribed in the native language of the sixteenth and seventeenth centuries.[8] This document preserves in very early written form some of the oldest remains of the extensive and valuable Russian popular poetry.

In the reign of the next sovereign, Aleksei Mikhailovich (1645–76), one can perceive a definite crystallization in the whole matter of foreign influence. Russia's contact with the West in the sixteenth century had been confined primarily to commercial and diplomatic relations. Except for such far-seeing rulers as Ivan and Godunov, the intelligent portion of the population in this century did not admit, in general, the crying need of Russia for the civilizing influence of the more advanced European nations. On the contrary, they were convinced of their own self-sufficiency and were inclined to regard any contact with the West with open hostility. At best the cultural efforts of Ivan and Godunov, valuable as they were, never got much beyond the pioneering stage. They prepared the ground, but it remained for future generations to sow the seed and reap the fruits.

In the seventeenth century, however, particularly in the latter half, an obvious change took place in the attitude of intelligent Russians towards foreign influence. They began openly to recognize the superiority of European civilization and the need of studying it, and, if necessary, of morally submitting to it. It was not mere intercourse they desired or a wholesale borrowing of worldly comforts. They were eager to learn everything about European ideas, customs, literature, and social relations. Here we have a basis for genuine, transforming influence. Serious-minded Russians, to a degree unknown in the sixteenth century, expressed discontent with the life and lack of culture in their own country, and they turned towards the West, not only for material aid, but for moral, spiritual, and intellectual enlightenment.

The appalling sameness of Russian life, which seems to be at the root of the pervading inertia of the people so often described in the national literature, was rarely disturbed in the early period by any conscious effort towards cultural reform. The peasants were chained to the soil, and the unvarying boredom of their life, seemingly symbolized by the dull, flat steppes they tilled, characterized likewise the social existence of the lesser nobles and the city middle class. But the Times of Trouble had wrought a change in the political position of the lesser nobles and the city middle class, leaving them with the chief influence in the state. With this increased responsibility their reactionary attitude towards the West diminished and they now welcomed, to some extent, the possibility of cultural advancement. Also, the new aristocracy, rising from the ashes of the old, which had been destroyed in the bitter struggle for power, saw in the obvious superiority of Western Europe an opportunity to improve their own position by learning and borrowing.

The results of this more enthusiastic regard for Western influence began to manifest itself in various ways in Russian society of the latter half of the seventeenth century. The doors were now opened wide to foreigners and their aid was sought in every direction. As yet the French were looked upon with suspicion. Their turn was to come later, and then in so powerful a fashion that it threatened to drive out all other foreign influence. But the Italians, Germans, Dutch, and English all received encouragement in the reign of Aleksei Mikhailovich.

The Germans in particular played an important part in this early drift towards the West. From the time of Ivan the Terrible enterprising Germans had settled near Moscow and built up a little colony with the express determination of accepting Russia as a new fatherland. Though they were subjected to hardships and persecution, the colony prospered, and by the time of Aleksei the German Suburb consisted of over a thousand Protestant families. These hardy colonists provided a model in miniature of European civilization for Russian imitation, and Moscow society began to adopt German furniture, costumes, household objects, pictures, and musical instruments. From this time German influence was to become a powerful factor in the political and cultural growth of Russia.

The movement acquired additional impetus from the fact that there now sprang up a number of outspoken advocates of cultural reform. Among these the most significant were Fedor Michailovich Rtishchev, Afanasi Lavrentevich Ordyn-Nashchokin, Artemon Sergevich Matveev, and Vasili Vasilevich Golitsyn. These men were intensely interested in the European systems of government, in social and economic ideas, and in all manner of foreign education and learning. They championed the cause of the new culture and their influence in this direction is everywhere evident. Matveev, a close friend of Aleksei, interested the tsar in European progress, and Golitsyn, who collected a library that would have done credit to a profound Western scholar of the time, advocated extensive reforms and became himself a man of great learning and progressive ideas.

Literature, the common carrier of culture, was slow to exert an influence on the dissemination of European thought in seventeenth-century Russia. Compared with such countries as England and France during this period, Russia was centuries behind in the matter of writing books. Nevertheless the first feeble attempts at literary production in the reign of

Aleksei were important in the spread of European ideas. Literature, like nearly everything else that pertained to cultural advancement at the time, was of a derivatory nature. But that translations should be freely allowed was a decided step forward. From 1550 to 1700 the total number of books translated into Russian was a hundred and thirty-four, a pitifully small figure, to be sure; but the great majority of these fell within the last half of the seventeenth century.

The educated inhabitants of the German Suburb took the lead in rendering works, mostly from Latin, German, and Polish, into Russian. The varied subject matter of the books translated indicates the trend of popular interest. For the most part they concerned religion, morals, *belles lettres*, history, geography, astronomy, and medicine. The tsar himself sometimes ordered the translation of certain works, and among those of special interest to England at this early date were translations of a book (the original is not known) on the life and execution of Charles I, and the *Argenis* of John Barclay, an allegorical Latin romance full of satirical hits at seventeenth-century life in Europe. A great many books in foreign languages were likewise imported, for natives now began to study Latin, German, and Polish. And this interest in literature is perhaps reflected in the establishment, at about this time, of higher schools of learning in Moscow. On the whole, the progress of influence through the medium of literature was slow, but the business of translating foreign books was to continue in ever-increasing volume, until Russia was deluged with a literature not her own.

Closely connected with the influx of Western European literature was the influence of foreign drama on the origin of the

Russian theatre. Folk drama and religious plays had existed in Russia for some time, but a formal attempt at the development of anything resembling a secular theatre did not take place until the reign of Aleksei. Court entertainments in general, in the seventeenth century, such as clowns, acrobats, and musical performances, found their inspiration in importations from abroad, especially from Germany. And it was a German Lutheran pastor, Johann Gregori, who gave the first real impetus to the Russian dramatic movement.

An English ambassador, the Earl of Carlisle, as early as 1664, had made an attempt at dramatic representation by staging a play in the ambassadorial residence in Moscow. The tsar's interest in drama was kindled by the reports of his envoys who had witnessed plays abroad, and under his patronage Gregori organized a troupe of amateurs in 1672 to perform before the sovereign. In his youth in Germany Gregori had come in contact with the so-called "English Comedy." Companies of English actors, with a repertoire of Elizabethan tragedies and comedies, had roamed over Holland and Germany in the closing years of the sixteenth century and exercised a considerable influence on the drama in these countries. The plays were originally given in English, but by the seventeenth century they had been translated into German, — and in the process nearly always mutilated; and of course the English actors were eventually displaced by natives. However, the companies retained the title of "English Comedians," and the plays were still largely English in substance if not in language. Consequently, when Gregori cast about him for material, he naturally helped himself to the printed collections of the German companies. He also started a school of the drama in Moscow where Russian youths were instructed in acting.

Among the plays selected by Gregori for translation and performance were two which pretty certainly derive from English sources. The first of these was *The Comedy of Queen Esther and the Haughty Aman*, which was acted before Tsar Aleksei in 1672. As is well known, plays on the theme of Esther were very common in Germany as early as the sixteenth century, and there is a slight possibility that the original of the Russian play was merely a reworking of German material. However, there is an English interlude, called *Esther, Queen of Persia*,[9] and it is very likely that this, or some later redaction of it, served as the original for the German version contained in the collection from which Gregori translated. Apart from the general similarity in action (which cannot be too much insisted on, since few of the Esther plays differ radically in this respect), there are turns of phrase and particular words which seem to indicate that the German piece was translated from the English interlude.

Concerning the other play there can be no doubt of its ultimate derivation from an English original. This is *Temir Aksakovo, a Play or "Small Comedy" on Bajazet and Tamerlane*,[10] which was acted in 1674. Marlowe's *Tamburlaine* had considerable vogue in Europe, and in its various wanderings over the Continent it underwent many changes. The loose nature of the plot laid the play open to alterations, and it was obviously some wrenched German version that Gregori translated into Russian. Consequently very few of the original features of Marlowe's play are preserved in the Russian drama. Tamerlane's bloody progress is reminiscent of the destructive course of Marlowe's famous protagonist. But the comic element is emphasized in the Russian version and a definite religious bias is worked into the play. Tamerlane becomes a Christian knight who rides forth to conquer the infidel. Indeed, the whole is a far cry from Marlowe's drama.

The tsar was enthusiastic over the performances and lavishly rewarded the participants. No one can deny that the foreign influence on the Russian stage in this first period of its development was mainly German. Nevertheless, in tradition and repertoire the influence derives in no small measure from English drama. It was perhaps fortunate that the heroic spirit of English drama, popular all over Central Europe at this date, should have been the first to come in contact with the Russian theatre. Later, in the reign of Catherine II, when the Russian theatre took another decided step forward, the predominant influence was French, although the English drama again played an important part, primarily through the great tragedies and comedies of Shakspere.

It must not be supposed, of course, that the vast cultural change that was taking place during the reign of Tsar Aleksei met with anything like undivided support. The old order was passing and a new one was slowly but surely taking its place. However, there was no lack of partisanship on both sides. Aroused by the rising tide of foreign influence, nationalism began to organize a powerful opposition. The seventeenth century, as a matter of fact, marks the origin of the two parties, the Westerners (Zapadniki) and the Slavophiles, which thereafter fought a long-drawn-out battle for cultural and often for political ascendency.

The cleavage was already discernible in the church schism of the time. The Old Believers wished to preserve the ancient national customs, both religious and domestic. For them Russia was a third Rome and its people a New Israel, and with burning zeal they predicted the downfall of the country if it tolerated innovations in the old beliefs of pure Russian Orthodoxy, or if it allowed apostates and traitors to introduce Western ideas and customs. On the other hand, under the leadership of the brilliant but harsh patriarch, Nikon, the innovators sought to reform the church services and to correct the liturgical books. The fight for reform by Nikon and his followers symbolized the spirit of revolt among the Westerners. They had begun the long struggle to lead the Russian people from their national isolation to a recognition of the West as the school in which Russia could learn, not merely industrial and economic efficiency, but how to live and to think. Reactionary forces, however, were powerful and the very inertia of the vast mass of Russian people was the strongest ally of those opposed to change. Even in this period of cultural advancement a strict censorship of literature was set up and a decree forbidding the circulation of books in the provinces was issued. The son of Tsar Aleksei, indeed, after his father's death, cleaned out, with a sense of purification, the court building where Gregori had staged his plays. But no opposition, however strong, could raise an effectual barrier against the force of Western enlightenment. The nations of Europe were now beginning to take a profound interest in the country, and especially in its vast unexploited resources. Foreigners came in large numbers, and though their principal motive was a desire for domination and power, they succeeded, while profiting by the weaknesses of the Russians, in deeply affecting the whole social structure of the country. Of the nations most interested, England, throughout the reign of Aleksei, stood in high favor with the tsar. Only when his envoys brought back the strange and terrible news of the revolution and the execution of Charles I did Aleksei waver in his devotion. In great anger he broke off relations, but after Cromwell proved his fitness to rule, this seventeenth-century tsar of the most autocratic of countries resumed relations with the Commonwealth of England.

The spirit of reform in the reign of Aleksei was soon to be caught up by a much more ambitious monarch, Peter the Great, who would not permit any nationalistic opposition to stand in the way of his violent innovations, many of which were inspired by his contacts with Western Europe. And here again England was to play an important part.

BIBLIOGRAPHY

SOURCES

K. Bestuzhev-Riumin, editor, *Pamyatniki diplomaticheskikh snoshenii moskovskago gosudarstva s Anglieiu, 1581–1604* (*Sbornik imperatorskago russkago istoricheskago obshchestva*, St. Petersburg, 1883, vol. XXXVIII).

N. Karamzin, *Istoriya gosudarstva rossiskago*, St. Petersburg, 1892, 12 vols. (First edition, 1818–29.)

A. Sobolevski, *Perevodnaya literatura moskovskoi Rusi XIV–XVII vekov*, St. Petersburg, 1903.

V. Kliuchevski, *Kurs russkoi istorii*, Moskva, 1904–10. (See Part III.)

S. Platonov, *Boris Godunov*, St. Petersburg, 1921.

INVESTIGATIONS

Russian Students Abroad

A. V. Arsenev, *Istoriya posylki pervykh studentov za granitsu pri B. Godunove*, St. Petersburg, 1887.

N. Golitsyn, "Nauchno-obrazovatelnyya snosheniya Rossii s Zapadom v nachale XVII veka" (*Chteniya obshchestva istorii i drevnostei rossiskikh*, 1898, II).

Early Russian Drama

A. Veselovski, *Deutsche Einflüsse auf das alte russische Theater*, Prague, 1876.

P. Morozov, *Ocherki iz istorii russkoi dramy XVII–XVIII stoletii*, St. Petersburg, 1888.

N. S. Tikhonravov, "Pervoe pyatidesyatiletie russkago teatra" (*Sochineniya*, Moskva, 1898, II, 93–119).

S. K. Bogoyavlenski, "Moskovski teatr pri tsaryakh Aleksee i Petre" (*Chteniya obshchestva istorii i drevnostei rossiskikh*, 1914, II).

CHAPTER III

Peter the Great and England; and the Period of the Favorites (1682–1762)

TOLSTOI might well have found Peter the Great a more suitable subject than Napoleon for the radical theory of history which he developed in *War and Peace*. For the accomplishments of no figure of importance in world history give quite the same impression of being controlled by sheer force of circumstances. Certainly if the motivating factors behind the significant events of history are pure chance, happy coincidence, Lady Luck, and an inability to understand the laws guiding one's own actions, then Peter the Great would prove Tolstoi's theory up to the hilt.

On the other hand, this giant of a tsar was not "a creature of mere instinct," [1] as one writer has recently described him. To be sure, he was preëminently a man of action, and in his restless roving over nearly all of Russia and most of Western Europe his many startling deeds betray the man of impulse rather than the calculating ruler with a well-planned campaign. However, impulsive actions do not necessarily argue a total lack of historical design, and when we consider the results of Peter's work with a large enough perspective, we see at once that they fit into a fairly definite pattern. Peter set out to Westernize Russia, and before he died he could claim this as an accomplished fact. The transformation, one must admit, was often concerned with mere externals, and much that he wrought with such great effort was soon swept away. But the fact remains that by dint of his own personal energy and genius he succeeded in modifying the whole social and political structure of his country.

Peter's work of reform, the greatest upheaval in the history of Russia before the coming of Communism, could never have been effected without the aid of foreigners. The Europeanizing initiated by his predecessors had concerned primarily the rulers and a few of the enlightened nobility. Now it was to enter vitally into the life of the whole nation.

During Peter's troubled boyhood the reformer V. V. Golitsyn, already mentioned in the reign of Aleksei and now the favorite of the regent Sophia, dreamed of a cultural *rapprochement* with the West. He had grandiose schemes for the improvement of Russia, such as religious freedom, the education of children abroad, and even a conditional freeing of the serfs. But unlike Peter, Golitsyn was more the visionary than the man of action and nothing much came of his reforms. Meanwhile the future ruler was already making contacts with the West and accumulating ideas and material for his own reforms.

The village of Preobrazhenskoe, where Peter spent his youthful days, was on the edge of the German Suburb, not far from Moscow. This famous settlement was now the center of a conglomerate collection of foreigners. Indeed the word *nemtsy* ("dummies"), which was first used as a name for Germans because they spoke no Russian, was eventually employed to designate all foreigners who lived in the *Nemetskaya Sloboda* ("German Suburb"). In Peter's youth the German Suburb represented a surprisingly variegated mixture of nationalities, religions, occupations, and costumes. Here lived French, Germans, English, Dutch, and Italians, who were engaged in all manner of industry and learning. There were physicians, apothecaries, merchants, manufacturers, artisans, and architects. The settlement possessed two Calvinist and three Lutheran churches, several schools, and many stone houses besides the customary Russian wooden dwellings.

Peter's natural curiosity and thirst for knowledge, which the foreigners so fully satisfied, and his love of jollity, which was not encouraged at the court or at Preobrazhenskoe, attracted him to the German Suburb. He was delighted with the whole new world, so different from the Russian, which he found there. And after he became sole ruler and no longer worried about the remonstrances of his foreigner-hating nobles and clergy, he openly associated with the residents of the Suburb, dining and carousing in their homes. He grew passionately fond of these foreigners and of their European manner of living, and his nature, which was extraordinarily imitative, quickly aped their customs and habits. More than anything he admired their technical proficiency and practical knowledge. From them he could learn geometry and shipbuilding and all matters pertaining to fortifications and military tactics, subjects which were of paramount interest to him throughout his life. With some of these foreigners of the German Suburb he formed a close friendship and their influence on his future policy of reform was considerable.

One of the earliest to win Peter's friendship was a Scotchman, Patrick Gordon, then a general in the Russian army. It will be of interest to digress a moment on the subject of the

Scots in Russia, for the part they played in introducing Western civilization is of consequence. Adventurous Scots had long ago made their way to Russia. When Ivan the Terrible had complained to Elizabeth about the corrupt practises of certain Englishmen in the employ of the Muscovy Company, the queen hastened to reply that the malefactors were no subjects of hers but Scotchmen. This unkind cut might suggest an apology for including the Scots in a study devoted to the English in Russia. However, their common heritage of language and culture is reason enough, and the Russians were not always so nice as Elizabeth in distinguishing between the two peoples of the island of Britain.

As a matter of fact there were many Scots in Russia in the latter half of the sixteenth century. Most of them had been soldiers in the Swedish army who were taken prisoners by the Russians. Nothing daunted they promptly took service in the Russian army and distinguished themselves in fighting against the Tatars and Poles. For the most part these Scottish soldiers of fortune settled in the country and married native women. Some of them bore the names of well-known families, such as Hamilton, Leslie, Gordon, and Bruce. Two sisters, descendants of a Hamilton among these early Scotch settlers, married into the famous families of Matveev and Narishkin. It was the pretty daughter of one of these marriages, Natalia Kirillovna Narishkina, who became the second wife of Tsar Aleksei Mikhailovich and thus the mother of Peter the Great. As a girl Natalia had been educated in the free manner of the Scots, so different from the half-Asiatic seclusion enforced upon the Russian women. And in her married life she leaned towards Western ideas, going about unveiled, riding in an open coach, and sponsoring the first theatrical performances in Moscow introduced by her royal husband. Peter dearly loved his mother and while she lived he submitted obediently, if sometimes reluctantly, to her wishes. There is, perhaps, some justification for the belief that her tincture of Western freedom and culture had more or less influence on her famous son.

Curiously enough another member of the Hamilton family, Mary Danilovna, became Peter's mistress while in the service of his wife, Catherine. She was condemned to death in 1719 for the crime of infanticide. Having refused her a pardon the tsar accompanied her to the scaffold. It is said that after she was beheaded he kissed the pale lips, threw down the head, crossed himself, and silently departed. Later, in 1735, a traveller to Russia writes of having seen the head preserved in a large crystal vessel in the Academy of St. Petersburg. "He [Peter] caused the head to be cupped and injected. The forehead is almost compleat; the face is the beautifullest my eyes ever beheld." [2]

The execution of Charles I also brought many of the exiled followers of the Stuarts into Russia to seek their fortunes. Tsar Aleksei was horrified at the downfall of the English king and welcomed these loyal Scots with open arms. Among them were Paul Menezius and Patrick Gordon. The former received much preferment and is said to have been the tutor of the young Peter for a time. Gordon, the younger son of a Catholic family, left his country after the overthrow of the Stuarts and travelled much on the Continent, fighting in several European armies. He came to Russia in 1661 and in campaigns against the Tatars and Turks gained rapid advancement in the Russian army. When Sophia attempted to oust Peter, Gordon threw in his lot with the tsar at the crucial moment, a service which Peter never forgot. Peter visited him often at his home in the German Suburb and the two became close companions. Though living in Russia, Gordon did not sever his connections with the West, for he was continually receiving from England books, maps, and scientific instruments. His knowledge of pyrotechnics especially fascinated the young ruler and Peter called upon him again and again to arrange elaborate displays of fireworks. The relationship between the two was that of master and pupil. Gordon's learning, seriousness, and honesty won for him an important place in the Suburb and in government circles. He served the tsar in various ways, helping to modernize the army, directing the siege of Azov, and offering advice on state affairs. When Peter was abroad Gordon protected his interests at home, successfully quelling the revolt of the Streltsi, which threatened the tsar's throne. At his death the grateful Peter stood weeping by his bedside, and he ordered a splendid funeral procession in memory of Gordon and his important services to the country.

Besides Patrick Gordon, among the Scots who stand out preëminently in Peter's great work of reform are Field Marshal George Ogilvy, Major-General James Bruce, and the physician Robert Erskine. Ogilvy distinguished himself in the tsar's Swedish wars and had a great deal to do with the introduction of German military methods into the Russian army.

A member of the Bruce family, Colonel William Bruce, had emigrated to Russia as early as 1650 and he and his descendants prospered exceedingly in the land of their adoption. His son, James Bruce, gained the reputation at Peter's court of being a chemist and astronomer of genius, although the natives of Moscow set him down for a sorcerer. His great powers of work recommended him to the energetic Peter. Though his career underwent many vicissitudes, he never lost the favor of his sovereign for long, playing a leading part in Peter's manifold activities. He helped to negotiate the highly successful Peace of Nystadt, which won for him the title of Count. He translated many foreign books into Russian and directed the tsar's schools of Navigation, Artillery, and Military Engineering. On the command of Peter he collected the codes of laws of other nations as a basis for legal reforms. In 1718 he was made a senator. Bruce's scientific work in astronomy savored much of astrology, but it served to gain him considerable renown. A whole legend grew up around the light which shone from the window of his lonely laboratory in the famous Sukharev tower. Brusovski Street in Moscow, where his house stood, was named after him.

But the services of the Bruce family did not end with James Bruce. Descendants of the original settler and other members of the clan from Scotland all filled positions of consequence under Peter and his successors.[3]

Dr. Robert Erskine was the first of the many Scottish physicians connected with the Russian court. Peter appointed him chief of the Ministry of Medical Affairs, and also used him in diplomatic services. He rose high in the favor of his sovereign, accompanying him on his travels through Europe. Erskine may be credited with establishing

a kind of precedent of Scottish physicians who stood close
to the Russian throne, having such notable successors as
John Rogerson, Matthew Halliday, Matthew Guthrie, and
Sir James Wylie in the reigns of Catherine II, Paul I, and
Alexander I. It was Sir James Wylie who, after the murder
of Paul I, so neatly cleared the troubled atmosphere by a
death certificate ascribing the emperor's violent end to
apoplexy. On the whole, the work of these Scotch physicians
in the development of Russian medicine was of the utmost
significance, and several of them were influential figures in
Russian foreign relations.

This by no means completes the beadroll of notable Scots
who formed part of the great army of foreigners that made
possible the far-reaching reforms of Peter's reign. And after
his death the procession of helpful Scots to Russia hardly
diminished. There was Admiral Thomas Gordon, a Jacobite
refugee, whom Peter, always on the watch for experienced
seamen, snapped up in Holland and placed in command of
a squadron in his growing navy. As a matter of fact, the
Russian navy owes much to Scots, such as Admirals Greig
and Elphinstone and many lesser officers, who under Catherine II raised the Russian fleet to a position of European
prominence. Then in the reigns of Anna and Elizabeth,
General James Keith rose to high honor in the wars. And
finally there was Prince Barclay de Tolly, descendant of a
Scottish family, who served Alexander I as Minister of War,
and to whom is credited the unique policy of retiring before
the French, which ultimately brought about Napoleon's
disaster in his Russian campaign.

Not only in the capacity of soldiers, sailors, doctors, and

diplomats did the Scots serve Russia, but many others of more humble origin worked as traders, artisans, and manufacturers. Perhaps it was out of regard for the number of Scots in his service that Peter contemplated the romantic scheme of reconciling the Jacobite Non-juring Episcopal Church of Scotland with the Orthodox Church of Russia. The project, of course, had no success, but it remains as a curious precursor of the attempted union of the Orthodox and Anglican churches in the nineteenth century.

The lot of the Scots, like that of most foreigners during Peter's reign, was not always a happy one. Their memoirs are filled with complaints of unjust treatment, the failure of the government to pay them their wages, and the frequent refusal to allow such valuable workers to leave the country. Nevertheless, the tsar esteemed these hard-working Scots and, as may be judged from the present account, they rendered him excellent service. Many of them married into the noblest families of the country, and long after Peter's death their descendants continued to play an important rôle in Russian affairs.

In 1689, at the age of seventeen, Peter entered Moscow as monarch, having relegated the ambitious Sophia to a convent. The old Russian elements regarded him with suspicion. His entourage was full of foreigners recruited from the German Suburb and his mind was clearly set upon innovation. The suspicion was fully warranted, for the young tsar soon astounded and horrified his subjects by his own personal actions and his reforms. After several years of ruling, however, he began to realize the inadequacy of his knowledge of foreign civilization. And when an embassy to certain

European courts was decided upon for the purpose of unit-
ing against the Turks, Peter seized the opportunity to
make his famous tour, which Macaulay describes as epoch-
making, not only in the history of Russia, but also in that
of the world. At Riga, Königsberg, Berlin, Zaandam, London, and other European cities Peter displayed an insatiable
curiosity about military organization, fortifications, state
institutions, technical inventions, science, manufacturing
processes, shipbuilding, dentistry, and medicine. Everything was of interest to him and his capacity for assimilating
a superficial knowledge, at least, of various trades, profes-
sions, and sciences amounted to nothing short of genius. His
naïve delight in the certificates of proficiency which his in-
dulgent teachers good-naturedly awarded him merely indicates his passionate desire to excel in those occupations
which stimulated his interest.

He met William III at The Hague and no doubt this English king of Dutch origin was somewhat flattered by Peter's
predilection for Holland. What Peter was really interested
in, however, was English shipbuilding. He had already imported English shipbuilders and their work pleased him
much more than that of the Dutch. He wished now to see
the English yards and to work in them. William extended
him a cordial invitation and on January 20, 1698, Peter arrived at Harwich and proceeded to London in the royal barge.

The tsar spent about three months in England and it is not
surprising that his visit created something of a sensation.
The London of the seventeenth century was not unaccus-
tomed to sights strange or barbaric, but the procession of the
plainly dressed tsar, six feet eight inches tall, followed by

his numerous retinue garbed in rich Oriental magnificence, apparently stirred the wonder of the Londoners. The Lord of Carmarthen, a famous wag and heroic drinker, was appointed to keep Peter amused during his stay. Historians have handed down entertaining accounts of the way in which Peter spent his time, a little highly colored perhaps in order to suit the traditional eccentric character of the tsar. We are told of the ravages he and his companions wrought in the houses provided for them; of Peter dressed as a workman, a pipe in his mouth, consuming huge potations of beer at the taverns; of his winning a large purse by matching one of his soldiers with an Englishman in a boxing bout; and of the classic reply to his English mistress, who resented the five hundred guineas he presented her as a parting gift: "What she gave me was not even worth so much as that."

But Peter did not neglect the serious purpose he had in coming to England. On the whole he snubbed the elegant society of London, exchanging visits only with the king. He sought out the places where he might satisfy his scientific interests, such as the Royal Society, the Observatory, and Greenwich Hospital. Likewise he witnessed Parliament in session and attended the theatre. The Society of Friends won his admiration and he visited one of the religious services, questioning the Quakers on their beliefs. William Penn wrote to him, and Burnet, Bishop of Salisbury, interrogated him on the possibility of a union of the churches. And always with an eye for raising money, he concluded a deal with Lord Carmarthen, selling him the monopoly of tobacco importation into Russia for twenty thousand pounds, meanwhile conveniently forgetting that his church still forbade the use of tobacco. The monopoly was subsequently the cause of diplomatic quarrels between the two countries.

Much of Peter's time was spent in serious work at the gun foundry of Woolwich and in the shipyards of Deptford. As at Zaandam he labored as an ordinary workman under the guidance of skilled instructors. He translated his love for the sea into a desire for a Russian navy, and any knowledge he could gain about ships he never failed to put to some practical use. The English taught him much in the matter of shipbuilding, and thereafter he was inclined to prefer their workmen and methods to those of Holland.

With a degree of Doctor of Laws from Oxford and the present of a yacht from King William, Peter left England, enthusiastic over what he had seen and learned. And he took back to Russia with him a large company of English gunners, artisans, doctors, men of science, and engineers who had agreed to enter his service.

In nearly all the countries he visited during his first journey abroad Peter hired scores of foreigners, most of them connected with the sea. Of the number he engaged in England, some sixty men in all, a few subsequently filled important positions in carrying out his building and educational schemes. One of these was a clever engineer by the name of John Perry, who was appointed by the tsar to direct the construction of canals and docks. Perry performed some notable engineering feats in Russia and has left an interesting account of his life and work there.

Another of the company, a Professor Farquharson (probably a Scot), was engaged by Peter to establish a School of

Navigation at Moscow. With the aid of two Englishmen he taught Russian youths arithmetic, geometry, trigonometry, geodesy, and astronomy. This seminary eventually provided teachers of mathematics for many of the provincial schools. In all matters pertaining to the sea, a subject dear to his own heart, Peter had the highest regard for English skill and knowledge. He requested and received from Queen Anne the privilege of placing Russian youths on English ships in order that they might learn seamanship. It may be that he carried his admiration too far, for the British government vigorously protested against his practise of persuading or impressing English sailors into the Russian navy. And when Queen Anne threatened to recall English shipwrights and carpenters in the tsar's employ, a serious diplomatic quarrel ensued.

Certain of the men whom Peter hired in England developed the manufacturing trades of Russia. Originally the buildings of the tsar's future capital, St. Petersburg, had to be glazed with glass procured in England. Now Peter had Englishmen build and direct a large factory at Moscow for the manufacture of glass. One of the principal manufacturing endeavors of the English, however, was the preparation of the raw tobacco which was shipped into the country after Lord Carmarthen had secured the monopoly. Here the English got into many difficulties, principally because of illegal shipments from the East which the Russian officials winked at.

It was in the time of Peter that Russia first seriously began to challenge the foreign trade of England and other nations that brought goods into the country. The tsar, ever eager to stock his own treasury with the vast sums needed for his many wars, turned merchant himself. He obtained monopolies of the most desirable products of his own country and sold them to the English and Dutch at a great profit. He also had his agents abroad buy up commodities in demand in Russia, thus seriously interfering with the business of the Muscovy Company. We find the English minister at Moscow, in a rather revelatory passage in his report, complaining that it will never do "to let the Czar and his subjects thus far into the mistery of trade, the sweets whereof will encourage them to more adventures and the increase of their navigation, which will prove no small damage to the english and others, who have hitherto enjoyed the benefit of their ignorance and all the northern commerce." [4]

While striving to bring the internal organization of Russia into line with European methods, Peter likewise sought to force his subjects to conform to the dress and manners of Western civilization. The characteristic Russian beard was abolished and an attempt was made to introduce European conviviality into the ordinary severity and almost Oriental exclusiveness of Russian upper-class social life. The tsar even commanded all nobles and those close to the court to dress in the English fashion. A coat of fine cloth, trimmed with silver and gold, according to the means of the individual, was to replace the long Russian kaftan. Models of the approved costume were hung on the gates of Moscow so that all might copy them, and penalties were decreed for failure to comply.

The women also, especially those connected with the court, were ordered to change their style of dress for the English.

They were now accorded the privilege of accompanying their husbands at court entertainments, but only if they were dressed in the new manner. According to some accounts the women were highly in favor of the change, and they quickly observed that the English styles made them more attractive to the men.

In the diplomatic relations between Russia and Europe during Peter's reign England occupied a significant place. While Russia was rapidly achieving the position of a world power, the nations of Western Europe looked on with deep distrust. By conquering the Baltic Provinces Peter·had at last realized the dream of Ivan the Terrible of opening up Russian ports which would give the country an easy access to the West. His alliances, diplomatic and by marriage, with European nations were all sought with the view of consolidating this position. England, naturally, looked askance at the utter defeat of Sweden in the Northern War and would have been more pleased if the Russian arms had not been quite so successful. However, she was willing to favor Peter, if for no other reason than to lessen the chance of a Russian alliance with France.

On his part Peter persistently sought the good will of England, and he was particularly eager that Queen Anne should act as a mediator between Russia and Sweden. His reign marks the beginning of a powerful English influence on Russian diplomacy. Previous to the eighteenth century the Russian diplomats sent to England had been men of insufficient training and with little interest in the structure of a government so radically different from their own. Peter's diplomats, on the other hand, such as Prince B. I. Kurakin, interested themselves in the organization of the English government. They studied appreciatively the British theory of national sovereignty, the organization of Parliament, the party system, and the nature of the cabinet. And their interest is reflected somewhat in Peter's administrative reforms. His diplomats began a long tradition of admiration for English political and judicial institutions, an admiration which often resulted in the advocacy of reforms based on English practise.

A fact that is often neglected in considering the work of Peter the Great is that he had no intention whatever of changing the fundamental nature of the governmental system he inherited. All his social and administrative reforms did not essentially alter the internal character of the autocratic Russian State. Only in the religious organization of the country did he make a decided break with the past. In this respect Peter may be correctly described as an extreme nationalist. All his reforms aimed simply at perfecting the existing order by infusing into it the dynamic spirit of Western efficiency and practicality. He merely poured the old wine into new bottles. The outward aspect of Russia bore a European cast, but the inner structure of the country remained virtually unchanged.

His cultural reforms clearly reflect this limitation. Veselovski compares the literary movement of Peter's reign to the situation in England at the time of the Restoration. That is, just as the return of Charles II marked the beginning of English literary subordination to France, so the accession of Peter witnessed a similar subserviency of Russia to the influence of European literature.[5] However, the relative cultural disparity between England and Russia at these periods, and the nature of Peter's own interests in literature, detract somewhat from the validity of this comparison.

To the end of his life Peter maintained the view that books were of great importance in his reforming efforts so long as they served a practical purpose, but he could not abide "mere tales that simply waste time." He could have more faith in a newspaper (he established the first Russian newspaper in 1703) than in most accepted types of literature as a medium for disseminating the kind of knowledge which he felt his subjects needed. For *belles lettres* he simply had no use, and this fact suggests very well the utilitarian type of culture which he favored. Under Peter a knowledge of the exact sciences received an honored place in Russia for the first time. With him and his associates the achievements of science were a never-failing subject of conversation, and all the original or translated literature in manuscript or book form concerned itself primarily with scientific works of a practical nature.

In the matter of establishing schools and insisting upon an elementary education at least, Peter accomplished more than any previous Russian sovereign. Not only in Moscow and St. Petersburg, but in nearly every provincial town both secular and religious schools were founded. Members of the nobility were now obliged to learn to read and to acquire some knowledge of mathematics or else they forfeited their right to marry and to advance in government employment. But for the most part the education he enforced aimed at producing navigators, engineers, technicians, artillerists, and diplomats, — that is, men fitted for war or civil service.

And it is worth noting that his most far-sighted attempt at promoting higher education, namely, the founding of an Academy of Science, which was actually established by Catherine I in the year of his death (1725), was inspired mainly by his desire to encourage the practical sciences.

Peter's utilitarian attitude towards culture, however, is by no means indefensible. To carry out his reforms he required men of practical knowledge. He also realized full well the widespread ignorance among the upper classes of society, to say nothing of the lower. Before poets and novelists and philosophers could be produced, some regular system of elementary education must be enforced. Of necessity, then, literature and the theatre stood on a lower level in his cultural scheme of things. He founded a theatre in which mystery plays, farces, and a few of Molière's dramas were staged, but at no time did the theatre thrive or encourage the growth of an original dramatic literature. Of the foreign books which he ordered to be translated we find only a few of any literary interest, such as *A History of the Destruction of Troy* and Ovid's *Metamorphoses*.

Though the literature of England, France, and Germany figured little in Peter's attempt to Europeanize Russia, it did not fail to interest many of the people he sent abroad. With much more success than attended Godunov's foreign educational scheme, Peter's students returned to the fatherland with something more than the technical knowledge for the sake of which they had been sent abroad. Western Europe was now definitely regarded by the Russian nobles, who were in sympathy with Peter's reforms, as a training school for all those who wished to acquire intellectual enlightenment and the more refined social graces. More than ever before, Russians began to evince a desire to travel, and the social necessity of the *grand tour*, which became so fashionable later, was already felt in Peter's time.

Comparatively speaking, however, there were few figures in Peter's reign who were so fully aware of the possibilities of a higher European culture as Ordyn-Nashchokin and Matveev in the time of Aleksei Mikhailovich. The most notable among these were Pososhkov and Tatishchev. The former, self-taught and devoted to his country and to Peter's reforms, pleaded in his works the great necessity of education for backward Russia, and in his economic studies he is credited with anticipating some of the ideas of Adam Smith. Tatishchev, like Pososhkov, was a man of great intellectual attainments. He travelled in Germany and Sweden and came in contact with the works of Machiavelli, Hobbes, Locke, and Bayle. The political and philosophical thought of these authors influenced his own historical studies. In his *Conversation concerning the Use of Books and Schools* he echoed his sovereign and even went beyond him in pointing out the crying need, not only of the nobles, but of all Russians, for education and culture.

On the whole, however, the age of Peter the Great was preëminently a period of preparation. Before Russia could absorb the finer features of European culture much elementary work had to be performed. The foundation was already in progress when Peter came to the throne. He simply accelerated it to an unbelievable speed, and by the time of his death (in 1725) Russia was nearly ready for the wholesale invasion of European literature and thought.

After this invasion a period of assimilation and imitation had to take place before Russian writers and thinkers finally ceased to be imitative and developed a culture of their own. In a sense the period of Peter's reign bears a striking analogy to the years immediately following the Bolshevik Revolution. Both periods felt the practical need of European scientific equipment, technical proficiency, and improved industrial methods to displace the old. The hiring of European technical experts on a large scale in Peter's reign is quite comparable to the procedure in Soviet Russia after the Revolution. Even Peter's habit of sending numerous students abroad to acquire a scientific education is a regular practise of the Soviet government. And presumably a new and independent Russian culture will be erected on this Soviet foundation, just as a Russian culture was built upon Peter's great reforms.

After Peter's death the expected reaction set in. His reforms had antagonized both the lower and the upper class, and once the tremendous personal power which had enforced the sweeping changes was removed, a tendency to slip back into the old ways soon manifested itself. Nevertheless, Russia's national isolation was definitely ended. Not only was the country now thoroughly aware of the advantages to be gained from its contact with Europe, but the nations of Western Europe had become vitally interested in Russia as the result of Peter's raising the country to a formidable position in world affairs. England, France, Austria, and Prussia now assiduously courted the new power, eager to interest Russia in their respective Continental policies. But in the period from Peter's death (1725) to the accession of Catherine

II (1762), events so shaped themselves that Germany and then France played the dominating rôle in the development of Russian politics and culture.

Although Peter had employed foreigners in nearly every capacity in effecting his reforms, it is a noticeable fact that the few favorites to whom he delegated any real power were, for the most part, Russians. And these, in exercising their power, never strayed far from the spirit and purpose of their sovereign. However, the rulers who immediately followed Peter, Catherine I (1725–27), Peter II (1727–30), Anna Ivanovna (1730–40), Elizabeth Petrovna (1741–61), and Peter III (1761–62), were nearly always controlled by favorites, and these were mostly foreigners. In his conquest of the Baltic Provinces of Esthonia and Livonia, Peter had acquired a part of Western Europe essentially Germanic in civilization, and the influence of Germans on the course of Russian history for the next twenty-five years was very significant. From the conquered provinces Russia obtained the services of a large number of German-trained statesmen, military officers, and teachers. The statesmen Ostermann, Münnich, and Biron in the reigns of Catherine I and Anna were Germans and the whole cast of court life became Germanic. Germans permeated the upper-class society and the powerful Guards regiments. German amusements and dress predominated at the court. Indeed, as Brückner puts it, Russian costumes appeared now only in masquerades. And German ideals and practise reigned supreme in the army and government.

In the diplomatic struggle that ensued among the nations of Western Europe to gain the influence and direct aid of

Russia, England gradually lost ground. She had great difficulty in protecting her powerful commercial interests and her
overland communications with Persia. Naturally, however,
when it became a question of France or England, the German favorites at the Russian court worked for the interests of
England. German domination did not come to an end until
the reign of Elizabeth (1741–61), who gained her throne largely
through the aid of the French ambassador and her French
physician and favorite, Lestocq. Her reign marks the real
beginning of French influence on Russia, which in the next
fifty years came very near to transforming the upper class into
Frenchmen and the court of St. Petersburg into a Versailles.

It may be judged from all this that Russia and Western
Europe had now grown very close together. To be sure,
there was never a time during the whole period of the favorites and later when there did not exist a strong nationalist
spirit which deplored and struggled against the all-pervading
foreign influence. But the wall between Russia and Europe
had been completely swept away and now there was no
stemming the tide.

In the period of transition from Catherine I to Catherine
II, a matter of thirty-five years, we can perceive the first
signs of a conscious literary development. Hitherto there
had been individuals with some pretensions to literary accomplishment, but they stand as isolated phenomena without any forebears or descendants. There was no continuity
and hence no conception of literary progression.

Apart from folk literature, no country ever develops a
sophisticated literature without first having recourse to
foreign models. Before Catherine I, foreign models, of course,

had existed in abundance, but Russia had not been prepared for the development of a literature of its own. Peter's practical kind of modernization had to take place first. Now the close relations between Western Europe and Russia and the increased practise of foreign travel revealed the higher cultural aspects of European life. The literature of France, Germany, and England began to be read and imitated.

The first writers in this period were men whose whole literary education was European and not Russian. Peter's Academy of Sciences, the universities established by Elizabeth at St. Petersburg and Moscow, and most of the newly formed preparatory and special schools in different parts of the empire, were staffed with foreign teachers and men of science, mostly German and French. And the foreign education begun in their own institutions was completed by these early writers in study abroad. Lomonosov, Kantemir, Tredyakovski, Sumarokov, and Volkov all travelled to the capitals of Europe to sit at the feet of renowned teachers and to associate with foreign literary masters.

In keeping with the fashion that prevailed at this time, French literature had the greatest influence on these early Russian authors, although German and the classics were by no means neglected. They were attracted by the brilliance of the French neo-classical school, unaware that this brilliance was fast fading, and they composed works in imitation of Molière, Corneille, Racine, Boileau, and later Voltaire and the Encyclopedists. The tradition they established was to dominate Russian letters for a long time.

There was a good deal of native originality, and certainly a wealth of versatility, in Lomonosov, but Tredyakovski and

Sumarokov were slavish followers of the French. Sumarokov wrote plays in imitation of the French and even assayed a neo-classical version of *Hamlet*. After the manner of Voltaire he regarded Shakspere as an inspired barbarian, — but more of that later. In his *Fifth Epistle* he lists Shakspere, Milton, and Pope among the great authors whom he would have his fellow-writers use as models, though there is no evidence that he himself was well acquainted with them.

Prince Antiokh Kantemir (1708–44), because of his residence in London as ambassador (1732–38), holds more interest for us. He belonged to that tradition, already mentioned, of Russian diplomats who were profoundly influenced by England, even to the extent of becoming forthright Anglophiles, as in the case of the Vorontsov brothers. Kantemir was very well educated and his inclinations tended much more to literature and science than to diplomacy. Essentially a monarchist, it was difficult for him to understand English political institutions. Thus when he protested on behalf of his government against an English pamphlet containing material offensive to Russia, he was told that freedom of the press was a fundamental British privilege. He could not avoid contrasting this attitude with the strict censorship in his own country.[6] Kantemir pursued his studies in England and associated somewhat with the political and literary circles of London. He was a great admirer of the works of Locke, and his ideas concerning education, which he introduced into his *Seventh Satire*, are borrowed directly from Locke's *Some Thoughts Concerning Education*.[7]

Kantemir's literary inspiration, however, was more directly French, and he lived in Paris for some time and was acquainted with the principal French literary figures of the age. Indeed, his *Satires* enjoyed the distinction, unusual in the case of Russian literary works of this period, of being translated into French. Yet it is perhaps of interest to note that one of his French contemporaries stresses his devotion to England rather than to France: "Il est plus à regretter pour la douceur de son caractère et les qualités de l'esprit que par rapport à son amitié pour nous, car *il étoit plus Anglois* que s'il fût né à Londres."[8] Certainly Kantemir's interest in things English continued to the end of his life. We hear of his writing to a friend in London to send him the productions of certain English authors, one of them being a collection of Swift's works.

This uncertain and rather predatory literary development towards the end of the period of transition was to blossom out in the reign of Catherine the Great into the first important era of Russian literature. The tendency then, to be sure, was hardly less imitative than in the early period. But the horizon was infinitely enlarged after the accession of Catherine, the production much greater, and the zeal for the creation of a purely national literature resulted finally in original works. French and German influence continued to play the largest part in the development of Russian literature in the Age of Catherine, but the instances of English influence were highly significant.

BIBLIOGRAPHY

SOURCES

Journal de Pierre le Grand, ed. M. Shcherbatov, Berlin, 1773.

A. Bolotov, *Zapiski, 1738–1794,* St. Petersburg, 1871–73, 4 vols. (See vol. I, 1738–60.)

Diplomaticheskaya perepiska angliskikh poslov i poslannikov pri russkom dvore, c 1704–1708 (Sbornik imperatorskago russkago istoricheskago obshchestva, 1884, XXXIX).

Pisma i bumagi imperatora Petra Velikago, St. Petersburg, 1887–1912, 7 vols.

Pavlov-Silvanski, *Proekty reform v zapiskakh sovremennikov Petra Velikago,* St. Petersburg, 1897.

Russki byt po vospominaniyam sovremennikov, XVIII vek (ot Petra do Ekateriny II, 1698–1761) sostavlenny P. E. Melgunovoi, K. V. Sivkovym, i N. P. Sidorovym, Moskva, 1914.

INVESTIGATIONS

Peter the Great and the Period of the Favorites

I. Sokolovski, *Petr Veliki kak vospitatel i uchitel naroda,* Kazan, 1873.

E. Schuyler, *Peter the Great,* New York, 1884, 2 vols.

A. Brückner, *Geschichte Russlands bis zum Ende des 18-ten Jahrhunderts,* Gotha, 1896, 2 vols. (See I, 535–638.)

K. Waliszewski, *Peter the Great,* New York, 1898.
L'Héritage de Pierre le Grand; règne des femmes, Paris, 1900.

M. Bogoslovski, *Oblastnaya reforma Petra Velikago* (Izdanie imperatorskago obshchestva istorii i drevnostei rossiskikh pri Moskovskom Universitete, Moskva, 1902).
Petr Veliki i ego reforma, Moskva, 1920.

S. Platonov, *Petr Veliki,* Leningrad, 1926.

The Scots in Russia

J. Perry, *State of Russia under the present czar,* London, 1716.

Memoirs of Peter Henry Bruce, London, 1782.

A. Brückner, *Alexander Patrick Gordon; ein Beitrag zur Geschichte Russlands im 17 Jahrhunderts,* Leipzig, 1879.

A. F. Steuart, *Scottish Influence in Russian History*, Glasgow, 1913. *Literature and Culture in the Period of Peter and the Favorites.*

Sochineniya pisma i izbrannye perevody Knyazya Antiokha Dmitrevicha Kantemira, red. P. A. Efremova, St. Petersburg, 1862.

A. Brückner, *Iwan Possoschkow: Ideen und Zustände in Russland zur Zeit Peters des Grossen*, Leipzig, 1878.

L. Maikov, *Ocherki iz istorii russkoi literatury XVII i XVIII stoletii*, St. Petersburg, 1889.

Arkhiv Kurakina, red. M. I. Semevskago, St. Petersburg, 1890–1902 (See I, 145; II, 261, 346–347; III, 294; IV, 35–36, 261, 278–279.)

A. Veselovski, *Zapadnoe vliyanie v novoi russkoi literature*, Moskva, 1896. (Fifth ed., 1916.) (See pp. 33–55.)

V. N. Aleksandrenko, *Russkie diplomaticheskie agenty v Londone v XVIII. v.*, Varshava, 1897, 2 vols. (See I, 376–395.)

P. Miliukov, *Ocherki po istorii russkoi kultury*, St. Petersburg, 1909–13, 3 Parts. (See Part III, 94–277.)

G. Alexinsky, *Russia and Europe*, London, 1917.

CHAPTER IV

ANGLOMANIA DURING THE REIGN OF CATHERINE II
(1762–1796)

THE comparatively unknown, sixteen-year-old German princess, Sophia Augusta of Anhalt-Zerbst, who married the future Peter III in 1745, was destined to complete the cultural work which Peter the Great had so vigorously begun. In a sense her historical position as Catherine II was paradoxical. Although a foreigner by birth and training, she sought to be more Russian than the Russians in order to protect her position on the throne. But the political and social reforms which she effected, and the cultural advancement which she furthered throughout her long reign were inspired by foreign example and foreign education.

However, there was a vast difference between the accomplishments of Peter the Great and those of Catherine the Great — a difference in kind and spirit which was accentuated by their utterly dissimilar natures and conceptions of sovereignty. Peter never tolerated an independent social criticism. The thoughts as well as the acts of his subjects were dictated by their emperor. Catherine not only encouraged the development of critical thought, but, until the French Revolution, she even tolerated a brand of popular opinion which deviated considerably from the customary notions of Russian autocracy. Peter, it has been said, created bodies for the Russians, and Catherine placed souls in them. Under Catherine, certainly, the country became for the first time intellectually conscious, and though her reign is notable for its achievements in war and for social reforms, its chief glory lies in the fact that culturally it marks the beginning of modern Russia.

French influence, which had begun in a formidable way in the time of Elizabeth, reached its height in the reign of Catherine. Artisans, lackeys, cooks, merchants, teachers, actors, artists, savants, and adventurers swarmed into the country from France. French architecture and furniture, French dress and manners, and French etiquette in eating and drinking prevailed among the nobility, and even in the provinces country gentlemen imitated French courtly graces. The business of learning French was entered into with enthusiasm and the French tutor became a fixture in most well-to-do families. In some circles the language came to be better known than the native speech. The French exploited their employers, a fact which the Russians did not seem to resent very much, but if they despised them they were careful not to show it. There are amusing tales of the Finn who for years taught his own language for French; and of the tutor, who, when asked about the "moods" of French verbs, blandly admitted that he knew them badly for he had been away from Paris a long time, and then, he explained, the "modes" there change very frequently. On the whole, however, the French got along with the Russians uncommonly well.

Paris now became the goal of all Russians who travelled for culture. They readily acquired a veneer of French *politesse*, and on their return they often associated with precious groups of Frenchified Russians who felt that what was *comme il faut* in Paris must be imitated at once in St. Petersburg and Moscow.

A Russian upper class, however, garbed in the dress and loose ornament of French civilization would have been a mere passing phase in a swiftly changing social development. But all this was only the outward aspect of a more significant internal revolution effected by the importation of French thought and culture. Much of the liberalism, humanitarianism, and critical attitude towards government, religion, and law which took root in eighteenth-century Russia was the result of French influence. Voltaire, Montesquieu, Diderot, and Rousseau were quickly accepted. Their works were translated, discussed, and lectured upon in the universities, and Voltaire especially gained such a following by his free-thinking and his attacks on religion and social institutions that his works were ultimately forbidden.

In the realm of *belles lettres* and literary criticism France again predominated. The young Russian theatre, pushing forward now in its first sturdy growth, was immeasurably indebted to the works of Corneille, Racine, and Molière. And as in the previous generation of Lomonosov, Tredyakovski, and Sumarokov, Russian poetry and criticism continued to be guided by the precepts of Boileau's *L'Art Poétique*. Even the light reading-matter of this time was largely supplied by France in the form of the *romans d'aventure*. Indeed, one critic estimates that three-fourths of the books read in Russia during the reign of Catherine were French. In view of such facts it is natural to conclude that if Russia now succeeded in making herself known to the intellectual consciousness of

Europe, then French culture was the chief influence in this intellectual awakening.

The reasons for this powerful influence do not require the elaborate explanations and apologies which we sometimes find in investigations of the subject. The Russians did not deliberately single out France for imitation because of her superior civilization. And there is a certain naïveté in attributing the influence to a supposed similarity in temperament between the two peoples, or to the *bon esprit* of the French and their ability to adapt themselves in foreign countries. The simple fact is that in the latter half of the seventeenth century French culture dominated the Western World, and the tremendous prestige of the Age of the *Grand Monarque* carried over into the reign of Louis XV. All the courts of Europe took the glittering Versailles for their model. Sophisticated society everywhere strove to imitate the manner and dress of the Parisians, and French thought, art, and literature permeated European culture to a remarkable degree. Hence it was only natural that eighteenth-century Russia, just emerging from a state of existence bordering on the primitive, should feel this influence, even though by this time its real force and effectiveness had been spent.

The reaction that followed was as profound as the subserviency had been all-pervading. England in the latter half of the seventeenth century and first years of the eighteenth did not rebel more indignantly against French domination in manners and culture than Russia in the Age of Catherine. The French were now blamed for corrupting Russian morals. Cheating at cards, affected gallantry, and dissolute living were charged to pernicious French influence. In the satirical journals of the time, especially those edited by Novikov,[1] a well-defined Gallophobia is the shaping spirit behind numerous articles attacking French abuses and Frenchified Russian coxcombs.[2] The drama likewise performed its part in ridiculing excessive admiration for everything French. In much the same fashion as Restoration comedies poked fun at English fops who affected a love for France, Russian satirical plays pilloried youths who returned from Paris swaggering their contempt for their countrymen. In the *Queer Fellows* of Knyazhnin (1742–93) one of the characters remarks: "I hold our language for a real jargon. When necessary I speak in this tongue with lackeys and coachmen, with all common people where one does not have to think." [3] And Firulina, in another play by the same author, is surprised that the people in her country-seat do not talk French. "Our village," she complains, "is so near the capital and yet nobody here knows French, but in France, even a hundred versts from the capital, everybody speaks French." [4] In Fonvizin's (1744–92) famous comedy, *The Brigadier*, native satire against the French invasion of Russian social life was immortalized in the notable characterization of Ivanushka, who, in default of his body, hoped that his soul might be French. Like Monsieur de Paris in Wycherley's *Gentleman Dancing-Master*, Ivanushka affects an exaggerated French *politesse*, an admiration for everything Parisian, and a fancy for interlarding his speech with French words and phrases. His classical description of the Frenchified Russian hits off the type for all time: "Everyone who has been in Paris already has the right, in speaking about Russians, not to include himself in their number, for he has already become more French than Russian." [5]

A more serious aspect of the reaction was the protest against the undermining influence of French liberal thought on Russian political and religious institutions. Montesquieu, Voltaire, and the Encyclopedists provided a far-reaching stimulation to incipient Russian liberalism, but the Revolution, the drastic dénouement of their thinking, was an extreme which the autocratically-minded Catherine could not sympathize with. Although she advocated and carried out enlightened reforms of her own, she was wary of any doctrine that struck at her absolute power. Besides, the bloody Pugachev revolt had filled her with a horror of rebellion. Accordingly, French liberalism was interdicted and its adherents were forced into underground activities. When time had somewhat mitigated the executions and devastation of the Revolution, France was once again regarded with favor, and the host of émigrés who poured into the country had a marked effect on Russian life and culture. France reached its second peak of popularity in the reign of Alexander I. In the first part of *War and Peace* Tolstoi gives us a brilliant picture of French success in the Russian capital during this period. Even Napoleon became something of a hero among the intelligentsia and the nobility, and Alexander himself admired the French emperor. But the march on Moscow ended all this, and it was many years before the Russians recovered from their hatred of France.

Probably as a reaction to the Gallomania, but by no means entirely so, many intellectual Russians in the second half of the eighteenth century turned to England and Germany for inspiration and models. In a cultural way the German influence was very pronounced and continued with increasing emphasis into the next century. German universities became the favorite haunts of Russian students abroad, and the *Sturm und Drang* movement and Hegel's philosophy exercised a powerful influence on much of the Russian literature and thought of the period.

It was England, however, that disputed with France for the premier position in the esteem of Russian society in Catherine's reign. Something that may be termed an Anglomania existed, although its circumference was less wide and its penetration less deep than the prevailing Gallomania. The admission must be made at once that Russia, in most essentials, was simply following a fashion that had taken root in France and Germany in the early years of the eighteenth century. Like the untaught child of civilization that she was at this time, Russia was almost bound to follow any cultural tendencies strongly advocated by her two closest and more advanced neighbors. And with no little irony the French craze "to do and think as the English" now communicated itself to the Russians, and in a large measure helped to undermine the Russian Gallomania. This French devotion to England requires no demonstration here. Scholars have long ago investigated every aspect of it.[6] However, it will be to our purpose to indicate the particular French writers who popularized English literature and culture in France, and who in turn were mainly instrumental in furthering Anglomania in Russia.

Previous to the Revocation of the Edict of Nantes in 1685, France had had practically no cultural contacts with England. In fact the French were inclined to regard their neighbors across the channel as barbarians, fiends, and parricides.

They never quite forgave the execution of Charles I, and in religion, politics, and literature England was held by cultivated Frenchmen to be beyond the pale of serious consideration. Very few Frenchmen visited England in the seventeenth century, and the language was little known or set down as a barbarous jargon.

After Louis XIV's historic Revocation, however, the whole situation changed. Thousands of French refugees fled to England, where they found political and religious security. Although they made their home in England, they did not sever their connection with the fatherland, and for over half a century the refugees, through numerous publications and visits to the Continent, were a means of disseminating a knowledge of English life, thought, and culture in France.

There now grew up in France an extraordinary admiration for everything English, which was to last for over sixty years. Throughout this whole period England herself was engaged in activities that served to increase her fame. The comparatively peaceful revolution of 1688, which had placed William and Mary on the throne, had impressed Europe. And the Continental successes of Marlborough, coupled with the long era of prosperity that followed, gradually won for England the prestige that had belonged to France. The latter country, meanwhile, was swiftly falling into the abyss of revolutionary turmoil. The English representative system of government and her judiciary, which appeared to insure the equality of all subjects before the law, gained a high reputation among the nations of Europe. Here was liberalism, but, paradoxically, a conservative kind of liberalism that made for law and order. And England's rapid educational development and achieve-

ments in science, philosophy, and literature in the last half of
the eighteenth century only served to enhance her growing
popularity.

French men of letters, — such as Prévost, Voltaire, Montesquieu, Rousseau, Diderot, and many other Anglophiles, —
sang the praises of England in numerous works. From Bacon
and Newton they learned science, from Pope deistic philosophy, and Voltaire, Rousseau, and Diderot popularized English literature. Shakspere, Milton, Pope, Addison, Young,
Thomson, and the English eighteenth-century novelists were
eagerly read and in many cases imitated in France. With no
exaggeration Gibbon could write in 1763: "Our opinions, our
fashions, even our games were adopted in France; a ray of national glory illuminated each individual, and every Englishman was supposed to be born a patriot and a philosopher." [7]
And from France Germany likewise caught the spirit of devotion to English culture.

The French and German admiration for England was slow
in penetrating Russia. We do not begin to discern its effects
until late in the latter half of the eighteenth century. The
French writers already mentioned were the first purveyors of
Anglomania. Prévost's novel, *Mémoires d'un homme de
qualité*, written during his residence in England, was translated into Russian. The story is entirely English, and nothing
could have been better calculated as an appreciative introduction to a foreign country. It is literally a guide book to
England, explaining in detail the life, customs, institutions,
and culture. The success of the book in Russia was considerable and it must have provided the readers of romances with
an altogether attractive picture of a land which they knew

little about. *Cléveland*, another novel of Prévost's, which is simply an exaltation of British virtue, was likewise translated into Russian and served the same end as the *Mémoires d'un homme de qualité* in furthering a good opinion of England. Even of greater significance, perhaps, was Prévost's *Le pour et contre* (1733–40), a magazine that naturalized the taste for English literature in France. And among the French-reading Russians it unquestionably performed a similar service in that country.

Literary historians have noted that no French writer was more widely read in Russia than Voltaire, and one of his most popular works, *Lettres philosophiques* or *anglaises*, provided the Russians with a fund of information concerning the philosophy, politics, and literature of England, all enthusiastically described and held up as models worthy of imitation. And throughout various productions of Montesquieu, Rousseau, and Diderot were scattered appreciative commentaries on English life and culture. Indeed, it is a curious fact that their Russian adherents, because of the radical tendencies of these great writers, were already beginning to shift their allegiance to the English thought and institutions which the Frenchmen praised.[8]   Finally, of prime importance in bringing about a knowledge of English culture in Russia were the numerous French and German translations of English books in the fields of *belles lettres*, political science, and philosophy. It must be remembered that as yet English was little known in Russia, whereas a knowledge of French, and to some extent of German, was very common. Hence it was mainly through these French and German translations that Russia first came into direct contact with English literature and thought. Furthermore, Russian translations of English works in the eighteenth century were, with few exceptions, made from French and German renderings.

The drift towards England was noted as early as 1772 in the pages of *The Painter*, a satirical journal. "The English have replaced the French," writes the author of this article. "Women and men nowadays strive to imitate everything English; and everything English seems to us fine and charming and attracts all of us." [9] But it must not be thought that the growing Anglomania drew its inspiration entirely from French and German sources. The English were numerous in St. Petersburg and Moscow and their industry, manner of living, and traditional virtues were much admired. These English were mostly of the merchant class and possessed their own houses, clubs, and parks. The eighteenth century in Russia was a time of considerable economic change, including the spread of free trade, and in these endeavors the English merchants led the way. Commercial contacts with Russia had been little interrupted since the time of Ivan the Terrible, and in the reign of Catherine England had this field pretty much to herself. English merchants not only shipped many of their own products into Russia, but they virtually took charge of Russian export trade, furnishing the ships and most of the capital.[10]

English houses, furniture, gardens, carriages, livery, and dancing now came into vogue, and we find the fashion journals praising the simplicity of the newly adopted English styles as superior to the ostentatious French dress.[11] To some extent, it would seem, the English were even able to usurp the preferred position of the French as tutors in Russian families.

At least, an Englishman, travelling through the country at the end of the century, remarks: "English taylors, and servants out of livery, and travelling valets frequently become the preceptors and governors of children. A fellow of this description said one day: 'In summer I be clerk to a butcher at Cronstadt, and in winter I teaches English to the Russian nobility's children.'" [12]

Russians travelling in England sent home to the journals enthusiastic accounts of English life. "I liked England more than any other country," writes one of these tourists. "Their government, education, manners, their public and private life, their machinery, buildings, and gardens, — all these are of the first order and far surpass the accomplishments of other people in similar undertakings. Likewise, the love of the Englishman for the Russian is naturally attractive to me." [13] It is also noticeable that the journals of the second half of the eighteenth century begin to display a strong interest in British politics, and much space is devoted to chronicling contemporary English history and to discussing the home and foreign policies of the government.[14] As a matter of fact, it was not long before satire, always an indication of excessive influence, was being employed to ridicule the Russian eagerness to imitate English styles and manners.[15]

In the practical affairs of life the English influence was of a more important and decisive nature than the French. Russia in the reign of Catherine began to concern itself with the still primitive methods of agriculture and industry, which had received little attention since the time of Peter the Great. England was admittedly the pioneer in developing improved methods in these fields, and it was to England that Russia now turned for practical advice and modern apparatus. The editor of the first Russian journal on economics writes in his introduction: "Concerning England, one should remember what everyone knows, — namely, in what manner this wise people, before all others, began to think about this useful business [i. e. agriculture]. It is well known what a great sum of money they put into agriculture from the beginning of the present century." [16] And the scientific and economic journals of the period contain many original and translated articles on English industrial and agricultural methods and discoveries.[17] Very much as we Americans were inclined to regard German manufactured goods before the World War as exceptional in quality, so the eighteenth-century Russian accepted the English stamp on scientific equipment and manufactured utensils as a guarantee of superior excellence. Russians who built their houses, laid out their gardens, worked their crops, and bred their cattle in the "English fashion" were considered very much abreast of the times. One can well imagine that Pushkin was not exaggerating when he described Muromski in his tale as an Anglomaniac who planted an English garden, had his groom wear English livery, hired a governess to give his daughter English lessons, and farmed his land on the English system.[18]

In this movement away from France towards England it is a fact worth noting that Catherine herself was one of the leaders. Born a German and a Lutheran, tutored in French literature, and an orthodox Russian by adoption, she was a truly cosmopolitan ruler. For Germany she cared little, but she had much reason to admire France. Her French governess inspired in her a love for Corneille, Racine, and Molière, and while still a Grand Duchess she occupied herself with Montesquieu and Voltaire, whose works had some influence on her thought and reforms when she became empress. Although Catherine sincerely endeavored to assimilate the spirit and character of a Russian, she remained at heart a Westerner. Her temperament seemed more Gallic than German or Russian. She fancied the French literary idols of the day, and her correspondence (in French) with Voltaire, Grimm, Diderot, D'Alembert, and others, which is distinctly her best contribution to literature, combined something of the intellectual clarity of Mme. de Sévigné with the wit of Mme. de Staël.

However, Catherine was intent on fulfilling her mission as the Semiramis of the North, and France and French liberal thought were not always congenial to her political schemes and her despotic conception of sovereignty. She made it clear that it was the "old France" which she admired and not the revolutionary-minded country of her own day. The politics of the Bourbons and the debauchery of Paris she detested, and the prestige of Versailles she envied. Catherine could coquette with French liberalism, since she desired to appear before the world as an enlightened ruler, but she wanted no more of it, as she indicated in her famous conversations with Diderot, than would enhance her intellectual reputation without endangering the absolutist principles of Russian autocracy. Essentially she had the same fear of France that characterized Peter the Great, and in keeping with the wave of Gallophobia, she lent her pen to satirizing French influence on Russian life. It is perhaps correct to say that Catherine had a high regard for certain great French thinkers and writers, but France as a nation she distrusted; and after the French Revolution her distrust turned into positive dislike.

"Moi," Catherine wrote to Grimm, "j'aime naturellement les Anglais." [19] And there is nothing in her words or actions that would make one doubt the sincerity of this statement. The sentiment was not simply a reaction to excessive French influence. Her devotion dates from the period before her reign, for English interests through the scheming of the ambassador to Russia, Sir Charles Hanbury-Williams, sometimes thought to have been in love with Catherine, helped to obtain the throne for her. Catherine's rule clearly marks the rise of English prestige over that of France, which had been current in Elizabeth's time. Austria and Prussia, to be sure, also enjoyed periods of high favor. England still continued to play the leading rôle in commercial relations with Russia, and even though Catherine grew extraordinarily crafty in the matter of foreign politics, the diplomatic correspondence between the two countries furnishes ample evidence of her warm regard for England. In the reports of the English ambassadors we find frequent statements of the following kind: "Russia to my predecessors, as their correspondence shows, appeared under French influence from inclination, custom, and education. Russia is now, by the Empress's firm, determined and declared opinions, and will be more so by all her institutions, *decidedly* English." [20] Whenever she approved of anything it was a common expression with her to say that "it was thought, said, or done like an Englishman." [21] After she witnessed a theatrical performance put on by some English actors from Copenhagen, she rewarded the manager of the company with a thousand roubles, remarking that she "thought herself at home amongst English people." [22] Even when the customary duplicity of foreign relations made her true feelings the subject of doubt, she warmly protested to the English representative: "Permettez-moi d'observer que la nation que j'aime le plus et de qui je croyais être le plus aimée, a été la dernière à avoir cette complaisance pour moi. . . . Je suis amie de l'Angleterre d'inclination ainsi que d'intérêt." [23]

England provided Catherine with invaluable naval assistance in her war with the Turks, and in return she contemplated furnishing twenty thousand of her troops for service against the rebellious American colonies. However, nothing came of this idea. An interesting repercussion of England's colonial difficulties was Catherine's hiring John Paul Jones to fight her naval battles against the Turks. But some personal scandal, combined with the vigorous protests of the British officers in her fleet, quickly brought Jones's tenure of service to a close.

In the field of medicine Catherine shared the traditional Russian esteem for British doctors. Her personal physician, John Rogerson (a Scot),[24] succeeded so well in gaining the empress's confidence that he became a highly important figure in court circles. Once when he departed for England on a vacation the French ambassador, Count de Ségur, notes with relief: "Comme il se mêle aussi souvent de politique que de médicine, et que c'est par lui qu'on prétend que se font les offres d'argent, je ne puis qu'être fort aise de son absence." [25] Dr. Thomas Dymsdale also won a high place in Catherine's favor, for it was he who performed the great service of introducing inoculation for smallpox into Russia. The empress allowed herself and the Grand Duke to be inoculated by Dymsdale in order to encourage the treatment among her suspicious subjects.[26]

Catherine was something of a pioneer in Russian enthusiasm for English governmental, legal, and educational institutions, an enthusiasm which was a part of the Anglomania in France and Germany.   Montesquieu's extraordinary panegyric on England in his *L'esprit des lois* [27] is an open avowal of his indebtedness to that country for many of his theories on government and legislation.   And Catherine in her famous *Mandate* (*Nakaz*) of 1767, which embodied the most advanced and humane ideas of her day on problems of legislation, leaned heavily on *L'esprit des lois*.   She could approve of Montesquieu because he advocated a monarchical system of government, yet a liberal and beneficent monarchy much after the fashion of the English.   And Diderot, another Anglophile, in his conversations with Catherine, advised the empress to model her government on the English.

On first consideration it might not appear that there was anything in common between the problems of English and Russian legislative procedure in the eighteenth century.   But in Blackstone's *Commentaries on the Laws of England* Catherine discovered problems identical with her own, and the result was that many of the most significant reforms incorporated in her *Institutions for the Administration of the Provinces* (1775) were profoundly influenced by the Englishman's work. When she came to the throne Catherine was faced with something like chaos in the organization and the administration of the law in the provinces.   The law-enforcing rôle of the British gentry as described by Blackstone suggested to Catherine the possibility of a similar structure in the Russian provinces. Her difficulty was concerned with the separation of power in which the various governments (*gubernias*) and districts (*uiezds*) should be made to assume the function of local administration directly responsible, as in England, to their own courts and governing bodies, and indirectly to the Crown. In the reorganization of the courts, and especially in the establishment of a Court of Equity, the first of its kind in Russia, Catherine learned a great deal from the *Commentaries*; and Blackstone's treatment of *habeas corpus* was also influential. Indeed, the whole legal ideology of the *Commentaries*, one of its less dubious contributions apart from the genuine literary merit of the work, produced a powerful impression on Catherine. Blackstone's plea that the law should be more humane and its punishments in special cases softened was the guiding spirit in the legal reforms of Catherine's *Institutions*. The great interest which she took in reading Blackstone is emphatically stated to Grimm: "Oh, ses commentaires et moi, nous sommes inséparables; c'est un fournisseur de choses et d'idée inépuisable." [28] It was a French translation of the *Commentaries* that Catherine read, but by her own command the work was finally rendered into Russian (1780–82). Nor did its influence cease with Catherine's interest. The rather impious suggestion of Radishchev's seminarist that "it would not be unsuitable to compel our courts to possess this book instead of the *Calendar of Saints*, and to oblige them to consult it more often than the *Calendar*," [29] achieved some measure of fulfillment in later reforms in the Russian judicial system.

In the matter of education Catherine, again, was inclined

to favor English methods, though it would appear that she did not have a very clear notion of them. It was primarily through Locke that Russia first became acquainted with English theories of education. As early as the reign of Peter the Great the historian Tatishchev had come in contact with the philosophical works of Locke, and Kantemir had been considerably influenced by his treatise, *Some Thoughts Concerning Education*.[30] This important work was first translated into Russian in 1760 and a second edition appeared in 1788. The popularity of the tract may be gauged by its frequent mention in the periodicals, and in the *General Plan* of the Moscow House of Education Locke's ideas are given a prominent place. Betski, one of the leading educational theorists of the Age of Catherine, was likewise indebted to Locke for part of his programme.

This general acceptance of *Some Thoughts Concerning Education* in Russia is no doubt a reflection of its success in England and on the Continent. It quickly won the position of a minor classic, and it may be remembered that even the discriminating Richardson introduced it into *Pamela* as a suitable present for a young mother. Five editions were printed in France within fifty years, and translations also appeared in Italy and Germany. In conjunction with Locke's *Essay Concerning Human Understanding* it strongly influenced the educational theories of Rousseau, Helvétius, and Basedow.

Locke's rational and primarily utilitarian approach to the purpose of education would have recommended him to Catherine. Like her future ambassador to England, Count S. Vorontsov, Catherine had little sympathy with the French type of education. Vorontsov was a partisan of the new specializing tendency in English schools which aimed to fit men for life rather than for the university. He protested against the encyclopedic education in France because it taught men to write and declaim verses but ignored the formation of character.[31] Indeed, Locke's prescription of the "manual arts" which he desired in a gentleman — gardening, woodwork, metalwork, varnishing, polishing lenses, and cutting precious stones — was a far cry from the customary accomplishments in Greek and Latin. But Catherine herself held few briefs for the classical type of education and the learn-by-rote methods of the pedagogues associated with this system. The new schools, she felt, must do something more than instruct; they must build character and relate their teaching to the practical problems of life. And in her instructions to Saltykov concerning the education of her grandchildren, Catherine borrowed whole pages out of Locke. The future Tsar Alexander I was brought up on the "English Plan," and for the empress this signified fresh air, liberal ideas, and instruction in practical as well as purely cultural subjects. The results of such training are clearly evident in Alexander's enlightened rule.

Although Catherine was unable to read English, the literature of England, through French and German translations, did not fail to come within the wide horizon of her intellectual interests. And as in the case of her legal and educational reforms, England again contributed in a marked degree to her literary accomplishments. In the development of the satirical journal and the drama, in both of which she played a prominent part, Catherine was influenced in form and content by English literature. But a discussion of this phase of her indebtedness must be left for later chapters.

The growing practise of sending students abroad to finish their studies had considerable bearing on the spread of new educational ideas in Russia. As already mentioned, the German universities were favored, and the liberal thinking taught at Heidelberg, Göttingen, and Leipzig was soon put to work when these students returned to their native land. Contemporary English liberalism, and especially English literature, had found their way into German instruction, and not a few of the Russian students of the time, notably Radishchev, owed their introduction to English culture to their studies in Germany.

The English universities, however, were not entirely neglected. The clever Princess Dashkova, who was so close to the empress, remained a long time in England and Scotland and was sufficiently impressed by this foreign culture to send her son to the University of Edinburgh. A number of Russian youths studied in Scotland, apparently because living was cheaper there. The most gifted of these was the seminarist Desnitski, who finished his education at Glasgow and returned to a professorship at Moscow University. He became thoroughly saturated with British ideas and soon began to advocate reforms that even went beyond those treated by Catherine in her *Mandate* and *Instructions*. England with its political institutions, its system of laws, and its freedom of thought was the model for Desnitski's projected reforms. What particularly impressed him in England was the broad spirit of self-development and the emphasis on individual liberty, national qualities which he tried to inculcate in his countrymen. Sometimes called the "Father of Russian Jurisprudence," Desnitski was the translator of Blackstone's *Com-*

mentaries, and he was also a pioneer in championing the freer position of women in Russian society.

Oxford and Cambridge were also patronized by Russian students in the reign of Catherine. In 1765 ten seminarists were sent to these institutions of learning in order to fit them for professorships on the staff of the theological faculty of Moscow University. Their visit lasted from seven to nine years, and, unlike Godunov's ungrateful students, they returned to Russia and occupied positions in society which did credit to their foreign training.

We find in the records between 1774 and 1786 a group of Russian students who made their way to English and Scottish universities more or less on their own initiative. Their favorite subjects were mathematics, law, medicine, history, and theology, and a few did special work in agriculture. By all accounts they were most zealous in the pursuit of knowledge, but we hear little of the use they made of their foreign education after they returned to Russia. The most noteworthy among them was Count N. Mordvinov, the future adviser of Alexander I, who studied in England for three years (1774-77). He was particularly interested in the sciences and the development of British political institutions. Like S. Vorontsov, Mordvinov was an enthusiastic admirer of *The Wealth of Nations* and of other English philosophical, scientific, and economic works. Many years after he had left England we find him writing to the brother of Jeremy Bentham: "I wish to reside in England and to be acquainted with your brother. In my eyes he is one of the first geniuses who have done and do most for the happiness of mankind, — Bacon, Newton,

Smith, and Bentham: each the founder of a new science, each a creator." [32]

The growth of freemasonry in eighteenth-century Russia was directly connected with the humanitarian aspect of the liberal movement. By 1732 there existed a number of masonic lodges established by foreigners, and in 1741 General James Keith [33] became the Grand Master of the brotherhood. Masonry was first organized according to the English system, and although various Continental systems were introduced later, the English achieved the greatest popularity and had the largest following. A close union was concluded with the parent Grand Lodge of London and Russian delegates were sent to conferences there.

A vast literature on the subject arose and the organization played a formidable part in the social and intellectual development of the time. Its doctrines of charity, mutual helpfulness, and freedom of conscience, advocated by such dominant figures as Novikov and Schwartz, contributed to the full spirit and practise of liberalism in Russia. By its very nature the movement was cosmopolitan, and from its contacts with Western freemasonry, especially with that of England and Germany, Russia again enjoyed the benefits of enlightened foreign influence.

In searching the records of Russian life in the reign of Catherine one is struck by the comparative absence of the species "Anglomaniac," of which one would expect to find a number in view of the persistent and widespread devotion to England. Such fervent acceptance of a foreign country, of course, is usually the result of long residence there. But the remoteness of England limited the possibilities of touring in an age when travel was not so simple as it is today. It was much easier to go to France or Germany, and most Russian tourists never got much farther.

There were few individuals like Prince A. B. Kurakin, who frankly admitted that if he were not a Russian he should prefer to be an Englishman.[34] Catherine's own devotion to England, however, set an example for certain of her subjects, especially among her ambassadors to England, who enjoyed a direct contact denied the empress. The important part that England played in the development of Russian diplomacy from the time of Peter the Great has already been commented on.[35] This influence reached its height in the reign of Catherine, when the ambassadorship became a position of the first rank.

A few of the most able of the ambassadors found in England a second fatherland. Early in the century Prince B. I. Kurakin, sent to London in 1710, became deeply interested in the organization of the government, and Prince Kantemir's strong affection for the country has been indicated.[36] But the love of the two Vorontsov brothers for England may fairly be described as an Anglomania.

The elder, Count A. Vorontsov, remained in England as ambassador only a short time (1762–64), but almost twenty years later, when his brother, Count S. Vorontsov, took over the same post, he wrote to him: "There is no people who in private life is more virtuous, moral, and hospitable than they; it is fine to live and to be born there." [37] Indeed, A. Vorontsov, after his return to Russia, lost none of his interest in England. He was continually receiving news of the country from his brother and from English books, such as *The Wealth of Nations*, which, after reading them, he sent to Radishchev, another admirer of England, who was in exile in Siberia. The influence of Vorontsov's knowledge of English political institutions on the reforms which he advocated at the beginning of the reign of Alexander I may be clearly detected.[38]

Before the younger brother was sent to London, the intervening ambassador, Count Musin-Pushkin, followed the example of the elder Vorontsov in his enthusiasm for England. He investigated English commerce and industry and their relation to agriculture. The reports of Musin-Pushkin provided Catherine with some interesting reading in the light of the reforms which she herself was then considering. He describes the English banking system, the industrial structure, and various political institutions, and his own discussion of the internal conditions of the country reflects his reading of Locke's two *Treatises of Government* and Hume's *Essays, Moral and Political*.[39]

It was in 1785 that S. Vorontsov took up his duties in London and two years later he wrote to his brother in Russia: "This excellent country presents as much interest as possible. Its government is the least imperfect of any that may be devised by a people. . . . Concerning commerce, manufacturing, agriculture, and science in its relations to physics and mechanics, I do not think that there exists in the world a country which may be compared with England." [40]

In the course of his long residence of forty-seven years in England, S. Vorontsov's high opinion of the country never changed and he came to love England with all the fervor of a native. The tenure of his service marks a high point in

Russian-English relations, and he labored most successfully to keep the two countries on friendly terms. His abilities as a diplomat were respected by the British government and when he died in London in 1832 England honored him as a sincere friend.

S. Vorontsov was a deep student of English political and economic thought, and in his voluminous correspondence [41] with relatives and friends in Russia he kept them informed of contemporary developments in English life and culture. In this way he was instrumental in disseminating English influence. To take one important instance: Vorontsov was a great admirer of the writings of Adam Smith, and upon hearing that his emperor was contemplating a new tariff law, he wrote to his brother, who was close to Alexander I, "to read, reread, and learn by heart the book of Adam Smith, *The Wealth of Nations.*" [42] From further remarks in his correspondence it is easy to see that S. Vorontsov had made a study of Smith and his predecessors in economic theory. [43]

The importance of such diplomats as Kurakin, Kantemir, the Vorontsov brothers, and Musin-Pushkin in creating a sentiment favorable to England was not inconsiderable. They were all men of consequence in their day and their position in the governing class enabled them to introduce, and, to some extent, to popularize a knowledge of English institutions and culture.

As we may perceive from the foregoing account, Anglomania in the reign of Catherine was largely centered in a group of individuals, the chief of whom was the empress herself. In this period society did not capitulate so completely to England as it did to France. The acceptance of English fashions and outward manner of life was not so widespread and lasting as in the case of French fashions; but Russian devotion to the more serious accomplishments of England, — to her governmental structure, legal system, education, industry, agriculture, commerce, and science, — was of far greater consequence in the development of the country than any mere imitation of dress and etiquette. And now, as a definite and most important phase of this interest in England, we must consider the rôle of English literature in eighteenth-century Russia.

BIBLIOGRAPHY

HISTORY: STUDIES AND CONTEMPORARY DOCUMENTS

Arkhiv Knyazya Vorontsova, Moskva, 1870–95, 31 vols.

Pisma imperatritsy Ekateriny II k Grimmu (1774–96), izd. Ya. Grota, St. Petersburg, 1878.

A. Brückner, *Katherina die Zweite*, Berlin, 1883.

Arkhiv Knyazya Kurakina, St. Petersburg, 1890–1902, 8 vols.

K. Waliszewski, *Romance of an Empress: Catherine II*, New York, 1894.

V. Ikonnikov, *Znachenie tsarstvovaniya Ekateriny II*, Kiev, 1897.

V. Bilbasov, *Istoriya Ekateriny Vtoroi*, Berlin, 1900, 12 vols.

Memoirs of Catherine the Great, translated by Katharine Anthony, New York, 1927.

FRENCH INFLUENCE ON RUSSIA

D. Kobeko, "Ekaterina II i J. J. Rousseau" (*Istoricheski vestnik*, 1883, XII, 603–617).

L. Pingaud, *Les français en Russie et les russes en France*, Paris, 1886.

C. Larivière, *La France et la Russie au XVIIIe siècle*, Paris, 1909.

E. Haumant, *La culture française en Russie*, Paris, 1910.

DIPLOMATIC RELATIONS WITH ENGLAND

Diplomaticheskaya perepiska angliskikh poslov i poslannikov pri russkom dvore (*Sbornik russkago istoricheskago obshchestva*, St. Petersburg, 1873, XII, 1876, XIX).

V. N. Aleksandrenko, *Russkie diplomaticheskie agenty v Londone v XVIII v.*, Varshava, 1897, 2 vols.

V. Timiryazev, "Russkie diplomaty XVIII stoletiya v Anglii" (*Istoricheski vestnik*, 1898, LXXII, 243–266, 567–581).

Correspondence of Catherine the Great when grand-duchess with Sir Charles Hanbury-Williams, and letters from Count Poniatowski, edited and translated by the Earl of Ilchester and Mrs. Langford-Brooke, London, 1928.

CATHERINE'S EDUCATIONAL REFORMS

P. Maikov, *I. I. Betski. Opyt ego biografii*, St. Petersburg, 1904.

S. Rozhdestvenski, "Proekty uchebnykh reform v tsarstvovanie imperatritsy Ekateriny II do uchrezhdeniya komissii o narodnykh uchilishchakh" (*Zhurnal ministerstva narodnago prosveshcheniya*, 1907, XII, 172–228).

MASONS IN RUSSIA

T. Sokolovskaya, "Masonstvo, kak polozhitelnoe dvizhenie russkoi mysli" (*Vsemirny vestnik*, 1904).
Russkoe masonstvo i ego znachenie v istorii obshchestvennago dvizheniya, St. Petersburg, 1908.

A. Pypin, *Russkoe masonstvo XVIII i pervoi chetverti XIX v.*, Petrograd, 1916.

RUSSIAN STUDENTS IN ENGLAND

V. N. Aleksandrenko, "Proekt bogoslovskago fakulteta v moskovskom universitete pri Ekaterine" (*Vestnik Evropy*, 1873).
"Iz zhizni russkikh studentov v Oxforde v tsarstvovanie imperatritsy Ekateriny II" (*Zhurnal ministerstva narodnago prosveshcheniya*, 1893, Yanvar, CCLXXXV, 1–15).
Russkie diplomaticheskie agenty v Londone v XVIII v., Varshava, 1897. (See I, 270–275.)

CULTURAL DEVELOPMENT IN CATHERINE'S REIGN

A. Kleinschmidt, *Katherina II als civilisatorin*, Hamburg, 1891.

A. Veselovski, *Zapadnoe vliyanie v novoi russkoi literature*, Moskva, 1896.
(Fifth ed., 1916. See pp. 74–126.)

A. Arkhangelski, *Imperatritsa Ekaterina II v istorii russkoi literatury i obrazovaniya*, Kazan, 1897.

P. Miliukov, *Ocherki po istorii russkoi kultury*, St. Petersburg, 1909–13, 3 Parts. (See Part III, chapters IV–VIII.)

Russkii byt po vospominaniyam sovremennikov XVIII veka, sostavlenny P. E. Melgunovoi, K. V. Sivkovym, N. P. Sidorovym, Moskva, 1923.

CHAPTER V

ENGLISH LITERATURE IN THE EIGHTEENTH-CENTURY RUSSIAN JOURNALS

HITHERTO this study has been concerned primarily with contacts of a non-literary nature between England and Russia. Such an exclusion, of course, was dictated by the fact that modern Russian literature did not really begin to bloom until the reign of Catherine. The literary production in the time of Elizabeth, though extremely significant in the incipient cultural development, had not become a moving force in the intellectual consciousness of the nation. The audience it appealed to was small — the people connected with the court at St. Petersburg and a circle of literary devotees at Moscow. Throughout the eighteenth century the reading public in Russia was never very large. Indeed, until comparatively recent times literature was more or less a closed book to the vast majority of the population, a fact that must always be kept in mind in studying the history of Russian culture. But in the Age of Catherine we begin to perceive the first definite signs of the growth of an intelligentsia. A class was coming into existence whose interests were devoted to things of the mind, to a conscious intellectual advancement, and such a class provides the necessary impulse to native literary production. Poets and prose writers in large numbers now rapidly entered upon the cultural scene, not only in St. Petersburg and Moscow, but in

many of the larger towns of the provinces. Literary form
and substance became a matter of discussion, and literary
criticism in general showed by its first stumbling attempts
at discrimination and appraisal that an intellectual consciousness had been born. The long, slow, arduous task of
creating a national literature now began in earnest.

It will be the chief business of the remainder of the book
to study this literary growth in its relation to English literature. Various other contacts of a cultural nature will not be
neglected, but they will be considered more as a foundation
on which a knowledge of English literature was built in
Russia.

The Russian journals of the eighteenth century were
largely instrumental in acquainting the reading public with
the works of foreign writers and they constitute a very important part of the literary movement in the reign of Catherine. We find in them an excellent cross-section of social
customs and literary tastes, and to some extent a record of
public opinion on some of the live questions of the day.
Many of the foremost authors, as well as a host of minor
writers, contributed to the journals, and literary animosities
and personal quarrels were threshed out in their pages. They
range from mere weekly newspapers to monthly moral, satirical, critical, scientific, economic, and fashion journals.

However, perhaps nothing is so calculated to convince one
of the purely derivative nature of Russian literature and
culture in the eighteenth century as an investigation of the
journals, numbering well over a hundred, which were published during this period. Not only in initial inspiration and
form were the majority of the journals indebted to foreign

models, but the contents of some of them, running to several volumes, are made up entirely of translations from English, French, German, Danish, Swedish, Dutch, and Polish periodicals and books. As a matter of fact, the declared purpose of certain of the journals was to acquaint their readers with foreign literature in translation. A few of the best journals achieved some originality, though the articles were rarely informed with the penetrating observations and charm of style which we find in the best of the English periodicals. On the whole they are depressingly dull, though occasionally relieved by what Addison would call a "sprightly dullness."

Journal publication had begun very early in the century, but it was not until 1750 to 1760 that the periodicals took on a definite literary cast. The pioneer of the group, *Monthly Papers for Profit and Entertainment*,[1] had a double purpose: to provide historical information in special articles, and to acquaint its readers with foreign literature in translation. The general model is obviously the English journal of the *Spectator* type. Indeed, some twenty-one tales and essays from the *Spectator* alone were translated for this journal, with the professed intention of teaching the control of mind over passions and of setting an example of proper behavior in social intercourse. The only original material consisted of the historical articles and the poetry.

The periodicals that immediately followed, — bearing such fetching titles as *Idle Time*,[2] *Industrious Bee*,[3] *Profitable Entertainment*,[4] *Harmless Exercise*,[5] *Leisure Hours*,[6] and *Good Intentions*,[7] — were all of the same type as *Monthly Papers for Profit and Entertainment*, depending mainly on foreign journals for their material. German periodicals were frequently laid under contribution, and occasionally French, but a large part of the borrowings are from English. In the case of *Good Intentions*, nearly the whole of the first volume is composed of direct translations from the *Spectator*.

The popularity of English periodical literature in Russia at this time is indicated by the publication of a book made up entirely of translations from English journals. This is the *Amusing Philosopher*, which appeared in 1766. In an interesting preface the translator, who must have had a good knowledge of English, expatiates on the literary excellence of Addison, Steele, Swift, Johnson, and Tillotson, whose works, he informs us, "provide attractive morality and kindle in the heart of youth an inextinguishable flame of virtue." [8] The contents of the book consist of some of the finest essays and tales selected from the best of the eighteenth-century periodicals. The tales, which predominate in the collection, are of the regular moral type, and it is noticeable that several of them became favorites in later Russian journalistic literature. The *Amusing Philosopher* was well received and achieved the distinction of a reprint in 1784.[9]

The vogue of the English periodical literature was greatly extended in the next phase of the development of the Russian journals. The general European trend towards satire in the eighteenth century profoundly affected the form and contents of Russian literature, and much of the verse and prose in the reign of Catherine was satirical. In the journals already mentioned a few examples of satirical essays occur in the borrowed matter, but the moral tale and essay, also typical of eighteenth-century taste, were by far the favorite material for translation. Between 1769 and 1774, however, a whole series of journals of the *Spectator* variety, devoted chiefly to satire, flourished in Russia.

England has often been dependent upon foreign models and incentive for the creation of literary forms, but the origin of the satirical journal of the *Spectator* type is one of the few great exceptions to the rule. And in its turn the *Spectator* inspired a host of imitations in Western Europe. Even before the journal came to an end in 1714, imitations began to appear in Germany, where it is estimated that in the eighteenth century some five hundred moral and satirical journals were published. France, Denmark, and Poland soon adopted the fashion, though not quite so enthusiastically as Germany.

With the possible exception of Germany, Russia's devotion to the *Spectator* and the type of literature it represented was as pronounced as the devotion in any of these countries. No doubt the reading public first became acquainted with the *Spectator* through French and German translations. Thus we hear of a French version's being bought by a Russian as early as 1725,[10] and a very early manuscript translation of *Spectator*, Number 139, is preserved in the library of the Russian Academy of Sciences.[11] In 1731 a friend, writing to the poet Tredyakovski, remarks: "Do you desire a better small collection of jests or tales, or some sort of travel book, or the discourses of our favorite *Spectateur*?"[12] In this same year translations from the *Spectator* began to appear in *Notes in Journals*,[13] and in nearly all the literary periodicals published in the 1750's and 1760's the *Spectator* was a favorite source of material.

In view of this obvious popularity of the *Spectator* in Russia about the middle of the eighteenth century, it is not at all surprising that the English periodical should have been used as a model when the creation of a purely satirical journal was contemplated. Such a relationship undoubtedly exists between the *Spectator* and *All Sorts and Sundries*,[14] the first satirical journal in Russia, published in 1769. It was issued every Friday at the price of one and a half kopeks.

The origin of *All Sorts and Sundries* is shrouded in mystery. Its declared editor was G. Kozitski, the secretary of the empress, a man of wide literary knowledge. But Catherine herself was certainly a leading contributor, and there exists not a little evidence that she was the originator of the journal. The enterprise represents one phase of her attempt to foster a spirit of criticism (provided it did not become too searching), as part of the cultural development of her subjects; besides, Catherine was always on the alert for an opportunity to occupy her facile pen.

The purpose of *All Sorts and Sundries* and the *Spectator* is virtually the same. The Russian editor writes: "We have no doubts concerning the speedy correction of morals, and we expect the prompt extirpation of all vices; for already they [the readers] have begun to learn by heart *All Sorts and Sundries*."[15]   In the same strain Addison tells us that the purpose of the *Spectator* is "to banish Vice and Ignorance out of the Territories of Great Britain."[16]   And the method of the *Spectator* for banishing vice and correcting morals — the satirical essay with its kind and gentle humor — was adopted by the Russian journal. Even the pleasant familiarity and the confidential tone which give the *Spectator* essays this special flavor are effectively reproduced in *All*

Sorts and Sundries. "Gentle reader," writes a contributor in good Addisonian fashion, "I have undertaken to report to you all that which appears to me to be of interest, without any particular order. Sometimes I shall give you useful instructions, sometimes you will be amused." [17]   In external features, such as the form and kind of article, we can observe the patent influence of the English journal. A letter sent by the reader to the editor, the moral Eastern tale, and the vision are narrative devices and forms employed by the Russian contributors, and these were no doubt suggested by the *Spectator*.

Of course the possibility should not be ignored that this kind of influence may well have been exerted indirectly by French and German imitations of the *Spectator*. An abundance of such German satirical periodicals and a few French ones were well known in Russia at this time. However, the debt of *All Sorts and Sundries* to the *Spectator* amounts to something more than mere influence on the forms and types of essays and tales. Contributors to the Russian journal translated and paraphrased a large number of the *Spectator* articles. It is true that only a few of these are direct translations. Something of the skill of artful plagiarism is employed. A rough paraphrase of the whole contents of a *Spectator* essay will be made, or the general theme will be appropriated and developed in a pseudo-original fashion with an occasional sentence lifted *in toto* from the source. And in certain instances two numbers of the *Spectator* will be combined to make a single essay in *All Sorts and Sundries*.

The editors were rather evasive in the matter and few acknowledgments were made as to the source of these borrowings. Contemporary journals twitted *All Sorts and Sundries* about its affectation of originality. Thus the editor of *The Idler*, another satirical journal, writes: "This [*All Sorts and Sundries*] substitutes for its own efforts articles from the renowned English *Spectator*, representing them as products of its own wisdom." [18] But the whole important question of the debt of the Russian journal to its English model has been fully investigated, and nineteen numbers are listed by V. Solntsev as direct translations or paraphrases.[19] And the investigator goes even farther than this in tracing the dependence of the first Russian satirical journal on the *Spectator*. While not refusing *All Sorts and Sundries* a certain claim to originality in its satire, he proves that the tone, manner, purpose, and the very significance of this satire derive from the English periodical.[20] Even the themes of satire, he points out, — such as the defective education of children, the lazy and wasteful life of landowners, the foppery of town dandies, and many other foibles and vices, — were suggested by the *Spectator*.[21] Finally, he concludes his study with this significant statement: "Almost all the articles of *All Sorts and Sundries* recognized as important for a history of the accomplishments and morals of society in the Catherine epoch have been borrowed from the English journal." [22]

As in England after the publication of the *Tatler*, a number of satirical journals came into existence in Russia after *All Sorts and Sundries*, and flourished until their prohibition in 1774.[23] Owing to its primacy in the field it is only natural that *All Sorts and Sundries*, — the "grandmother" of them all, as Catherine fondly called her journal, — should have served as the immediate model for these periodicals. Actual translations from the *Spectator* did not figure in them so largely as in the case of *All Sorts and Sundries*, but their purpose and general makeup were the same as those of the English journal. We find in them a Russified Addisonian humor, the comic correspondence of the fop, the diary of the provincial in the capital, the advice of the editor to the public, literary reviews, and attempts at character sketches after the fashion of Sir Roger de Coverley, with the customary conversations on such subjects as life and love. With considerable success the satirical journals also imitated the eclectic and humane satire of the *Spectator*, genially ridiculing misdirected education, foppery, superstitions, hypocrisy, ignorant pedagogues, and violations of the law. It is noticeable that many of the abuses they satirized, though real enough in England, had little significance in Russia. This fact may be justly regarded as an indication of the slavishness with which they imitated their English model. Certain historians of the satirical journals have refused to accept this judgment. Afanasev writes: "This influence of foreign satirical publications on our journals we admit only in the matter of the form and tone of the articles, but the contents of our satirical journals were drawn from our own national life." [24] Nevertheless, such vital questions as peasant slavery, the wholesale plundering of the nobles, and the extreme injustice of the social system came in for comparatively little attention in the Russian satirical journals. The simple fact is that Catherine herself indicated quite clearly what were the proper subjects for satire, and the journals that succeeded hers followed her example, apparently unwilling to criticize the real evils around them. And Catherine's notion of satire, as Solntsev points out, was borrowed from the *Spectator*. He writes: "The views of *All Sorts and Sundries* on the problem and limits of satire did not belong to the Empress Catherine herself; they did not issue from her principles of discretion, nor were they the result of the influence of materialistic ideas appropriated by her from the French philosophy: rather they were entirely borrowed from the *Spectator*." [25] Only such fearless editors as N. Novikov in *The Idler*,[26] *The Painter*,[27] and *The Purse*,[28] and F. Emin in his *Infernal Post*,[29] dared to satirize in a straightforward manner the real social evils of the time, and the zeal of these writers quickly brought to an end the literary movement which the satirical journals represented. Catherine would not permit such outspoken criticism of the country which she ruled with a stern hand.

To judge from the indebtedness which has just been described, it is perhaps no exaggeration to affirm that the *Spectator* was the most significant factor in the origin and development of the Russian satirical journals of the eighteenth century. Furthermore, as material for translation, the *Spectator* was laid under contribution again and again by Russian journals of a non-satirical nature in the remainder of Catherine's reign, and by a few in the early part of the nineteenth century. The Oriental tales and the purely moral and philosophical essays were the favorites, and literally scores of these were translated.[30]

The *Spectator*, of course, was not the only English periodical known to Russian journal writers of the eighteenth century. They found an abundance of material for translation in the *Tatler*, the *Guardian*, the *Gentleman's Magazine*, the *Universal Magazine*, the *Rambler*, the *General Magazine*, the *Mirror*, and the *Patriot*.[31] Considerable detective work is required to run down definitively the many translations and paraphrases from these periodicals. The Russian editors had something of the Elizabethan's simple unscrupulousness in wholesale borrowing and plagiarizing. Often they are at pains to conceal their originals, or a veiled hint as to the source in question is regarded as sufficient acknowledgment. And the difficulty is further complicated by the fact that not a few of the essays and tales are represented as translations from the German or the French when in reality they are German or French translations from the English. In general the editors of the non-satirical journals drew upon the English periodicals for the same kind of material which the *Spectator* had already made popular: that is, the moral Eastern tale of the type of the *Vision of Mirza*, and the philosophical essay. One can hardly turn the pages of any of these rather numerous Russian journals without finding one or more translations from English periodicals, and their debt to them in the matter of form was also considerable.[32]

It must not be supposed, however, that English literature apart from the periodicals escaped the intellectual curiosity of the culture-seeking Russians of Catherine's reign. The English language, of course, was little known in Russia at this time, but the numerous translations of English works into French brought them within the range of the French-reading Russian intelligentsia. The vanguard of native critics of English literature fumbled badly at first, forcing their way into a dimly comprehended field, like the *parvenu* in a brilliant salon, totally unaware of the insufficiency of their training. The example of French criticism, from which they borrowed most of their facts and theory, availed them little at first. They ignored the fundamental condition that before one can write literary history, one must have a thorough knowledge of the individual authors and their works. Consequently, the critical appraisals of English literature in introductions to translations and in periodicals in the first half of Catherine's reign are pitifully inadequate. Thus, in 1762, an anonymous critic attempts a survey of poetry in the journal, *Profitable Entertainment*.[33] With amusing insufficiency he dedicates three pages to the whole field of English verse. He begins somewhat surprisingly with the statement that "English poetry first becomes worthy of notice with Shanger in the fourteenth century"[34] — meaning, of course, Chaucer. Then he makes a swift transition to the seventeenth century and Milton, who is summed up as "the glory and wonder of England." In this section Dryden likewise comes in for his meed of praise, which is curiously qualified by the following judgment: "If Pope, who came after him, had not written, towards the end of his life, the *Essay on Man*, then he could not even be compared with Dryden."[35] This sounds almost like an independent conclusion born of careful study of the relative merits of both authors, for Pope was consistently reverenced by eighteenth-century Russian readers. With characteristic neglect, however, the critic has failed to acknowledge his source, for this strange discrimination is translated literally from Voltaire.[36] At this chronological point, by sheer inadvertency, so it would seem, our historian of literature introduces and dis-

misses Shakspere in one sentence: "Shakspere wrote tragedies, many of which are very fine and many are very bad." [37]
Such critical aplomb on the part of this anonymous critic
might be commended were its source not patently French.
Finally, with a word or two of praise for Swift and Addison,
he concludes his survey with a paragraph of critical finesse on
the highly moral, meditative, and allegorical character of
English literature. In extenuation it must be added that
French literature comes off hardly a whit better and German decidedly worse. It remained for Karamzin, a generation later, to give his countrymen a truer perspective of
English literary history.

This shreds-and-patches effort at tracing the development
of our poetry, however, is no real indication of the extent to
which English literature was read and appreciated in Russia
in the reign of Catherine. And to estimate the variety of interest we must again turn to the Russian journals of the
period.

Shakspere early won the attention of the Russian editors.
It was through French translations that Shakspere was first
introduced into Russia, and hence it is curious to find one
of the earliest translators repudiating a French rendering.
In a translation of the "To be or not to be" soliloquy in
Hamlet, this contributor, belligerently signing himself "Anglomaniac," takes Voltaire to task for his version of this
same speech. He says in his introductory remarks: "Not all
Russians know French. Therefore in comparing this translation with the original, I saw that Voltaire had labored more
with Shakspere than with his translation, and that if anyone should turn the translation back into English, nobody

would recognize it as Shakspere's work." [38] Such critical discrimination was rare at this time. There are other fragmentary translations in prose and verse from *Hamlet, Romeo and
Juliet, Henry IV*, and *Henry VIII*, [39] but a critical appreciation of the plays, which we might expect in the journals,
is quite lacking. Such criticism, however, was to come in
abundance in the early part of the nineteenth century under
the impetus of German interest in Shakspere during the
Romantic Movement.

Of the older English authors of high rank Milton was perhaps the first to gain considerable attention in Russia. A
manuscript translation of *Paradise Lost* by A. G. Stroganov
had been circulating since 1745, and Novikov's printed
version made the poem accessible to a large circle of readers.
Furthermore, the early practise of group-reading increased
the popularity of *Paradise Lost*, and translations multiplied
throughout the latter half of the eighteenth century and the
first half of the nineteenth. Indeed, few Western classics
were better known in Russia during this period than *Paradise
Lost*.

The appearance of Milton in the journals reflects this popularity. The Continental fame he won as a great Latinist and
the champion of liberty did not filter into Russia. The journals were interested in his minor poetry and, critically, in
his renown as a writer of epics. There are two complete
translations in prose of *Il Penseroso* in the journals and one
fragmentary version, the earliest dated 1763. And in the
same year we find a prose translation of *L'Allegro*. That
prose was an unhappy medium for rendering such poems
never seemed to occur to these Russian translators. They

keep close enough to the originals in sense, but a similar prose version of *Lycidas* in 1801 goes badly astray. The opening, more faithful than the rest of the attempt, reads, when translated back into English: "Green laurels, tender myrtles, and thou, ivy blighted by frost, allow me once again to pluck your unripened fruit." [40]

In view of the rather elementary state of Russian literary criticism at this time, Milton fares pretty well. In the journal *Harmless Exercise* (1763), the author of an article on epic poetry devotes considerable space to Milton.[41] He displays an unusual awareness of documentary material relating to *Paradise Lost*, and shows that he has carefully read the poem as well as the English and French criticisms of it. "I cannot understand," he writes, "how *Paradise Lost*, considering the nature and inclination of the English people, was for such a long time not only unhonored, but almost entirely unknown, in England." [42] With real insight he goes on to say: "The observations of Mr. Dryden on Milton do not please me at all; he wrote eulogistic verses to him [43] in which he not only puts him on a level with Homer and Virgil, but gives him a preëminence over them. And then, in his own foreword to his translation of the *Aeneid*, he honors Milton equally with Chapelain and Le Moine, two of the most abominable poets. The manner in which he elevates Milton in his verse and debases him in his prose is for me an incomprehensible riddle." [44] It is Addison, he insists, "the best critic and writer of his age, who revealed the treasured beauties of *Paradise Lost* and acclaimed forever the glory of its composer." [45] Having finished with the previous critics of Milton, the author enters into a detailed analysis of *Para-*

dise Lost, commenting on its merits and faults with genuine appreciation. He concludes his study with an enthusiastic tribute to the minor poems.

On the whole, this all-too-brief criticism reflects more credit on its author than the unequal essay on Milton in the *Lives of the Poets*, published some sixteen years later, reflects on Johnson. I have mentioned it at length because it was a unique attempt at this time, and we have to wait until 1802 before anything comparable on the same subject was published in Russia in a literary journal. This was an elaborate and complete study of Milton and his works which measures up to the best European standards of criticism and scholarship.[46] There is nothing more of importance concerning Milton in the eighteenth-century journals, except occasional references to him and an amusing story how a beautiful young lady inspired the creation of *Paradise Lost*.[47]

The other purely seventeenth-century authors who appear in the Russian journals of this period are Waller, Cowley, and Dryden. It is surprising enough to find the first two, for they were little known on the Continent, and as a matter of fact they come in for but passing mention. There is a translation of a letter of Waller to Lucy Sidney, sister of the famous "Sacharissa" of the poems,[48] and a rendering of Cowley's *Ode on Brutus*. Dryden, on the other hand, was frequently mentioned in eighteenth-century French criticism, and such attention would lead us to expect an ample consideration of him in the journals. Yet only a fragmentary translation of his *Essay on Dramatic Poetry* was published. At the turn of the century, however, Dryden came to be more admired in Russia.

Naturally enough, English authors of the eighteenth century predominate in the journals, and in some cases their popularity was truly widespread and occasionally significant in the literary development during the reign of Catherine and later. Of works which belong to the very early part of the century we find translations of a scene from Vanbrugh's *Provoked Wife*, an eclogue of Parnell, and a series of Prior's poems. Prior's elegant verse, with no more taste than in the case of Milton's minor poetry, is rendered into prose in most of the selections. The translator is pretty successful in following the sense, though he makes an occasional slip, as in *A Better Answer*, where "Odds life! must one swear to the truth of a song?" becomes "Life of odes! who must swear to the truth of a song?"

Swift appeared very early in the journals, a translation of *Esquire Bickerstaffe's Most Strange and Wonderful Predictions* being published in *Compositions and Translations for Profit and Entertainment* in 1758. Other translations followed and Swift became something of a permanent adornment in the journals of the later eighteenth century. His real popularity in Russia, however, dates from the translation of *Gulliver's Travels* in 1772–73. Swift's masterpiece was admired and imitated,[49] and other translations were made of it.

From what has been said of the influence of the *Spectator*, it may be inferred that a good many of Addison's papers, and to some extent those of Steele, found a prominent place in the journals. The anonymity consequent upon this type of publication served to render Steele's name practically unknown among the journal-readers. But Addison was well known apart from the *Spectator*, perhaps because of his *Cato* and the fame he enjoyed as an arbiter of literary taste. Thus the *Vision of Mirza* from the *Spectator*, which was a favorite and was translated at least four times,[50] was usually connected with his name in the journals. Even such little-known works of Addison as the dissertation *On the Christian Religion* [51] and the *Pax Gulielmi* [52] were honored with separate translations, and in one of the journals we find a rendering of the rhymed *Letters from Italy to Charles Montagu*. No doubt French criticism had a great deal to do with the lofty position which Addison achieved in Russian letters. In an age which had not learned to appreciate Shakspere, it is easy to understand why Voltaire's unique judgment, that Shakspere would have been "un poëte parfait s'il avait vécu du temps d'Addison," [53] was readily accepted in Russia. For it was Addison's *Cato* which exalted him in Russian eyes as a poet and a dramatist. The play, which suited admirably the prevailing neo-classical taste in Russian drama, was translated, once completely and once partially, in the journals.[54] And if we may judge from the numerous testimonials of its greatness by Russian writers of the time, there is reason to believe that they fully agreed with Voltaire's conviction that *Cato* was "la seule tragédie anglaise écrite avec une élégance et une noblesse continue." [55] Finally, as a literary critic, Addison again gained a high place in the esteem of Russian writers of the eighteenth century, a fact which has been indicated in the references already made to his critical insight.[56]

Pope's misbegotten philosophical fame was enhanced in Russia with a largesse past all accounting. A comparison with Shaftesbury, or even with Pope's philosophical father, Bolingbroke, would have pleased the poet mightily. But the Russian translator who paid him the following extraordinary compliment would have won Pope's eternal gratitude: "He united the charm of verse to a sincerely useful and extremely important and sane philosophy, both of which are found in him alone and only in Plato and Homer combined." [57] For such an encomium one is tempted to believe that Pope would have forgiven the same translator's shoddy rendering of the neat rhymes of the *Essay on Man*.

It was an age of compliments, and Russian writers were more inclined to praise since as yet they had few standards of their own by which to condemn. Nevertheless Pope gained an entirely disproportionate place as a philosopher in eighteenth-century Russia. The fact may be partly explained by the general drift towards deism, influenced largely by French philosophical thought and by Shaftesbury, whose theories were taught in Moscow University. Pope, introduced as a deist by the French, came on the ground rather early. His *Essay on Man* was translated in 1754, and its great popularity may be judged by the fact that there were at least six editions and another new rendering within the next fifty years. The Russian readers of the *Essay on Man* failed to find the "penury of knowledge and vulgarity of sentiment" which Dr. Johnson attributed to the poem. Pope became enshrined as a great thinker and his moral aphorisms and pseudo-philosophical ideas were mouthed by the young Russian deists of the time, and the intellectual heroes of the Russian eighteenth-century romances were often represented as deep students of Popian thought. So significant was this devotion to the poet's deistic beliefs that he was considered a menace in religious circles — a fact which would have immensely flattered him. The clergy regarded him as a free-thinker and the *Essay on Man* aroused heretical discussion among students of religion. Veselovski tells how the Archbishop Ambrosius, fearful of the effect which the unapproved teachings of the poem might have on his seminarists, deleted certain of the more dangerous passages, unhesitatingly substituting more orthodox verses of his own composition.[58]

However, Pope's fame in Russia as a philosopher did not detract from his reputation as a poet. In his introduction the translator of the *Essay on Man*, after admitting somewhat naïvely that Pope's version of the *Iliad* and *Odyssey* "is more original than Homer" (Pope's worst enemies would hardly quarrel with this judgment), goes on to say that as a poet, "in his own material and thought, he has gained the greatest preëminence." [59] No less than in England during his lifetime, Pope was regarded in Russia as an exponent of perfect taste in form and expression in verse. Besides the *Essay on Man*, there were complete translations, in the latter half of the eighteenth century, of the *Rape of the Lock* and the *Temple of Fame*.[60] In 1806 the Russian translator *par excellence*, Zhukovski, did *Eloisa to Abelard*, and the *Pastorals* were published in Russian garb in 1809. The journals show even a more varied interest in Pope's poetry. In their pages we find translations of the *Ode for Music on St. Cecilia's Day*, *Essay on Man*, *On Silence*, *Pastorals*, *Lines on Newton*, and two each of the *Messiah*, *Universal Prayer*, and *Eloisa to Abelard*. These translations are from both French and English and in prose and verse, and the popularity they indicate is fully borne out by the readiness with which contributors to the journals quote from Pope's works. He was imitated, and occasionally inspired native productions, as in an article on "The Dressing Table of the Fashionable Belle." The author quotes relevant sections from the *Rape of the Lock* and speculates on the brilliant satire the poet might have written on the toilet of the modern damsel.[61]

In the rather sparse criticism of Pope scattered through the journals there is rarely any descent from the heights of exaggerated appreciation to the level of common-sense appraisal. The worship of the French, especially that of Voltaire,[62] was the inevitable touchstone for the Russian critical estimate of Pope. In truth, the enthusiasm of neo-classical French criticism for Pope undoubtedly had much to do with his vogue in Russia, but after he had been translated he secured his popularity on his own merits.

English authors belonging to the middle of the century and to the Age of Johnson likewise appeared in the Russian journals, but, with a few exceptions, not with the frequency of the earlier writers. English literature of this period was too close in point of time, and not many of the authors had obtained the Continental popularity which would have made their works more accessible to the Russian editors. Dr. Johnson's great fame in England, for example, because of its peculiar insularity, was quite lost on the Russians. Some of the *Rambler* essays were used, and it was in an early journal in 1764 (only five years after its English appearance) that *Rasselas* was first translated into Russian.

Russia was no exception to the universal appeal of the *Vicar of Wakefield* and Goldsmith's fame was assured with

the translation of his novel in 1786. But even before this
the journals had borrowed from the *Citizen of the World* and
the *Cultivated Nature*. And of the essay writers Lord Chesterfield also found a place in the journals.

We should hardly expect to find such little-known poets
as Shenstone and Collins in Russian dress, but the former's
Pastoral Ballad, and his *Ode to a Young Lady*, and the
latter's *Ode on the Death of Thomson* were served up to the
journal-readers in translation. And a poet with none of the
talent of Shenstone and Collins and entirely forgotten today, was warmly appreciated in two Russian periodicals at
the turn of the century. This was Robert Bloomfield, whose
poem *The Farmer's Boy* was published in 1800. With questionable taste the Russian journals praised the poem highly,
and one contributor translated part of it into prose. Perhaps the fact that twenty-six thousand copies of the work
were said to have been sold in England in three years had
something to do with its quick reception in Russia.

The eighteenth-century novelists Defoe, Richardson,
Fielding, Sterne, and Mackenzie come in for more or less
attention in this journal literature. There are fragmentary
translations of some of their works, but most of the material
is concerned with criticism and letters of appreciation sent
to the editors. However, several of these authors were to
play a significant part in the development of the Russian
novel, and hence it will be more convenient to postpone a
consideration of this material to the next chapter.

For the same reason I must omit a detailed discussion of
Young, Thomson, Gray, and Ossian. In a later chapter we
shall study the whole important question of their influence

on the sentimental movement in Russian literature. It is
enough to say here that no two English authors are mentioned so frequently in the journals as Young and Ossian,
and their extensive popularity is clearly reflected in numerous translations and criticisms. Imitations and translations
of Thomson's *Seasons* appear, and besides the six separate
renderings of the *Elegy in a Country Churchyard* in the
journals, there are also two translations of Gray's *Ode on
Adversity* But more of this later.

This brief survey will give some idea of the English authors
and works that were made accessible to the Russian journal
readers of the last fifty years of the eighteenth century Furthermore, as may have been inferred from the previous
chapter, belles lettres did not constitute the entire material
considered worthy of translation in the journals. English
philosophical, historical, and economic thought found a
place, although a rather modest one, through discussion and
partial translations of the works of Bacon, Locke, Bolingbroke, Gibbon, Robertson, and Hume.

It would be uncritical, however, to draw any positive in-
ferences from this parade of authors as to the influence of
English literature on Russian in the latter half of the eighteenth century. In the first place, many of the translations
were made, not to satisfy an established demand for certain
types of literature, but merely to fill up space when originality
was lacking. It was rare that any well-defined method of
selection obtained. We are not to suppose that these editors
or the occasional contributors had a thorough knowledge of
English literature and combed the field for works which
should meet a standard of taste or supply a popular demand.

The usual situation, no doubt, was that an editor, in looking through the pages of a contemporary German or French periodical, would come upon a translation from English literature and appropriate it. Likewise, French criticism must have provided hints as to desirable authors, and book translations of certain English works in Russian, French, and German suggested the possibility of rendering other compositions of these authors for the journal-readers.

Nevertheless, in a proper sense the journals may be regarded as a kind of index to the popularity of several English authors, and in a few cases they unquestionably reflect the influence of certain English works on the development of Russian literature throughout this period. Thus the admitted popularity in Russia of Addison, Pope, Young, Thomson, Gray, and Ossian is clearly indicated in the translations from these authors in the journals, and also, though to a lesser extent, the popularity of Richardson, Fielding, and Sterne. Nor can we question the fact that the journals as a whole, and the satirical variety in particular, show the extensive influence of the *Spectator* on their origin, form, and contents. And the part that English sentimental literature and the eighteenth-century novels were to play in the corresponding Russian movements is clearly foreshadowed and aided by the attention the journals paid to the English poets and novelists connected with these movements. Finally, this investigation of the eighteenth-century journals enlarges our perspective of the extent to which English literature was known in Russia during this period.

BIBLIOGRAPHY

EIGHTEENTH-CENTURY RUSSIAN PERIODICALS
BIBLIOGRAPHICAL STUDIES

A. Neustroev, *Istoricheskoe rozyskanie v russkikh izdaniyakh i sbornikakh, 1703–1802*, St. Petersburg, 1875.

N. Lisovski, *Russkaya periodicheskaya pechat*, St. Petersburg, 1915.

INVESTIGATIONS

V. Miliutin, "Ocherki russkoi zhurnalistiki" (*Sovremennik*, 1851, XXV–XXVI).

P. Bulich, *Sumarokov i sovremennaya emu kritika*, St. Petersburg, 1854.

N. Dobroliubov, "Russkaya satira Ekaterinenskago vremeni" (*Sovremennik*, 1859, X).

A. Afanasev, *Russkie satiricheskie zhurnaly*, Moskva, 1859. (Latest edition, Kazan, 1871.)

P. Pekarski, *Redaktor, sotrudniki i tsenzura v russkom zhurnale, 1755–1764* (Sbornik II, otdeleniya II, 1867).

A. Nezelenov, *Nikolai Ivanovich Novikov, izdatel zhurnalov, 1769–1785*, St. Petersburg, 1875.
Literaturnyya napravleniya v Ekaterinenskuiu epokhu, St. Petersburg, 1889.

V. Solntsev, "*Vsyakaya vsyachina* i *Spectator*" (*Zhurnal ministerstva narodnago prosveshcheniya*, Yanvar, 1892, pp. 125–156).
"Smesi" (*Bibliograf*, 1893, I).

A. Veselovski, *Zapadnoe vliyanie v novoi russkoi literature*, Moskva, 1896. (See last edition, 1916, pp. 56, 78–90.)

L. Maikov, *Ocherki iz istorii russkoi literatury XVII i XVIII stoletii*, St. Petersburg, 1899. (See pp. 369–424.)

P. Miliukov, *Ocherki po istorii russkoi kultury*, St. Petersburg, 1909–13. (See Part III, chapters II–III.)

N. Antonomov, *Vsyakaya vsyachina. Satiriko-nravouchitelny zhurnal*, Moskva, 1913.

V. Semennikov, *Russkie satiricheskie zhurnaly, 1769–74*, St. Petersburg, 1914.

TRANSLATION FROM ENGLISH PERIODICALS AND AUTHORS IN THE
RUSSIAN EIGHTEENTH-CENTURY JOURNALS

(Complete bibliographical details of separate book translations of
English authors mentioned in this chapter are easily accessible in the
Ukazatel k opytu rossiskoi bibliografii V. S. Sopikova, sostavil V. N. Rogozhin, St. Petersburg, 1908, and accordingly they will not be repeated here.
However, there exists no itemized bibliography of translations from English in the journals. The list appended here is not entirely complete, for
some of these eighteenth-century journals are very rare. Nearly all of
them have been examined, however, and the list is complete enough to
serve practical purposes. The English periodicals are arranged chronologically, and likewise the authors and the order of translations from them in
the Russian journals. Full bibliographical information concerning the
journals may be found in N. Lisovski, *Russkaya periodicheskaya pechat.*)

I. TRANSLATIONS FROM ENGLISH PERIODICALS

Tatler

Ezhemesyachnyya sochineniya k polze i uveseleniiu sluzhashchiya, 1757,
II, 503–515; (No. 100), *Sochineniya i perevody k polze i uveseleniiu
sluzhashchiya*, 1761, I, 413–423; (No. 107), *ibid.*, II, 278–287;
(No. 23), *ibid.*, 1762, I, 283–287; (No. 13), *Moskovskoe ezhemesyachnoe izdanie*, 1781, I, 1–9; (No. 25), *ibid.*, II, 15–24.

Spectator

(No. 374), *Primechaniya v vedomostyakh*, 1731, IV, 2; (No. 7), *ibid.*,
VII, 1; (No. 296), *ibid.*, XLII, 2; (No. 8), *ibid.*, XLVIII, 2; (No.
201), *ibid.*, LXI, 1; (No. 111), *ibid.*, 1732, X, 5; (No. 520), *ibid.*,
XXVI, 2; (No. 513), *ibid.*, LX, 5; (No. 587), *ibid.*, 1733, II, 5;
(No. 210), *ibid.*, LVI, 6; (No. 471), *ibid.*, 1735, XVI, 5; (No. 159),
Ezhemesyachnyya sochineniya k polze i uveseleniiu sluzhashchiya,
1757, I, 345–353; (No. 626), *Sochineniya i perevody k polze i uveseleniiu sluzhashchiya*, 1759, I, 265–273; (No. 621), *ibid.*, I, 539–550;
(No. 392), *ibid.*, II, 351–356; (No. 391), *ibid.*, II, 357–362; (No.
404), *ibid.*, II, 378–384; (No. 450), *ibid.*, 1760, I, 75–86; (No. 447),
ibid., I, 185–192; (No. 408), *ibid.*, I, 230–237; (No. 449), *ibid.*, I,
237–244; (No. 464), *ibid.*, I, 244–250; (No. 487), *ibid.*, I, 470–477;
(No. 519), *ibid.*, I, 478–486; (No. 543), *ibid.*, I, 487–494; (No.
559), *ibid.*, 1761, I, 362–372; (No. 587), *ibid.*, I, 373–378; (No.
605), *ibid.*, 1762, I, 71–90; (No. 598), *ibid.*, I, 187–190; (No. 11),
ibid., II, 469–476; (No. 93), *Prazdnoe vremya v polzu upotreblennoe*,

1759, I, 29–35; (No. 447), *ibid.*, I, 36–42; (No. 111), *Trudoliubi-vaya pchela*, 1759, pp. 180–187; (No. 139), *ibid.*, pp. 229–231; (No. 474), *Poleznoe uveselenie*, 1760, II, 22–23; (No. 275), *ibid.*, II, 193–196; (No. 281), *ibid.*, II, 209–213; (No. 411), *Svobodnyya chasy*, 1763, II, 579–584; (No. 605), *ibid.*, II, 621–623; (No. 517), *Dobroe namerenie*, 1764, I, 16–23; *ibid.*, I, 38–47; (No. 92), *ibid.*, I, 91–94; (No. 524), *ibid.*, I, 113–128; (No. 330), *ibid.*, I, 129–135; *ibid.*, 135–138; (No. 1), *Vsyakaya vsyachina*, 1769, No. 1; (No. 7), *ibid.*, No. 6; (No. 11), *ibid.*, No. 14; (No. 328), *ibid.*, No. 27; (No. 27), *ibid.*, No. 36; (No. 193), *ibid.*, No. 45; (No. 253), *ibid.*, No. 65; (No. 447), *ibid.*, No. 71; (No. 17), *ibid.*, No. 74; (No. 335), *ibid.*, No. 75, (No. 818), *ibid.*, No. 94; (No. 5), *ibid.*, No. 103; (No. 40), *ibid.*, No. 117; (No. 130), *ibid.*, No. 123; (No. 108), *ibid.*, No. 131; (No. 141), *ibid.*, No. 137; (No. 28), *ibid.*, No. 139; (No. 90), *ibid.*, No. 147; (No. 96), *ibid.*, No. 170; (No. 98), *Poleznoe s priyatnym*, 1769, No. XIV; *ibid.*, No. XVII; (No. 35), *Opyt trudov, Volnago rossiskago sobraniya*, 1774, No. VI; (No. 159), *Utrenni svet*, 1777, III, 285–297; (No. 373), *Detskoe chtenie dlya serdtsa i razuma*, 1789, XX, 97–101; (No. 411), *Chtenie dlya vkusa, razuma i chuvstvovani*, 1793, X, 183–199; (No. 412), *ibid.*, XII, 3–28; (No. 413), *ibid.*, XII, 207–226; (No. 375), *Priyatnoe i polez-noe preprovozhdenie vremeni*, 1794, I, 129–139; (No. 477), *ibid.*, I, 237–245; (No. 215), *ibid.*, I, 307–314; (No. 558), *Muza*, 1796, pp. 204–215; (No. 35), *Ippokrena, ili utekhi liubosloviya*, 1798, I, 88–92; *ibid.*, 1800, I, 240–245; (No. 159), *ibid.*, I, 401–412; (No. 558), *ibid.*, 1801, VIII, 321–332; (No. 564), *ibid.*, VIII, 337–344; (No. 562), *ibid.*, VIII, 345–352; (No. 571), *ibid.*, IX, 49–59.

Guardian

(No. 24), *Sochineniya i perevody k polze i uveseleniiu sluzhashchiya*, 1762, I, 456–461; (No. 52), *ibid.*, I, 465–476; (No. 135), *ibid.*, I, 537–543; (No. 34), *ibid.*, II, 61–66; (No. 126), *ibid.*, II, 184–191; (No. 93), *Ezhemesyachnyya sochineniya k polze i uveseleniiu sluzh-ashchiya*, 1763, pp. 548–551; (No. 93), *Ippokrena, ili utekhi liubosloviya*, 1801, X, 161–164.

Gentleman's Magazine

Sanktpeterburgski vestnik, 1780, VI, 17–24.

Universal Magazine

Sochineniya i perevody k polze i uveseleniiu sluzhashchiya, 1758, I, 197–202; *ibid.*, I, 253–260; *ibid.*, 1759, II, 429–457; *ibid.*, 1760, I, 151–

162; *ibid.*, 1762, I, 172–180; *Prazdnoe vremya v polzu upotreblennoe,* 1760, I, 254–259; *Sanktpeterburgski vestnik,* 1778, II, 353–360; *Lekarstvo ot skuki i zabot,* 1787, pp. 122–132.

Rambler

Sochineniya i perevody k polze i uveseleniiu sluzhashchiya, 1759, I, 539–550.

General Magazine

Sochineniya i perevody k polze i uveseleniiu sluzhashchiya, 1760, I, 265–272.

Mirror

Sanktpeterburgski vestnik, 1779, V, 340–354; *Panteon inostrannoi slovesnosti,* 1798, II, 1–32.

Patriot

(III, 142), *Prazdnoe vremya v polzu upotreblennoe,* 1758, I, 61–67;. (III, 216), *ibid.*, I, 68–76.

II. TRANSLATIONS FROM ENGLISH AUTHORS IN THE EIGHTEENTH-CENTURY JOURNALS

Bacon

(*The Wisdom of the Ancients*), *Utrenni svet,* 1780, IX, 28–84; *ibid.*, X, 146–173.

Shakspere

(*Romeo and Juliet,* V, 3, "In faith I will. — Let me peruse this face," etc.), *Vechera,* 1772, pp. 14–16; (*Hamlet,* III, 1, "To be or not to be," etc.), *Opyt trudov, Volnago rossiskago sobraniya,* 1774, No. 10, pp. 257–261; (*Hamlet, ibid.*), *Lekarstvo ot skuki i zabot,* 1786, I, 195–199; (*Hamlet, ibid.*), *Ippokrena, ili utekhi liubosloviya,* 1801, VIII, 17–19; (*Henry IV,* Part I, III, 2, "God pardon thee, yet let me wonder Harry," etc.), *ibid.*, VIII, 19–21; (*Henry VIII,* III, 2, "So farewell to the little good you bear me," etc.), *ibid.*, VIII, 21–22.

Waller

(Letter to Lucy Sidney), *Aglaya,* 1808, IV, 46–49.

Milton

(*Il Penseroso*), *Sanktpeterburgski vestnik,* 1780, VI, 115–124; (*Il Penseroso*), *Novosti,* 1799, II, 150–159; (*L'Allegro*), *ibid.*, II, 160–168; (*Il Penseroso,* fragment), *Ippokrena, ili utekhi liubosloviya,* 1800, VII, 62–63; (*Lycidas*), *ibid.*, 1801, IX, 241–252.

Cowley

(Ode to Brutus), Ippokrena, ili utekhi liubosloviya, 1801, VIII, 51–56.

Dryden

(An Essay on Dramatic Poetry, fragment), Utrennyaya zarya, 1805, III, 121–125.

Locke

(Reasonableness of Christianity), Vechernyaya zarya, 1782, III, 19–42.

Defoe

(Robinson Crusoe, fragment), Ippokrena, ili utekhi liubosloviya, 1800, VII, 319–320.

Vanbrugh

(Provoked Wife, I, 2), Sanktpeterburgski vestnik, 1778, II, 375–378.

Prior

(An Ode), Ippokrena, ili utekhi liubosloviya, 1800, VII, 26–32; (The Garland), ibid., VII, 33–35; (Cloe Jealous), ibid., VII, 88–90; (A Better Answer), ibid., VII, 91–95; (Cupid Mistaken), ibid., VII, 95–96; (Venus Mistaken), ibid., VII, 141–143.

Swift

(Esquire Bickerstaffe's Most Strange and Wonderful Predictions), Sochineniya i perevody k polze i uveseleniiu sluzhashchiya, 1758, II, 551–558; (Saws and Epigrams), Sobranie novostei, 1775, pp. 155–156; (Meditations on a Broomstick), Priyatnoe i poleznoe preprovozhdenie vremeni, 1794, I, 81–91.

Addison

(Cato, V, 1, Cato's monologue), Vechera, 1772, p. 196; (Cato, ibid.), Utrennyaya zarya, 1800, I, 65–67; (Letters from Italy to Charles Montagu), Ippokrena, ili utekhi liubosloviya, 1801, VIII, 40–51, (Cato), ibid., VIII, 90–229.

Bolingbroke

(Letters on the Study and Use of History), Beseduiuschi grazhdanin, 1789, II, 91–98; III, 156–165; (Essays on Human Knowledge, selections), Ippokrena, ili utekhi liubosloviya, 1800, X, 115–121, 136–142.

Parnell

(Eclogue, Health), Chtenie dlya vkusa, razuma i chuvstvovani, 1791, III, 136–142.

Young

> (*Night Thoughts*, Night II), *Vechera*, 1772, pp. 105–136; (*Force of Religion*), *Utrenni svet*, 1777, III, 297–352; (*Night Thoughts*, Night I), *ibid.*, 1778, IV, 229–251; (*ibid.*, Night II), *ibid.*, V, 251–286; (*ibid.*, Night III), *ibid.*, 1779, V, 161–189; (*ibid.*, Night IV), *ibid.*, VI, 175–217; (*ibid.*, Night V), *ibid.*, VI, 217–271; (*ibid.*, Night VI), *ibid.*, VII, 1–41; (*Letters of Young*), *ibid.*, VII, 93–158; (*Night Thoughts*, Night VII), *ibid.*, VII, 269–343; (*ibid.*, Night VIII), *ibid.*, 1780, VIII, 99–172; (*On Marriage*), *ibid.*, VIII, 195–205; (*To Voltaire*), *ibid.*, VIII, 264–266; *Ot vsego pomalenku*, 1782, II, 10–13; (*Night Thoughts*, Night III), *Irtysh prevrashchaiushchisya v ippokrenu*, 1789, I, 1–22; (*ibid.*, Night I, fragment), *Ippokrena, ili utekhi liubosloviya*, 1799, IV, 389–396; (*ibid.*, Night III, fragment), *ibid.*, IV, 401–410; (*Letters*), *ibid.*, 1801, XI, 65–85; (*Night Thoughts, Night III*), *Novosti russkoi literatury*, 1802, IV, 245–256.

Gay

> (*Sweet William's Farewell to Black-eyed Susan*), *Ippokrena, ili utekhi liubosloviya*, 1800, VII, 85–87.

Pope

> (*Messiah*), *Moskovskoe ezhemesyachnoe izdanie*, 1781, IX, 203–208; (Messiah), *Ot vsego pomalenku*, 1786, II, 3–7; (*On Silence*), *ibid.* II, 7–10; (*Universal Prayer*), *Zerkalo sveta*, 1786, I, 129–132; (*Pastorals*), *Raspuskaiushchisya tsvetok*, 1787, 166–189; (*Eloisa to Abelard*), *Novyya ezhemesyachnyya sochineniya*, 1786, III, 78–103; (*Lines on Newton*), *Chtenie dlya vkusa, razuma i chuvstvovani*, 1793, XII, 227; (*Essay on Man*), *S. Peterburgski merkuri*, 1793, III, 151–190; (*Eloisa to Abelard*), *Ippokrena, ili utekhi liubosloviya*, 1800, I, 337–357; (*Universal Prayer*), *ibid.*, VII, 17–19.

Chesterfield

> (*Common Sense*, No. 14), *Sanktpeterburgski vestnik*, 1779, III, 199–208; (*Common Sense*, No. 54), *ibid.*, 1780, VI, 187–193.

Thomson

> (*The Seasons*, Summer, ll. 1269–1370), *Chtenie dlya vkusa, razuma i chuvstvovani*, 1793, XII, 28–35; (*Hymn on the Seasons*), *Ippokrena, ili utekhi liubosloviya*, 1800, VII, 3–10; (*Hymn on Solitude*), *ibid.*, VII, 10–13.

Johnson

> (*Rasselas*), *Dobroe namerenie*, 1764, pp. 167–192.

Sterne

> (*Sentimental Journey*, Calais), *Sanktpeterburgski vestnik*, 1779, IV,
> 24–32; (*Tristram Shandy*, History of Le Fevre), *Satiricheski vestnik*,
> 1792, II, 203–234; 335–340; (*ibid.*, Trim's Catechism), *Priyatnoe
> i poleznoe preprovozhdenie vremeni*, 1794, II, 43; (*ibid.*, Le Fevre),
> *Muza*, 1796, II, 143–155; (*Beauties of Sterne, Tristram Shandy*,
> chapter XLIII), *Ippokrena, ili utekhi liubosloviya*, 1800, V, 193–
> 224; (*ibid., Tristram Shandy*, chapter LXIV), *ibid.*, VI, 536–540;
> (*ibid.*, from *Sentimental Journey*), *ibid.*, VII, 117–141.

Shenstone

> (Eclogue, *Solicitude*), *Trudoliubivy muravei*, 1771, pp. 122–125; (*Ode
> to a Young Lady*), *Ippokrena, ili utekhi liubosloviya*, 1800, VII, 149–
> 150.

Hume

> (*Essay on Trade*), *Opyt trudov, Volnago rossiskago sobraniya*, 1774, I,
> 87–112.

Gray

> (*Elegy*), *Pokoiushchisya trudoliubets*, 1785, pp. 187–193; (*Elegy*),
> *Beseduiushchi grazhdanin*, 1789, III, 138–144; (*To Adversity*),
> *Chtenie dlya vkusa, razuma i chuvstvovani*, 1792, V, 4–7; (*Elegy*),
> *Ippokrena, ili utekhi liubosloviya*, 1798, II, 2–12; (*To Adversity*),
> *ibid.*, 1800, VI, 150–153; (*Elegy*), *ibid.*, VI, 440–448; (*Elegy*),
> *Vestnik Evropy*, 1802, VI, 319–325; (*Elegy*), *Utrennyaya zarya*,
> 1803, II, 103–114.

Collins

> (*Ode on the Death of Thomson*), *Ippokrena, ili utekhi liubosloviya*, 1800,
> VII, 145–148.

Robertson

> (*History of America*, Part III), *Akademicheskiya izvestiya*, 1780, IV,
> 19–42, 185–207.

Goldsmith

> (From *Citizen of the World*), *Ezhemesyachnyya sochineniya i izvestiya o
> uchenykh delakh*, 1763, No. 3, 348–353; (*Animated Nature*, On
> Fish), *Akademicheskiya izvestiya*, 1780, III, 175–187; (*Story of
> Alcander and Septimius, Bee*, No. 1), *Novosti*, 1799, I, 81–92.

Ossian

> (*Ossian*, "Oina-Morul"), *Zritel*, 1792, pp. 145–152; (*Ossian*, "Dar-thula"), *ibid.*, pp. 184–215; (*Ossian*, "Dar-thula"), *Chtenie dlya vkusa, razuma i chuvstvovani*, 1792, V, 14–15; (*Ossian*, "Comala"), *Priyatnoe i poleznoe preprovozhdenie vremeni*, 1794, V, 385–388; 1795, VI, 117–119; (Ossian, "Oina-Morul"), *Novosti*, 1799, II, 106–109; (*Ossian*, "Death of Oscar"), *Novosti russkoi literatury*, 1802, I, 121–128, 358–364; (*Ossian*, "Conlath and Cathona"), *Utrennyaya zarya*, 1806, IV, 42–57; 1807, V, 181–185.

Mackenzie

> (*Man of Feeling*, chapter XX), *Sanktpeterburgski vestnik*, 1779, III, 286–291.

Bloomfield

> (*The Farmer's Boy*, fragment), *Novosti russkoi literatury*, 1802, IV, 209–233.

CHAPTER VI

The English Novel in Eighteenth-Century Russia

THE journal, however, was not the most popular literary *genre* in Russia in the eighteenth century. This distinction belongs to the novel, or the romance, as the type was familiarly called, which was a powerful force in the cultural growth of the younger generation between the years 1775 and 1800. The rapidly growing reading public began to manifest a taste for those "mere tales that simply waste time" which the practical-minded Peter the Great had scorned.

As in the case of the periodical, the initial impulse for novel writing came from abroad, and perhaps to an even greater extent were the first results unoriginal and imitative. Yet the movement contained the seeds of a significant growth. The fruit of this early planting was the realistic novel of the nineteenth century, Russia's greatest contribution to world literature. But for the time being the tendency was to follow rather than to lead, and it was not until the appearance of Gogol's *Dead Souls* in 1842 that Russian writers finally overthrew foreign domination in the novel and proceeded to the creation of a body of literature purely native in content and execution and unexampled in the whole course of the country's development.

The insane devotion of Western Europe to the many-volumed heroic romances of the seventeenth and early eight-

eenth centuries did not become prevalent in Russia until
the latter part of Elizabeth's reign and the beginning of
Catherine's. Russia's enthusiasm for the numerous French
progeny of *Amadis,* — particularly *Cassandre, Faramond,
Artamène, Clélie,* and *La Princesse de Clèves,* — was scarcely
less than that of England. Russian maidens wept over the
trials of these much tried heroes and heroines, and like their
English cousins they

> to Love an altar built,
> Of twelve vast French romances, neatly gilt.

Even the almost contemporaneous popularity of the very
unromantic *Gil Blas* failed to break the charm of the inter-
minable works of La Calprénède, Scudéry, and La Fayette.

At first the dissemination of these tales of adventure was
greatly hindered by the lack of printing facilities, and manuscript versions often filled the want of the printed book.
But one of Catherine's earliest improvements affected the
press. In 1767 a special "translating department" was established in the Academy of Science and printing was directly
encouraged. The results were very apparent in the tremendous increase in publications during Catherine's reign, and
by far the majority of books issued from the press were
romances.

The craze for these courtly tales did not escape the satirist's lash in Russia any more than it did in England. The
satirical journals poked fun at the impossible heroes with
their grandiose conceptions of love and duty, and serious
critics warned the fair sex of the harmful teaching latent in
the *romans d'aventure.* "O dear beloved women!" pleads one
erstwhile reformer, "you whose natures are gifted with such

feeling spirits! Beware of the danger of reading romances, and especially those which already please you." [1]   However, devotees were not lacking who came stoutly to the defense of their favorite reading material. In the middle of the century Bolotov writes: "It is customary to condemn the romances because the reading of them does more harm than good, and because they frequently afflict young people with a kind of poison. I, however, may solemnly say of them that they never did me any harm." [2]   On the whole, there can be little doubt that they must have served a serious cultural purpose, stimulating the feelings and awakening an intellectual interest among a people which up to this time had not come in contact with any extensive narrative literature. One critic goes so far as to maintain that the romances and the love poetry of the time created the first school of Russian idealism.[3]

The chief fault found in the heroic romance was its creation of a purely imaginative world, totally unrelated to real life. Probability, reality, anything which pertained to normal background and actual existence was neglected. Accordingly, a new and welcome note was sounded in the novels of Prévost and Marivaux.   The *Mémoires d'un homme de qualité, Cléveland*, and *Marianne*, which were translated in 1756, 1760, and 1762 respectively, all achieved considerable popularity by virtue of an emphasis on character development and of plots that did not entirely forsake reality for sensational adventures. Russian readers began to praise the psychological analysis of character which these novels of Prévost and Marivaux attempted with some small success. The stage was set for the appearance of the "English novel," which for the remainder of the century and the early part of the next was to sweep all before it.

Of all the creations of English literature during the eighteenth century the novel of middle-class life was undoubtedly the most original and important. Defoe, Richardson, Fielding, and Sterne effected a revolution in European letters by their accurate studies of contemporary society. The Spanish and French tales of adventure were laid aside for English novels which, untrammelled by any past traditions or rules of art, aimed to present a clear and realistic picture of modern life and modern man with all his faults, vices, absurdities, and fancies. It was a literature of the human mind and heart, faintly or powerfully touched with a moral purpose. Into the northern countries and Germany, into France and Italy the English novel made its way, and nearly all the bourgeois literature of modern times has its roots in the creations of Richardson and Fielding.

The part played by France, and, to a less degree, by Germany in introducing the eighteenth-century English novel into Russia was considerable. The Anglomania that swept France between 1700 and 1760 has already been mentioned, and the English novel of the period helped to keep bright the flame of worship. The profound influence of these writers, and especially Richardson, on French novelists has long been recognized. There had been some hesitation in the case of *Pamela*, but after the appearance of Prévost's translation of *Clarissa Harlowe* in 1751 the English novel reigned supreme in France. From every side came hysterical tributes, culminating in Diderot's extraordinary rhapsody, *Éloge de Richardson*. The endless stream of admiration was even sufficient to provoke the spleen of that sometime Anglophile, Voltaire, who protested sharply though ineffectually. Translations multiplied at a great rate and imitations poured from the press. Nearly every French writer of tales, from Prévost to Marmontel, Bernardin de St. Pierre, Pigault-Lebrun, Baculard d'Arnaud, and Mme. De Genlis, wrote in the tradition of Richardson or Fielding. The "English novel" became the fashion and it was long before French literature ceased to follow it. Nor was the submission of Germany less complete. "Unsere Romane," said Goethe to Eckermann, "unsere Trauerspiele, woher haben wir sie denn als von Goldsmith, Fielding und Shakespeare?" [4] The statement would have gained in veracity if he had included among the novelists Richardson and Sterne. Musaeus, Wieland, Gellert, and other German authors were indebted to the English, and their enthusiasm for the new type of fiction vied with the French. Of course the two writers who must be singled out for special mention are Rousseau and Goethe. *La Nouvelle Héloïse* and *Werther* were perhaps the most significant novels of the eighteenth century on the Continent, and though their authors advanced far beyond the inspiration furnished by Richardson, yet without *Clarissa Harlowe* it is hard to believe that Rousseau and Goethe would have written two such books. [5]

However, the whole matter of French and German indebtedness to the English novel is a story long grown cold. It has been necessary to touch on it here because the enthusiasm of these two countries for our fiction flowed over into Russia. Their translations, imitations, and criticisms of the English novels were well known in Russia, and in particular

La Nouvelle Héloïse and *Werther* won a wide success and did much to popularize the *idea* of the "English novel" among the Russians. It is only with these facts in mind that we can interpret properly the preponderating number of translations from French and German novels during Catherine's reign as compared with the small number from English. Thus in this period 350 translations have been listed from French novels, 107 from German, and only 6 from English.[6] In reality many of the novels described as French and German were in turn translations from the English or were written in the tradition, or in direct imitation, of Richardson, Fielding, and Sterne. With this fact in mind it is easy to understand why the "English novel" was the most important factor in the development of Russian fiction in the latter half of the eighteenth century.

The popularity of *Robinson Crusoe* all over Europe had its reverberations in Russia. Though the book was frequently imitated in France and Germany, Defoe himself gained little fame. Indeed, his name was often dissociated from his masterpiece, and occasionally ignored or forgotten by the very translators of the book. And few were the critics who perceived the real merits of the work. Defoe's amazing observation of details and his ability to give authenticity to imagined situations were quite lost on the critics. In France Rousseau alone seemed to appreciate Defoe's literary skill, and his enthusiasm was mostly wasted in an attempt to find in *Robinson Crusoe* an able treatise on natural philosophy. It was to be the only book in Émile's library, although Rousseau did not even trouble to name its author.

In Russia *Robinson Crusoe* was translated from French in

1762–64, and its popularity carried it through three more editions in the next thirty years.[7] As in France, however, the book was enjoyed as a tale of adventure in remote regions, gratifying the human yearning for a knowledge of unknown lands. Of the author himself or his artistic accomplishments we find nothing at all in the criticism of the time. So far as influence is concerned, Defoe's realistic fiction fell on barren ground, as in fact it did in England for some twenty years. The Russians even failed to accord him the dubious honor of imitation, for the numerous *Robinsonades* which sprang up in France and Germany are not paralleled in Russia.

The English novel was subjected to the usual delay which characterized the appearance of Western European literary productions in Russia. It was not until 1787 that *Pamela* was translated (with a second edition in 1796);[8] *Clarissa Harlowe* was published in Russian garb for the first time in 1791–92, and *Sir Charles Grandison* in 1793–94. No doubt in this instance, as in the case of other English works, the accessibility of earlier French translations accounts in some measure for the comparative lateness of the Russian renderings. And for the same reason a knowledge of many English novels probably preceded their earliest appearance in Russian.

From memoir-writers and periodicals of the times and from statements in the introductions to translated novels, we can form some opinion of the impression made by Richardson and other English novelists on the reading public in Russia. Madame Smirnova in her *Memoirs* tells a story about the daughter of the famous writer Karamzin. While a group of

friends was discussing an occurrence that happened to a
common acquaintance, Sophie, who "spent all her time de-
vouring English romances," broke in irrelevantly:

"That is exactly the situation when Arthur came to Mary."
We opened our eyes in astonishment and Poletika asked her:
"What Mary? what Arthur?" . . . Lerma burst out laughing.
"Ach, indeed, this is a romance in fifteen parts! Mademoiselle
Sophie is intrigued by it at the present time! It is longer and more
heart-rending than *Clarissa Harlowe*!" Sophie so lives in her Eng-
lish romances that she takes every possible personage in them for
her own acquaintance.[9]

Another well-known figure of the age, E. von Bradke, was,
no less than Karamzin's daughter, an admirer of Richardson.
As a youth he tells how he found in his father's library many
romances: "And I devoured with eagerness Lafontaine,
Kremer, *Grandison*, and *Clarissa* in many volumes." He
suffered the customary fate of youngsters too avid of light
reading — his parents tried to put a stop to it. "But," he
adds, "I continued it in secret." [10]

The journals likewise praised the novels of Richardson in
a fashion that would have provoked the honest indignation
of Fielding. A critic writes: "I should be surprised if one
book, such as *Clarissa* or *Grandison*, did not provide the
attentive reader with finer and nobler feelings than a whole
library of moral works brings to the learned." [11] Another
critic compares Richardson to Corneille. "Where," he asks,
"is there a better philosophy of morals than in his romances?" Then, striking a lyrical note, he continues: "How
my soul rises, grows tender, strives, so to speak, with Clarissa's!" Finally, having commented on her death and the vast
pity of it (this critic has evidently read the book through),

he makes the master himself the subject of his praise: "With what purity and nobility does love breathe in the productions of this author! Richardson has the gift of moving the heart in the interest of virtue." [12]

However, it is in the introductions to both translated and original novels that we find the fullest expression of Russian admiration for the new English fiction. And one should not forget that these familiar introductions were largely instrumental in forming the taste of the novel-reading public, and that they are invariably an indication of what was popular at the moment. In the preface to the 1787 translation of *Pamela* we get the full measure of devotion to Richardson and his creation. After informing the reader that he himself had experienced every terror of the heroine, and, "with the most tender compassion had wept continually over her unhappiness," the translator finally ranks Pamela among the great forces for good in the world. "Every family will want to have a Pamela in their home who may serve as a shining example of honor and unyielding virtue." [13]

The very name "Pamela" came to have a special significance among Russian writers and readers of romances. Though Russian nobility cannot parallel the enthusiasm of the duc d'Orléans, who is said to have named one of his natural daughters after Richardson's heroine, yet a "second Pamela" and a "virtuous Pamela" are the descriptive epithets applied to a character in one of the original novels of the time,[14] and another is hopefully entitled *A Russian Pamela*. As in France, the name became a synonym for a young lady of impeccable virtue.

Grandison, too, occupied a place in the hearts of the Rus-

sian maidens, whose affections were now transferred from
the old heroic romances to the new English novel. "The
ordinary sergeant of the guard," says one critic, "appeared
to the romantically-minded damsel a Grandison." [15] Pushkin, who came to the reading of Richardson in an age that
was already turning its back on the sentimental, thought
Clarissa rather fatiguing. "Such a boresome fool is not possible," he writes.[16] But he was too fine a critic not to recognize the genius of Richardson's total accomplishment. In
discussing *Clarissa Harlowe*, he wrote: "The whole theme
of Richardson's romance has unusual merit." [17] And his
own unfinished novel, *A Romance in Letters*, draws its inspiration from this work. The three novels of Richardson
in the original found a place in his library, and he was fond
of nicknaming his friends "Clarissas" and "Lovelaces." In
Eugene Onegin Pushkin very properly attributes to his
heroine, Tatyana, and her mother a prevailing characteristic
of the women of the day. They are both omnivorous readers
of novels, and especially those of the English variety. One
of Tatyana's favorites is *Clarissa*,[18] and her mother well-
nigh goes out of her mind reading the works of Richardson.
In this respect it is curious to note the difference of a generation between Karamzin and Pushkin. The former, on his
visit to England, was shocked on talking with his chambermaid to learn that "Lovelace seemed to her incomparably
more favored than Grandison. Such are London serving
girls!" [19] he exclaims. But Pushkin, writing some years
after Karamzin, represents Tatyana's mother as sharing the
preference of the London chambermaid:

She so adored her Richardson,
Though not because she'd read him through,
Nor did she like his Grandison,
Because his Lovelace was untrue. [20]

So thoroughly was Russia deluged with translations of foreign novels that at first there was little incentive to original production. Gradually, however, native writers attempted to imitate and, as we might expect, Richardson's works exerted a patent influence on these early Russian novels.

Only two years after the appearance of the translation of *Pamela*, Lvov published his *A Russian Pamela, or the History of Marie, a Virtuous Peasant Girl*.[21] It is the story of the love of a young nobleman for a beautiful peasant girl. The machinations of the nobleman's cynical friend keep the hero and heroine apart for a long time, but everything turns out right in the end. In his foreword Lvov declares very patriotically:

My zeal and my very devotion to my beloved fatherland have constrained me to write the *History of Marie, a Virtuous Peasant Girl*, who was as much honored in her actions, as, for example, *Pamela*, written by the glorious Richardson, may have been. For this reason I have called her a "Russian Pamela," for there are among us such tender hearts of noble sensibility in lowly circumstances.[22]

In the person of Marie, the lovely peasant girl, we have a sedulous imitation of Pamela. She is modest to a fault and shares her English sister's conviction that virtue is a pearl of great price. Her lover, however, leans more towards the Grandison type, whereas his friend plays the part of a Mr. B with something of the craft of a Lovelace. Like Pamela and Clarissa, Marie is given to moralizing at great length, continually fortifying herself with a specious kind of Christian ethics. With his model too much in mind, the author failed to observe the native life around him, or what he did observe he idealized. Yet the book was popular and influenced succeeding writers to some extent.

The novels of Emin, one of the more original writers of the time, show obvious indebtedness to Richardson. His early work, *Roza*,[23] follows the epistolary fashion. The hero advises Roza to read Richardson and Fielding,[24] and he himself is clearly modelled on Lovelace. The death scenes of both Roza and Vetrogen are very reminiscent of the death scenes of Clarissa and Lovelace. Another of his novels, *The Game of Fate*,[25] while indebted to Richardson for certain small details, is, on the whole, a more original performance.

Poor Liza,[26] an extremely popular short novel of Karamzin, has the same general theme as the *Russian Pamela*. Liza's love affair, however, takes a tragic turn and she commits suicide. Karamzin was an admirer of Richardson, whose notions of social equality in marriage are preached in *Poor Liza*, and the heroine herself is a curious combination of Pamela and Clarissa.

Despite the vogue that Richardson's works obtained in Russia, their actual influence on the novel was not nearly so great as it might have been under other circumstances. For example, Richardson did not have the host of disciples and imitators that he had in France and Germany after the publication of *Clarissa Harlowe*. The reasons are not difficult to ascertain. In the first place, the production of original fiction in Russia in the last forty years of the eighteenth century was very slight in comparison with the large num-

ber of translated novels.[27] The translated works were so
much better than the native attempts, and so accessible,
that Russian novelists received little encouragement. Then,
too, the direct influence of Richardson was partially pre-
empted by an earlier acquaintance with his French and German followers, whose works, in fact, were often described
as "English novels." *La Nouvelle Héloïse* had been translated
as early as 1769, and *Werther* in 1781; and whereas, of all
Richardson's works *Pamela* alone achieved a second edition,
the novels of Rousseau and Goethe ran into several editions
each. Their popularity dimmed the star of the Englishman.
Richardson's novels never created a school of pure imitation
in Russia as did *La Nouvelle Héloïse* and *Werther*. But if
Rousseau and Goethe succeeded in stealing something of the
popularity of the master, it was largely on the strength of
the peculiarly "English" features of their novels, such as
the psychological development of character, the portrayal of
family life, and the background of Christian idealism. And
these were features most consistently imitated by Russian
novelists of the time. But perhaps more than anything else
it was the sentimentality of Rousseau, and more especially
of Goethe, and their imitators, — somewhat different in
kind and much more pronounced than the sentimentality of
Richardson, — that won them a large Russian following.
This sloppy sentimentality carried all before it, and with the
increment of Sterne's special brand, a whole new school of
novel writers sprang up in Russia.

The history of Fielding in Russia during this formative
period in the development of the novel presents the paradox
of a writer's acquiring great popularity but no imitators. As

in the case of Richardson, the Russian attitude towards Fielding was somewhat dictated by France and Germany. Fielding was admired in France, but little understood. Some set him down as a poor disciple of Richardson, others as an imitator of Lesage, whose low picaresque adventures had now lost caste with a reading public in love with the moral and moralizing Clarissas and Grandisons. Only a few critics, such as La Harpe and Wieland, recognized the infinite truth and the rugged morality of *Tom Jones*. This mixed admiration had its counterpart in Russia, with the difference, however, that Fielding's position in relation to Richardson in the growth of the novel was critically understood and declared. The unvarnished realism of Fielding's works was ultimately to recommend itself to the peculiar genius of Russian novelists, and it is safe to say that if they had discovered him some fifty years later, he would probably have attracted a number of enthusiastic followers. But by that time Russia had learned to work the same mine which had provided the English writer with such rich ore, and with Gogol as their leader Russian novelists created their own school of realistic fiction.

It was unfortunate that the Russian translations of Fielding were based mainly on the emasculated versions of Desfontaines and La Place. The "prettyfying" of these Frenchmen had little of the justification and none of the art of Prévost's abbreviated renderings of Richardson's works. In consequence, much of the characteristic virility of Fielding's novels is lacking in the eighteenth-century Russian translations.

It is an interesting fact that Fielding was translated into

Russian before Richardson, a version of *Tom Jones* appearing in 1770–71. In 1770 also a translation of *Joseph Andrews* was published, and *Jonathan Wild* and *Amelia* followed in 1772. Later several novels appeared, which are not Fielding's although they were ascribed to him, — an unfailing indication at this time of the popularity of any translated author in Russia.[28]

With the exception of *Amelia*, all the translations ran into more than one edition,[29] and of Fielding's popularity in general there exists an abundance of evidence. An admirer writes a fervent letter to one of the periodicals in which he thanks Fielding "as a benefactor and a friend." Only after reading his novels, he confesses, has he "understood life." Finally, he exclaims:

> The power and inimitable art of thy pen and the correctness of thy principles incline my heart to everything that thou dost favor. . . . I should be cold to all thine instructions if they were otherwise joined with severity and bigotry. But why should I not love thee when thou, entering into the secret places of my heart and searching out its deepest motives, revealest the reason of my errors in a way that I, without thy help, should never have even thought of! . . . Great man, accept the offer of my gratitude and love which thou hast enkindled in my heart. I have felt all the importance, power, and charm of thy works, and my own defects![30]

Perhaps Fielding would have been more amused than pleased by this heartfelt and patient tribute from an eighteenth-century Russian reader, scented as it is with something of the eulogistic aroma that characterized the praises of Richardson's female devotees.

A more discriminating but no less enthusiastic tribute was offered by the translator of Joseph Andrews:

The author [he writes] is the renowned English dramatist, Mr. Fielding, whose fame is not merely local but is spread over all Europe. His writings are everywhere read with satisfaction, and the inhabitants of Great Britain were not at all indignant with him in that he selected, for the most part, the foibles of his own country on which to exercise his pen.[31]

Other equally laudatory appreciations could be added,[32] for in general Fielding's novels were regarded by Russian critics as the best realistic novels of manners. Furthermore, the critics showed little hesitation in rating Fielding as greater than Richardson, convinced as they were that his profound moral tone, arising from his healthy love of life, had more universal implications than the severe asceticism of Richardson.[33]

Yet, as already pointed out, despite his obvious popularity and recognized worth, Fielding had no imitators in Russia throughout this period. The reason lay in the all-inclusive literary convention in the matter of fiction. The reading public craved the sentimental; they wanted to see life through a veil of tears. Consequently, the whole-hearted optimism of Fielding, the humor of Parson Adams, the glorified crimes of Jonathan Wild, and the attractive rascality of Tom Jones, while genuinely appreciated, could not displace in favor the idealized virtues of the melancholy and lachrymose heroes of the eighteenth-century novel.[34]

Smollett received a vicarious reception in Russia. *Roderick Random* was translated in 1788 and ungenerously attributed to Fielding, and the same fate befell *Humphry Clinker*, which appeared the following year. The mistake must be laid at the door of the French translators of Smollett, who curiously and persistently confused him with the better known Fielding. But even in this gratuitous disguise Smollett's works played little or no part in the development of Russian fiction. As in France, his novels were felt to be too English, and hence were incapable of taking root in foreign soil. In the critical literature on the novel we find no mention of Smollett, and, in fact, it was only through the medium of German criticism that Russia finally identified him as the author of his own works.[35]

From what has already been said, it will come as no surprise that Sterne, of all the English novelists read in Russia in the last half of the eighteenth century, was perhaps the most popular and influential. In one respect his works contained an element of appeal not unlike that found in such different productions as *La Nouvelle Héloïse* and *Werther*, and largely because of this appeal Sterne vied successfully with Rousseau and Goethe for Russian favor. That is, all this fiction glorified sentimentality or sensibility to a greater or less degree, and this was the feature most often imitated by Russian writers until a very definite school of sentimental literature grew up and persisted into the nineteenth century. In this foreign literary competition, however, Sterne could stand his ground, for he had a brand of sentimentality all his own, and furthermore he popularized by the *Sentimental Journey* a literary form which inspired a whole library of "Journeys." But the essence of Sterne's influence in Russia was, in a sense, peculiarly unrelated to the development of the novel. *Tristram Shandy* was not even translated in the eighteenth century, though many Russians no doubt read it in the French version. It was the *Sentimental Journey* (translated in 1793) that the Russians grew enthusiastic

over, and this fact in itself indicates the kind and quality of
Sterne's influence. His fine sensitive intimacy and his "smile
mingled with tears" caught the Russian fancy and informed,
not so much the novel, but the whole literary atmosphere of
Russia during the last twenty years of the eighteenth century. In view of this it will be more appropriate to consider
Sterne in detail in the next chapter, which treats of the influence of English sentimentality on the corresponding
movement in Russian literature.

Goldsmith's rather early appearance in the Russian journals has already been mentioned, but his fame became widespread only after the translation of the *Vicar of Wakefield* in
1786. Though the details and execution are quite different,
Goldsmith's masterpiece has what might be called a spiritual
kinship with the novels of Richardson, Rousseau, and
Goethe, and hence its popularity in Russia at this time was
assured. The Christian idealism of the book and the long-
suffering vicar, who is a kind of sentimentalized Parson
Adams, were features that suited perfectly the growing
demand for idealized heroes and sentimental situations in
both the translated and the original Russian novels. The
critics wrote of him in terms of highest praise and the translator of the *Vicar of Wakefield* commented appreciatively:
"This novel may serve as a model for works of this kind.
. . . All must pay homage to the book. Since Russians
have manifested an inclination for the English and a respect
for their works, they can now contribute greatly to the ap-
proval of this book." [36] There were no forthright imitations
of the *Vicar of Wakefield*, but it had some influence on the
native novel, particularly in the matter of sentimental color-

ing and delineation of character. Thus the vicar seems to
have been the model for the Job-like old father of Marie in
Lvov's *A Russian Pamela*.

Curiously enough, scarcely one of the English novelists we
have been discussing achieved quite the astounding vogue in
eighteenth-century Russia that fell to the lot of Ann Radcliffe. And it is a tribute to the unique service performed by
France in disseminating a knowledge of English literature in
Russia that the novels of Ann Radcliffe were known primarily
through French translations, for I have been unable to find
a single Russian rendering of her works in the eighteenth
century, although a few appeared in the early years of the
nineteenth. The frequent and often unrestrained encomiums
of her many Russian admirers leave no doubt as to the
startling effect produced by her novels. So well established
was her fame that booksellers, as in the case of Fielding, un-
ceremoniously ascribed to her the works of other foreign
writers in order to increase their sales.[37] M. A. Dmitriev in
his memoirs, after remarking on the popularity of Voltaire,
La Nouvelle Héloïse, and the novels of A. Lafontaine, Genlis,
and Kotzebue, concludes: "But no one gained such glory as
Mrs. Radcliffe!"[38] He tells how in the country the family
gathered together in the parlor of an evening and someone
"read and others listened, especially the ladies and girls.
. . . What horrors the famous Mrs. Radcliffe spread!
'Famous' was sometimes printed before her name in translations of her works."[39] Indeed, her romantic tales seemed to
have a particular fascination for the "ladies and girls" of
the time. In one of Pushkin's stories the heroine is described
as an impulsive, sentimental girl, "nourished on the mysteri-

ous horrors of Radcliffe." [40] And an account of a high-born lady of the age informs us that "she read very little: in her hands they saw only the romances of Mrs. Radcliffe." [41] Nor did the men scorn this type of reading. F. Vigel, a famous memoir-writer, commenting on the occupations of his early youth, remarks: "Frequently I was out of my wits from the horrors of Mme. Radcliffe, whose tormenting agreeable forms acted upon the irritated nerves of my companions." [42] A native novelist of the period, feeling the powerlessness of his own language, interrupts his narrative to exclaim: "O Mistress Radcliffe, why have I not thy divine talent? How by thine own agreeable, charming manner wouldst thou have apprised my readers of the sight and sound of my heroine!" [43]

For the most part the critics reflected the enthusiasm of the reading public. The imaginative power which Mrs. Radcliffe possessed to an enviable degree, notes one critic, is precisely the quality lacking among the native novelists. "The creations of Mrs. Radcliffe," he writes, have enriched our literature. I say 'enriched,' because, not having them, we should be obliged to read such things as *Prince Bova* and *Eruslan Lazarevich*." [44] Another contributor to the periodicals tells how he sits down at night with the novels of Radcliffe. "Dear Mistress Radcliffe plays on my imagination as it pleases her. I have never read romances with such dreaminess, such enthusiasm, as those of this dear and unique writer." [45] And the Russian novelist Shalikov went so far as to hold up her works as a good educational influence:

No matter what may be said about romances, the magic brush of the incomparable Mistress Radcliffe paints, more life-like than the cynical pen, charming pictures of virtue and hideous caricatures of vice! Her romances, in which, contrary to the ordinary romances, love does not always play the leading rôle, are more edifying than dry moral tracts. Read *la Fôret!* [46]

Even as late as the middle of the nineteenth century we find the critic A. Grigorev reminiscing about the great popularity of Mrs. Radcliffe in his early youth.[47] Critically, perhaps, her fame reached its height in Russia with the translation of Scott's wholly appreciative essay on her life and works in 1826.[48]

Nevertheless, throughout this period she was not lacking in detractors who objected to her novels primarily on the score of their harmful effect on the imagination of the young. Thus one critic questions the usefulness of her tales and condemns them for "not having any purpose, for not bringing to light any positive knowledge of society, and for not revealing any new moral truths." But especially, he says, "they can be harmful. They act on the nerves. The continual impression of horror sometimes results in bad consequences, — all physicians will testify to this. We know women who for three nights were not able to sleep after having read the *Mysteries of Udolpho!*" [49] Another critic refers to the "absurd nonsense of Mrs. Radcliffe," [50] while a third slightingly comments on her "childish tales." [51] Her mysterious backgrounds and naïvely rationalized supernatural agencies, while delighting the general reading public, did not always escape the satirical barbs of the Russian critics. One of them, falling into doggerel, thus humorously describes the "Plan of a Romance à la Radcliffe":

> Robbers a few and a dungeon at night,
> With a half dozen owls on a tower;

Then down the passage a thin ray of light,
While the wind roars and wolves howl by the hour;
Now to the hero in dreams must appear
Griffins a-flying, a dragon or two;
Horror on horror and fear piled on fear. . . .
That, à la Radcliffe, is romance for you![52]

The essential appeal of Mrs. Radcliffe's works is patent enough. Her novels, with their pure and perfect heroines and mysterious heroes, and their sensational plots that have something of the attraction of a detective story, needed nothing more to gain a favorable reception anywhere in Europe in the late eighteenth century and the early nineteenth. If Russia had been a little farther advanced in the development of the novel, Mrs. Radcliffe's great popularity might have inspired a "School of Terror" in fiction such as existed in England and Germany. However, she had no direct imitators and, as in the case of Fielding, this is not surprising, for the invariable goal of the few aspiring native writers was the sentimental novel. In fact, much of the adverse criticism of her works was the result of her partial divergence from the popular sentimental *genre*. Her novels lacked realism and the psychological development of character, features which Richardson, Rousseau, and Goethe had taught the critics to expect. But she had something in common with this *genre* which no doubt facilitated her ready acceptance. Such tales as *The Romance of the Forest*, *The Mysteries of Udolpho*, and *The Italian* are by no means devoid of tears, and their exaggerated, romantic descriptions of nature were settings just suited to the taste of the Russian sentimentalists. In reality, however, Mrs. Radcliffe had little or no influence on the development of the

Russian novel. Her significance, if any, was as a harbinger of one phase of the romantic movement, which at the end of the century was already beginning to make itself felt in Russian literature.

Other English writers of fiction, whose names still count for something in literary history, were translated by 1800, but their works were pretty much lost in the host of novels served up to the Russian reading public at this time. Translations were made from the works of Aphra Behn, Sara Fielding, Dr. Johnson, Beckford, Mrs. Sheridan, Fanny Burney, and Mrs. Inchbald.[53]

However much the Russian critics may have differed on the relative accomplishments of individual authors, they were all agreed that the English novelists had created a definite type of fiction and that the type bore the patent of originality and excellence. Their own observations, as well as the opinions of French and German critics, supported them in this conviction. "We should wish, preferably," declares one of these critics, "that better and more useful romances might be translated into our language, — the works of Richardson, Fielding, Goldsmith, and those like them." [54] The popular interest aroused by the English novel is reflected in the very titles of critical articles on fiction, such as "Concerning Certain of the Newer English Romances," [55] "Concerning Tales, and Especially Those of English Writers," [56] and "Concerning the Reading of Romances in General and the English in Particular." [57]

On the whole, despite the confusing mass of translated novels in the eighteenth century, it is not difficult to trace the lines of influence and to define the predominant taste of

Russian readers. The French pseudo-classical *romans d'aventure* continued to enjoy some popularity until the very end of the century and, as a matter of fact, inspired a few Russian imitations. But gradually interest in them diminished and for the most part they were relegated to readers of the lower class. With the appearance of the works of Richardson, Fielding, Sterne, and Goldsmith, a new kind of fiction was recognized and this was generally designated by the Russian critics as the "English novel." Its acceptance among the intelligentsia was immediate, and long before the century had ended the English novel was imitated by native writers. The features consistently connected with the new type were the individualized hero and heroine, the psychological development of character, Christian idealism, realism, sentimentality, and the epistolary form. It must be admitted that native writers had but little success in imitating these features. Their characters, though often cast in the mold of Pamela, Clarissa, Lovelace, Grandison, and the Vicar of Wakefield, remained bloodless types, lacking all individuality. And the realism of Fielding, though much praised, was scarcely employed with the effectiveness of the master in depictions of Russian life. Of all the features of the English novel, however, it was the Christian idealism and the sentimentality that the native writers copied most successfully. To be sure, the brand of sentimentality they favored was that made popular by *La Nouvelle Héloïse* and *Werther*, both of which were directly or indirectly indebted to Richardson. Through the Russian novels of the time moped lachrymose heroes and heroines who wept copiously on the slightest provocation. For the time being Russian novelists were interested in portraying the idealistic rather than the realistic side of life.

The part played by foreign disciples of the English novel in popularizing the type in Russia has already been indicated. By the end of the century and in the early years of the next the authors who had somewhat displaced Richardson and Fielding, and to a large extent, Rousseau and Goethe, were Marmontel, Baculard d'Arnaud, Mme. de Genlis, Meissner, and Gellert. But these French and German authors were students in the school of Richardson, Fielding, and Sterne, and their works recommended themselves to the Russian reading public because of their "English" features. The Russian critics made no mistake about the line of descent. "It is worthy of note," wrote Karamzin, "that this country [England] has produced the best romancers. . . . Richardson and Fielding have taught the French and Germans how to write romances as the story of life." [58] And his Russian contemporaries shared this belief.

The influence of this translated fiction on the society of the time was perhaps of much greater consequence than its influence on the growth of the native novel. Young men and women affected the attitudes, actions, and occupations of their favorite heroes and heroines. They tried to live the idealized life which they found in the sentimental variety of the "English" novel, and pure love, an admiration for nature, and ready tears were characteristics of the sensitive youth of the day.

The original fiction inspired by the "English" novels soon ran its course, no doubt because it was too far removed from reality. The sentimental works of Emin, Lvov, Gorchakov,

Galinkovski, Popov, and Karamzin were quickly forgotten in the enthusiasm for a new type of fiction, the historical novel, which came in with the romantic movement. Not even Narezhny's rather fine realistic performance, *A Russian Gil Blas* (1814), could compete with this new interest, and the book was undeservedly ignored. But when the popularity of the historical romance had somewhat subsided, the English novel of the eighteenth century and its successors were once again admired in Russia. And their principal contributions, realism and the psychological treatment of character, have left their trace on all the great Russian novelists of the nineteenth century.

BIBLIOGRAPHY

BIBLIOGRAPHICAL STUDIES

V. V. Sipovski, *Iz istorii russkago romana i povesti*, St. Petersburg, 1903. (Contains a descriptive bibliography of all the original and translated fiction in eighteenth-century Russia).

V. Sopikov, *Ukazatel k opytu rossiskoi bibliografii* (sostavil V. Rogozhin), St. Petersburg, 1908.

INVESTIGATIONS

"O nekotorykh noveshikh angliskikh romanakh" (*Liubitel slovesnosti,* 1806, II).

"O skazkakh i romanakh" (*Avrora,* 1806, II).

"O skazkakh i ob angliskikh pisatelnitsakh" (*Vestnik Evropy,* 1807, XXXIV).

"O sternakh ili puteshestviyakh sentimentalnykh" (*Aglaya,* 1808, I).

"O chtenii romanov voobshche i angliskikh v osobennosti" (*Rossiski muzeum,* 1815, IV).

"*Tom Dzhons* Fildinga i *Klarissa Harlov* Richardsona" (*Syn otechestva,* 1834, CLXVII).

N. Karamzin, "O knizhnoi torgovle i liubvi ko chteniiu v Rossii" (*Sochineni*, izd. A. Smirdina, St. Petersburg, 1848, III, 545 ff.).

A. Pypin, *Dlya liubitelei knizhnoi stariny*, Moskva, 1888.

N. Belozerskaya, "Vliyanie perevodnago romana i zapadnoi tsivilizatsii na russkoe obshchestvo XVIII v." (*Russkaya starina*, 1895, LXXXIII).

Vasili Trofimovich Narezhny, St. Petersburg, 1896.

V. V. Sipovski, *Ocherki iz istorii russkago romana*, St. Petersburg, 1909–10, 2 vols. (The classical investigation on Russian fiction up to 1800.)

CHAPTER VII

ENGLISH SENTIMENTALISM IN RUSSIAN LITERATURE
(THOMSON, YOUNG, OSSIAN, STERNE)

UNTIL the time of Pushkin Russia was unusually susceptible to those movements in Western European
literature which, because of their chronological concurrence
and sameness in form and subject-matter in the various
countries, suggest a kind of law and order in literary development. Like France, Germany, Italy, and England, Russia
had its neo-classical period, and the several phases of this
movement in criticism, poetry, and the drama were closely
duplicated, although with little originality and few contributions to the formation of a purely national literature. The
satirical journal and the eighteenth-century novel were also
reproduced, and soon the Romantic Movement of Western
Europe was to establish itself and inspire a literature hitherto
unequalled in Russia. To be sure, the country was always a
generation or more behind in reacting to the literary tendencies of its neighbors, but the reason for this — Russia's
long isolation and her consequent slow cultural development
— has been brought out in the early chapters of this study.

In the light of these facts it is not surprising that Russia
also experienced a counterpart to what has been called the
Pre-romantic Movement. Native literary historians rarely
accept this designation, perhaps because it is difficult to
circumscribe its limits or indicate its precise tendencies.

Certainly there are no ostensible extremities, such as the introduction of the new nature poetry in England and the publication of the *Lyrical Ballads*, to provide us with convenient points of departure. Nor was there any declared revolt against existing literary forms and subject-matter. Neo-classical poets could continue to write their highly formal odes and satires and at the same time produce poetry that embodied indubitable romantic tendencies. And the fact that the inspiration for these defections from the literary traditions of the day came largely from foreign productions that sporadically filtered into the country prevented the movement from taking any concrete form and direction. All that can be said is, that in the last twenty years of the eighteenth century and in the first few years of the next there were evinced among Russian writers a willingness to submit to certain pre-romantic, foreign, literary influences, and a desire to experiment with forms and subjects different from those established by neo-classical tradition. And among the foreign authors most significant in effecting this change were Thomson, Young, Ossian, and Sterne. It is not suggested that there was any conscious purpose working towards romanticism among the Russian writers thus influenced. Still, their productions show a persistent attempt to break away from the prevailing neo-classicism along lines that characterized the nascent romantic tendencies of their English models.

Some explanation may be necessary to justify this grouping of English authors in a chapter dealing specifically with sentimentalism. For I do not wish to distort the significance of sentimentalism, remote as that significance may be in its

connection with romanticism. That a literature of sentimentality existed in England in the eighteenth century is an accepted fact, but critics have not always agreed that Thomson, Young, and Ossian contributed anything to it, or if they
did, that their contributions in this respect had anything to
do with the Pre-romantic Movement in England. The problem, however, becomes less a problem and more a matter of
simple definition if we consider the effect that these writers
had on the Continent. For the works of Thomson, Young,
Ossian, and Sterne were first subjected to French and German translations and criticism before they ever reached
Russia.

The Seasons, *Night Thoughts*, and the *Poems of Ossian*
achieved a wide popularity in France and Germany, primarily because of their quality of *feeling*, which Rousseau
and his disciples were glorifying in opposition to the *reason*
of the fast-waning literature of neo-classicism. Although it
would have surprised the contemporary English reader,
Thomson's Continental admirers were more interested in
his philosophy and his love of humanity than in his descriptions of nature. Not that they were blind to the latter quality, however. They praised his accurate descriptions of the
more picturesque aspects of nature. But what they really
grew enthusiastic over in *The Seasons* was the emotions
aroused by thoughts of eternal life, conjugal happiness, and
the simple pleasures of the peasant. In short, Thomson's
admirers were concerned mainly with his treatment of the
sentiment of the individual man in contact with nature.
And the occasional sentimentality in *The Seasons* was mag-
nified and considered characteristic by French and German

readers. Nor is the author entirely irresponsible for this interpretation. After all, a poet who could describe so feelingly a fish, "weak, helpless, uncomplaining wretch," beguiled by the "agonizing folds" of the "tortured worm" [1] was not far removed from the tearful excesses of a Sterne. At all events *The Seasons* contributed to the sentimental rhapsody and deep melancholy of man before the wonders of nature which found faithful reflection in *La Nouvelle Héloïse* and *Werther*.

Likewise it was the sepulchral philosophy of Young peering darkly through the "enchanting sadness" of the *Night Thoughts*, a melancholy closely allied to the sentimental, that brought about his incredible vogue in France and Germany. And of a piece were the gloomy reflections of Ossian, the poet's hallowed feelings before aspects of nature sombre and sublime. Such were the features of Macpherson's *Fragments* and *Fingal* that particularly recommended themselves to readers on the Continent.

Obviously sentimental confession, the turning of man's mind upon himself, runs through all these works. It is the quality of subjectivity, an unfortunate but necessary word, that gives a unity of sentiment to *The Seasons*,[2] *Night Thoughts*, and the *Poems of Ossian*, and subjectivity will generally be admitted by the nicest of critics to be a quality of romanticism. Sensibility, feeling for nature, and melancholy are merely three phases of the same disposition of the soul. To the resultant sentimentality Sterne added his own special brand and thus crystallized a literary tendency that had started with Richardson. French and German disciples emphasized the sentimental quality in all these works, and hence this quality was most highly regarded by the Russians.

Although there are scattered instances of contacts with the originals, most of the Russian renderings of Thomson, Young, Ossian, and Sterne were based on French and German translations. Furthermore, such foreign periodicals as the *Journal Étranger* and the *Gazette Littéraire* helped, with enthusiastic articles, to popularize in Russia the literary tendency to sentimentalism growing out of these works. The West now began to pour into Russia an antidote for the poison of unbelief, reason, and materialism which the country had imbibed so eagerly from the same Western sources only a few years before. What might be described as a "philosophy of feeling" took hold of Russian writers at the end of the century and soon exerted a powerful influence on literary production.

Generally speaking we may discern two main groups in the Russian Sentimental Movement, a differentiation no doubt inspired by the *Sturm und Drang* school between 1760 and 1780. One group put absolute faith in the teachings of innate genius. Genius may slumber in every one of us, as Young and Sterne thought. It is only necessary to bring it out into the open and nurture it. The rule and line of neoclassicism must be abandoned and free genius must return to healthy nature, to feeling, and to the idealization of one's native land. Such a conception amounted to the glorification of *self*, a search for the realization of the individual consciousness against the background of the universe. Once aware of its own soul, genius must express itself in exalted, passionate feeling.

The other group, by far the larger, consisted of peaceful devotees of sentimentality, men who were concerned with a quiet analysis of their own feelings rather than with the *Weltschmerz*. Lulled to a sense of subdued rapture and tears by a presentiment of life's sadness, they preferred to shun society for nature and wrap themselves in the security of their own tiny ego. They may grow sentimental while contemplating nature, music, ideal friendship, or beautiful virtues, but essentially their feeling is within them. Self-observation reaches a degree of scrupulosity, and the *schöne Seele* becomes the chief object of meditation. Love feeds on sadness, and the love of friends is deeper and more sacred than the love of man for woman. The "joy of grief" which Sterne apotheosized became a virtue of the highest order among these Russian sentimentalists. One could scarcely hear the sweet sound of music, behold the moon, look into a beloved one's eyes, or listen to the soft murmur of pine trees without bursting into tears.

The contemplative melancholy of the *Night Thoughts* or the *Poems of Ossian* was the favorite mood of the sentimentalists, who were the sworn enemies of jollity. For them the joy of sadness was to be found while sitting at night in the cell of some ruined monastery with the moonlight streaming through the window. The sentimentalist fairly revels in melancholy, and death becomes an escape pleasant to contemplate.

On such themes and moods was constructed a sentimental literature in Russia with such famous writers as Karamzin and Zhukovski as its chief exponents. And this literature was the natural prelude to the Romantic Movement which soon followed and, indeed, included among its disciples several of the authors who received their early training in the lachrymose productions of the earlier movement. It will be of interest, then, to consider individually the history of Thomson, Young, Ossian, and Sterne in the inception and development of Russian Sentimentalism.

The Seasons was not introduced into France until 1759, but its success was immediate and numerous translations and imitations followed during the next fifty years. Voltaire, Rousseau, Diderot, Grimm, and many lesser authors were warm in its praise. Germany, too, succumbed, and Gessner's *Idyllen*, which so completely caught the spirit and sentiment of *The Seasons*, served by its great popularity to reflect additional credit on Thomson's work. Continental critics, ignoring the splendid nature passages in Shakspere and Milton, regarded Thomson and Gessner as the creators of nature poetry. Thomson's success, of course, was not a little aided by the fact that his treatment of nature was in complete harmony with that of Rousseau.

Although the first Russian translation of *The Seasons* was not made until 1798, there is evidence of a much earlier knowledge of the poem in fragmentary renderings and imitations in the periodicals.[3] That is, as so often happened in the transmission of English literature, some familiarity with the work was gained through French and German translations and criticism before it was made generally accessible in Russian. A second edition of the 1798 version appeared in 1803, and there was a fresh rendering in 1808. That the poem was regarded with considerable favor scarcely requires more support than the mere fact of these translations. However, it is not difficult to accumulate testimony in the form of tributes, critical appreciations, and imitations.

Before *The Seasons* had gained anything like a general reading public in Russia, N. Karamzin (1766–1826) had already probed its beauties and praised the poem to his own literary circle. This author, known to Western Europe chiefly as an historian,[4] was one of the first great men of letters in Russia, and his name looms large in the Sentimental Movement, to which he was the first to give full expression. A true cosmopolitan, Karamzin knew well the literatures of France, Germany, and England. In his youth he came under the influence of the pietistic group of Masons, indulging a natural bent for philosophy and religious mysticism. Such associations turned him against French satire and Voltairean impiety. His mind was naturally receptive to English sentimentalism and to those German writers, such as Klopstock, Gessner, and Kleist, who were most in sympathy with it. Karamzin soon became the high priest of the literature of feeling, which sought in poetry pure love, lofty idealism, and a melancholy worship of nature. Joined to his devotion to German thought and culture was his strong regard for England. He had grown up with an admiration for that country and on his visit there, when he came in sight of it, he exclaimed: "The shore! the shore! We are in Dover, and I am in England — in that land which in my childhood I loved with such warmth, and which, by the character of its inhabitants and the nature of its education, is surely one of the chief governments of Europe."[5] Among his exact contemporaries in Russia there were few, indeed, who knew English literature so well or could appreciate it with such sympathetic understanding. And as to the four writers treated in this chapter, — Thomson, Young, Ossian, and Sterne, — no author, certainly, was more instrumental in furthering their popularity in Russia than Karamzin.

In a long unrhymed production called *Poesy*, composed about 1787, Karamzin attempts to conceive imaginatively the birth of poetry and comments on some of its most famous names.[6] After hailing Britain as "the mother of the greatest poets," and extolling Shakspere, Milton, Young, and Ossian, he turns to Thomson:

> Nature adored and deeply contemplated,
> Searching the yearly cycle's every phase,
> Thomson proclaimed to us the charms of Nature,
> The joy of seasons. Nature's worthy son,
> O Thomson! I shall praise thee for all time!
> For Nature hast thou taught me to enjoy,
> And in the forest's shade to praise its Creator![7]

This was written quite early in Karamzin's literary career, and despite its rhapsodic tone, a mannerism entirely characteristic of the sentimentalists, there is no reason to doubt the sincerity of his devotion. For throughout his future works in both prose and verse Karamzin often pays tribute to Thomson, and *The Seasons* played an important part in his literary development. There is good reason to suppose that he read the poem in the original,[8] a unique accomplishment for a Russian at this time. That he knew English there can be little doubt,[9] and he more or less clinches the fact by quoting from the works of English authors in the original, among them *The Seasons*.[10]

Karamzin connected Thomson's merit as a poet of nature with a special phase of English literary genius. In the *Letters of a Russian Traveller* he writes: "The literature of the English, like their character, has many peculiarities, and is excellent in different ways. Here is the fatherland of descriptive poetry (*poésie descriptive*): the French and Germans have imitated this trait of the English, who are able to note the most minute features of nature. Up to this time nothing can be compared to Thomson's *Seasons of the Year*; one may call it the mirror of Nature." [11]

Karamzin is not merely echoing French and German criticism here, for before he made these observations (1790) he had come in contact with Thomson in a practical way in his translation of *A Hymn on the Seasons*.[12] Thomson's accurate descriptions of nature, as well as those of his German imitators, taught Karamzin to observe the splendor of forest and field, of mountains and the heavens. "Spring," he says, "would not be so beautiful for me if Thomson and Kleist had not described all her beauties." [13] But to a degree greater than in his model, he found a quiet, sentimental joy in communing with nature. He tells us how he set out for the city with a copy of Thomson's poems in his hand. After meditating upon the verses, the still spring evening filled his soul with an "idyllic harmony." [14] And again, while walking in a garden at night he sees the ribbon of the Elbe shimmering under the moonlight and weeps, "which usually happens when I am very joyous at heart." [15]

In a small prose piece called *The Country*, which resembles Thomson's juvenile poem, *Of Country Life*, Karamzin attempts a contrast of village and city life, a theme much favored by Russian sentimental writers as well as by English pre-romantic and romantic authors. The inspiration of

Thomson becomes even more obvious when Karamzin, in describing how he spends his day, remarks at one point that from all his books he selects the works of the English poet. "I go with him into the meadow and read. Then I lay the book down under a raspberry bush and look up at the lofty trees, at the thick green branches through which the shining sunbeams filter; hearing the manifold sighing of the leaves, so different from the noise of such cities as Paris and London, I fall into meditation and then again take up the book." [16]

The influence of Thomson and his German disciples is everywhere in evidence in Karamzin. In certain of his poems, in such tales as *Julie*, *Poor Liza*, and the *Thick Forest*, and in various parts of the *Letters of a Russian Traveller*, he endeavors to look upon nature with a discerning eye and to describe its beauties great and small, — an altogether new note in Russian literature. He was quite conscious, however, of his inability to equal his model as a poet of nature. In some Anacreontic verses he admits his limitations:

> While strolling through a wood
> And watching Philomel,
> I thought to be with Thomson
> And sing of golden summer;
> Alas! for me 'twas needful
> To say unto myself
> That Thomson's thrilling voice
> I ne'er possessed at all.[17]

In reality Karamzin was not a very good nature poet. The landscape which he preferred to describe was not always characteristic of the Russian countryside. He was not entirely free from the native literary vice of imitation, and it is noticeable that he often found in nature only those features which his models described. And more particularly, it was Nature in the abstract, as so frequently with Rousseau (who also influenced him) that called forth his admiration and tears. Thus conceived, the abstract loveliness of Nature could more suitably form a sentimental background for his tales. In short, it was not so much a keen observation of nature that concerned Karamzin as the sentimental rhapsodizing of the *schöne Seele* about Nature and the necessity of being in complete harmony with its varying manifestations. Thomson had revealed to Karamzin the possibilities of nature as a genuine subject for poetry, and Karamzin, while not ignoring this fact, preferred to regard nature as an object of sentimental worship. And it was pretty much this attitude that was adopted by those of his contemporaries who looked upon him as their literary preceptor.

If one turns, for example, to Dimitrevski's translation of *The Seasons* (1798), the inflated language of his introduction, punctuated by ecstatic periods of sentimental adoration, recalls at once the similar address of Karamzin. The poem becomes an "organ made up of strong and soft, high and low tones." And of Thomson the translator writes: "Nothing is dead, nothing dumb. The fiery force of his variegated imagination enlivens all things; his eye everywhere contemplates inimitable beauties; his ear hears harmonies everywhere, and his heart pours itself out in sentiments of praise and devotion." [18]

But it was in the periodicals that Thomson's popularity was chiefly reflected. Besides the fragmentary translations already mentioned, we find scattered through their pages a large number of compositions, mostly anonymous, which were patently inspired by *The Seasons*. Spring, summer, autumn, and winter now became fashionable themes for both prose and poetic exercises.[19] In an essay on "Village Life" one contributor, like Karamzin, finds in nature a retreat where he can indulge himself in meditation and sentimentalize over the works of Thomson, Young, and Ossian.[20] Indeed, two of the periodicals, *Ippokrena* and *Time Passed Agreeably and Usefully*,[21] were especially devoted to sentimental contributions suggested by these English authors. It is in *Ippokrena*, for example, that we find a translation of Collins's "Ode on the Death of Thomson," a rendering that must have been suggested primarily because of the subject. And the same journal contains extraordinarily far-fetched tributes to Thomson. One admirer dedicates a poem to the "Beloved sweet singer of *The Seasons*"; [22] and another likens Thomson to a "tender thrush crying out in the valley, and sweet as the sweet-tuned nightingale." [23]

Among Karamzin's most illustrious followers in the Sentimental Movement was Zhukovski (1783–1852), who likewise came under the influence of Thomson, though not to the same extent as his predecessor. We read in Zhukovski's *Diary* for 1804 that he was applying himself to *The Seasons*,[24] and in 1808 he translated *A Hymn to the Seasons*, which seems to have been a favorite. Imitations of *The Seasons* were produced in France and Germany and in turn won recognition in Russia. In the nature of things such attempts offered irresistible temptation to Russian authors. Karamzin was scarcely capable of a sustained imitation of Thomson's work, but this was well within the province of Zhukovski, who, unlike Karamzin, was primarily a poet. Such an effort, however, was made by a comparatively unknown writer, A. Ivanchikov, in his *Four Seasons of the Year*.[25]

It would be a little extravagant to claim that Thomson inspired a new nature poetry in Russia. Among certain poets who came under his influence we can perceive an attempt to observe and describe nature in a way hitherto unknown in that country. But, as in the case of Karamzin, they kept their eye too much on their model and too little on their native landscape. We have to wait for the Romantic Movement and Pushkin's beautiful descriptions of Caucasian scenery before we have a genuine Russian nature poetry. And here the inspiration came, not from Thomson, but from Byron. However, the sentimental worship of Nature which Karamzin distilled from *The Seasons* and the works of its German imitators was passed on to his disciples and became closely related to the popularity which Young and Ossian enjoyed in Russia. For the sentimental feeling for nature now took on a melancholy cast under the influence of these two English poets.

In France the *Night Thoughts* was regarded as the noblest elegy ever written on the miseries of human existence. A whole legend was built up about Young. Long after he had been quite forgotten in England the French clothed him in the dark robes of a sepulchral philosopher, compared him to Pascal, and liked to believe that his famous poem was written at night by the light of a candle burning in a human skull. The first *Night* was translated for the *Journal Étranger* in 1762, and numerous partial renderings followed, culminating in Letourneur's translation of the complete work in 1770.

Young inspired a vogue of death and moonlight in literature, and the spell of the *Night Thoughts* became universal.
The French public completely submitted. Robespierre kept
the book under his pillow during the Revolution, Camille
Desmoulins read it through more than once, and Chateau-
briand paid it frequent tribute. It was twice translated into
German and caused a furor in Klopstock's circle. And many
of the French and German, as well as English, romantic
writers were warm admirers of the *Night Thoughts*.

Despite this extensive Continental popularity, it is rather
surprising, in view of the usual slowness with which English
works made their way, that Young's fame reached Russia so
early. Just ten years after the first French translation appeared (1762), we find a rendering of part of the *Second
Night* in a Russian periodical.[26] And in the next decade many
fragmentary translations from the *Night Thoughts*, and various selections from the minor works of Young, appeared in
the periodicals.[27] One of them ran a series of eight of the
nine *Nights*.[28]

The first translation of the *Night Thoughts* in book form
was published in 1778, and four more separate renderings
followed in 1785, 1799,[29] 1803, and 1812. Two of these versions went into three editions, and Young's unusual popularity was sufficient to create a demand for the little-known
Satires, which were turned into Russian in 1792. In truth,
the frequency of translations, imitations, discussions, and
tributes leaves no doubt as to the strong hold Young obtained on the Russian reading public from 1780 to 1815. The
old opposition between the social and the natural man, the
main theme of the *Night Thoughts*, was a philosophical prob-

lem that much concerned Russian thinkers of this period. And the other elements of the poem — man's fellowship with nature, an appeal to the human conscience, and the sad conviction of man's wretched condition on earth — were subjects which the sentimentalists found much to their taste.

Although Karamzin was by no means a pioneer in the craze for Young, he was among his earliest devotees. In his *Poesy* he thus apostrophizes him:

> O Young, the friend and comforter of hapless man!
> Thou pourest balsam in the heart and tears dost dry,
> And with thy friend's death thou befriendest us with life! [30]

As a youth Karamzin read Young and the memory of the experience remained with him in his old age.[31] Wrapped in sentimentality the author of the *Night Thoughts* avoids life in a studied preoccupation with his own soul. Karamzin found rest in the Christian religion of the poem, as he did, more or less, in the nature poetry of *The Seasons*. He felt that Young, "the terror of the happy and the comforter of the unhappy, and Sterne, the original painter of sensibilities, closed the phalanx of the immortal British bards." [32] In a melancholy scene Karamzin compares himself to Young, and in a prose piece entitled *Night*, he rhapsodizes over nocturnal pleasures in the fashion of his model.[33]

The singular barrenness of ideas which characterizes the *Night Thoughts* was scarcely noticed by Russian admirers, any more than by the French and Germans. The tolling bells, tombs, mournful dirges, and phantoms of the poem were the proper setting for the enchanting sadness that pervades it, and this melancholy was what particularly captivated Russian readers. In the tributes that appeared with frequency in the periodicals, Young is invariably praised as the singer of sadness. A poet advises those who would discover genius

> To hearken to the spirit of the storm
> In Ossian's mournful verses, or with Young
> To pour forth tears.[34]

On his "Morning Walk" a graveyard is the favorite destination of another writer. There he sits, and Young and Gray are his constant companions, and "holy melancholy" comforts him.[35] In a poem, "Thoughts about Death and Eternity," the unknown author begins with an apostrophe to his inspirer:

> O Young, in converse with me, bard divine!
> Whose pleasant numbers stir me as some wine. . . .[36]

And then he continues with an exhortation to the poet to animate his muse with the proper spirit for a contemplation of death and eternity. Another journal contributor, in the introduction to a fragmentary translation of the *Night Thoughts*, repeats the lugubrious legend, which Young invented, of the death of his wife, step-daughter, and her husband within a few months of each other. "Thus, in the course of three months," writes the translator, "he was deprived of everything that he had any love for. . . . Conceive what must have been the unhappiness of this man who had a great talent and a feeling soul. . . . And where did he write? Over the graves of the churchyard in the village where he was minister." [37] And in a pretty verse "Envoy to Young's *Nights*," he is hailed as:

> That poet sad, both of the lyre and soul,[38]

who sings of griefs and the miserable destiny of mortal man.

Sufficient examples have been noted to suggest the nature

of Young's influence in Russia. Nevertheless, the extraordinary popularity of the *Night Thoughts* would be difficult to understand if we did not know that these anonymous or little-known contributors to the periodicals, as well as such authors as Karamzin, F. Pokrovski, A. I. Turgenev,[39] and Zhukovski,[40] had already been subjected to the tearful effusions of Rousseau and the sentimentality of the early German *Sturm und Drang* group. Hence their susceptibilities were prepared for the moody philosophy and melancholy mouthings of Young. The youthful experience of S. N. Glinka (1776–1847), a minor writer of the period, is not at all an exaggerated example of the effect that Young had on these "feeling" souls. "In my youth, he writes, "dreaming of Young, I wandered into remote places, into deep woods. Once, while dreaming under the pouring rain, and composing in the strain of the *Nights* of Young, I was aroused by a clap of thunder; returning home I transferred my gloomy thoughts to paper." [41] Tales have been told of the once great popularity of Young's masterpiece in England, but surely these melancholy verses never furnished forth poetic inspiration on their native heath under such discouraging circumstances.

It will come as no surprise that the *Night Thoughts* provided atmosphere and favorite reading material for the heroes and heroines of the sentimental novels discussed in the last chapter. In Emin's *Roza* the friendship between Milon and the heroine ripens in a common love for the poetry of Young. One day the hero comes upon Roza while she is reading the *Night Thoughts*. She is bathed in tears. He filches her copy, which has her name written in it, and later the theft results in his making her acquaintance. Milon rejoices that Roza cares for Young. "What!" he exclaims, "at such an age Young occupies thy time. . . . Young calls forth tears! Young, O rare heart! heart worthy of adoration!" [42] Indeed, Milon himself is cast in the very mold of the moody, moaning, melancholy philosopher of the *Night Thoughts*. "Young," he writes to his friend, "the refuge of the unhappy, fills my soul with joyous exaltation!" [43] And the hero of an anonymous tale, *The Flute*, turns to Young in his misfortunes and cries: "O Young! immortal Young! how justly, then, has it been said, 'Qu'un cœur sensible est un cruel présent de la Divinité!'" [44] Furthermore, the worship of "night" became a veritable cult with these sentimental heroes and heroines. The occasion permitting, which was frequently enough, they take up a comfortable position under the moonlit heavens, and in the bombast of Young tearfully praise the beauties of night.[45]

This deep-rooted admiration for the *Night Thoughts*, however, resulted in something more than heartfelt tributes and the creation of novel characters endowed with the pessimistic philosophy and unrelieved melancholy of the poem. Both prose and verse were written in frank imitation of the *Night Thoughts* or directly inspired by it. The periodicals in particular, as in the case of *The Seasons*, gave much space to descriptive poems or poetical prose pieces on the single theme of "Night." Most of them are sentimental, and nearly always the authors meditate in sublunary settings on death, the tomb, and man's wretched state.[46]

Nevertheless, none of these works has anything like the scope and few of them anything of the genius of Young's poem. Indeed, no attempt was made at an extensive imitation or at an original work employing the broad sweep and sustained imagery of the model. Like *The Seasons*, Young's poem was regarded by Russian readers as a source of inspiration and solace from which they imbibed long draughts when the sentimental or melancholy thirst came upon them. The mental attitude he popularized became an integral part of the sentimental frame of mind in which they lived. If they did not feel an urge to imitate, they were content to pick up the *Night Thoughts* and read and think with Young that Time

> In Nature's ample ruins lies entomb'd·
> And Midnight, universal Midnight reigns.

Young's melancholy, however, was subjective, and his plaint was for man's suffering in the present. The poet's *memento mori* was always for the benefit of his contemporaries, and their sad fate inspired him to write those long passages on the blessings of immortality. But Young never permits his imagination to wander over the vanished glories of ancient civilizations. He is quite insensible to that peculiar, but most legitimate, strain of Teutonic melancholy, — the sorrow that comes from a sense of the passing of things.

The eighteenth century surrendered itself completely to this strain, to the sweet yet bitter recollection of departed happiness. And it was Macpherson's Caledonia and its poet, Ossian, that filled the hearts and minds of men with the melancholy of regret for glories that once were.

There is no need to repeat here the history of that development in England, of which the *Poems of Ossian* was only one factor, although a most significant one, which drew the attention of many distinguished authors and scholars to a past, mysterious and little known. The development has become a commonplace in the study of literary history, and is now considered a definite phase of the Pre-romantic Movement. And the unique popularity and influence of Ossian among the peoples of Western Europe likewise requires no rehearsal. But the course of Ossian in Russia has received little attention from Western scholars. Although I shall indicate the general course of Russian Ossianism, only the very important part it played in the development of the Sentimental Movement will be considered in detail.

The first appearance of Ossian in Russia was in the fragment quoted in *Werther*, which was translated in 1781. Karamzin, at an early date (1787), hailed him in his *Poesy* as Britain's most ancient bard, the moody son of Fingal —

> Grieved for his friends, heroes in battle fallen,
> And from the grave the bard evoked their shades.
> Just as the roar of ocean waves that sounds
> Through forests far from shore, and bearing sadness
> To hopeful hearts: so are the songs of Ossian,
> Pouring sweet anguish into languid minds,
> Preparing us for sombre images;
> Afflicted was this dear and gentle soul.
> O Ossian, thou art great, inimitable! [47]

It was not, however, until 1788 that a substantial rendering of Ossian was published. This was the *Poems of the Ancient Bards*, translated by A. I. Dmitriev.[48] Other translations in periodicals and book form followed,[49] the best known being that of Kostrov in 1792,[50] made from the French version by Letourneur. As a matter of fact, translations, imitations, and critical articles on Ossian did not cease to appear in considerable numbers until 1830.

As in France and Germany, it was the melancholy in the prose-poetry of Ossian that the Russians seized upon at once. The bard's contemplative sadness against a background of awful images brought tears to the eyes of the sentimental Russian writers. It would be wearing a commonplace threadbare to point out the similarity between the indigenous sadness of these so-called Gaelic songs and the sad temperament characteristically associated with Russians. Native critics, however, have labored the point.[51] But an insatiable appetite for the Ossianic scenery of remote and dismal regions, with mountain mists and the wind soughing among the crags, becomes everywhere apparent in imitations and tributes. What might be termed "melancholy imaginativeness" was the Ossianic imprimatur among the Russian sentimentalists.

Karamzin read his Ossian with loving care, and like the ancient British bard, he, too, affected the title of "bard of the Neva." [52] In his *Letters of a Russian Traveller* Karamzin finds inspiration in the *Poems of Ossian*. With a copy of *Fingal* (in English), which he had bought in a Leipzig bookshop, he sits on a moss-covered stone by a rushing stream with "wild, gloomy banks," and reads the poem.[53] Again, while sitting by the banks of a stream, he grows sad at the thought of ancient beauty passing away and hurrying humanity's indifference to it. But Ossian comforts him. "Thou didst feel deeply," Karamzin writes, "this sorrowful fate of all sublunary things, and because of this thou movest my heart with thy sad songs." [54] On board ship during a storm he turns to Ossian and translates *Carthon* amid the roaring of the elements.[55] "What a holiday for my imagination filled with Ossian!" he exclaims.[56] Concerning this very translation he later wrote: "All lovers of poetry have felt its beauties." The peculiar merit of the work, he believes, consists in its "inimitable and excellent simplicity. . . . Profound melancholy, — sometimes tender, but always touching, — runs through all [Ossian's] creations, guiding the reader into sadness; but our soul loves to abandon itself to sadness of this kind, loves to cherish it, and in its own gloomy imaginings is pleased." [57]

So completely and appreciatively had Karamzin entered into the spirit of Ossian that his own works show the pronounced influence of these Macphersonized Gaelic tales. This is particularly true of his short novels.[58] Besides his assimilation of the elegiac mood of Ossian, we may observe a direct indebtedness in many descriptive passages. Not only does Karamzin show a fondness for the wilder aspects of nature, but he attempts to harmonize his descriptions, in Ossianic fashion, with the actions of his characters, especially in the more melancholy and tragic scenes.[59] In his verse, on the other hand, much of which was devoted to the lighter themes of French neo-classical tradition, there is little influence of Ossian. Only in a few poems in the vein of the English and German sentimentalists do we find Ossianic echoes.[60]

It is a well established fact that Karamzin's interest in Ossian was most marked in the youthful period of his literary development. As he grew older and submitted to a changing taste in literature, he brought a maturer judgment to an evaluation of the productions of Macpherson. Though his admiration for Ossian scarcely diminished, he did begin to complain of "too much sameness." [61] And something of a defection from his youthful enthusiasm may be discerned in the fact that in his later years Karamzin took the "Homer side" of that strange controversy that raged about the respective merits of Ossian and the Greek poet. Russian critics followed the English, French, and German into the blind alley of trying to prove the authenticity of the Gaelic prose-poems.[62] As may be expected, they achieved no more success than their predecessors in establishing whether or not Macpherson was an impostor. The tendency in Russia was to accept the works as genuine ancient fragments, and as such worthy of comparison with the Homeric epics. Karamzin was astute enough to eschew the well-nigh unsolvable riddle of authenticity, but with all his admiration for Ossian he was not ready to regard him, or the vicarious Macpherson, as a "second Homer."

As in the case of *The Seasons*, Karamzin's interest in Ossian no doubt helped to infect his group of close literary friends and disciples with a similar enthusiasm. Reference has already been made to the translation of A. I. Dmitriev. His brother, I. I. Dmitriev, likewise came under the spell and published a series of poetical paraphrases of Ossian.[63] And it was to this latter poet that N. Grammatin dedicated his version of *Carthon*.[64] Derzhavin, one of the older and chief poets of the period, forgot his neo-classical traditions long enough to read the Ossianic translations of A. I. Dmitriev and Karamzin's *Songs of Selma*.[65] The results were soon apparent. Derzhavin's poems *The Taking of Ismail, Warsaw,* and *On Crossing the Alps* [66] contain names and forms taken from Ossian, and in the last of these three poems he hails his inspirer as "the singer of mists and sea." And his long and famous ode, *The Waterfall,*[67] is shot through with Ossianic influences. Sometimes images and whole poetic conceptions are appropriated by Derzhavin from Dmitriev's translation.[68] Finally, two other literary friends of Karamzin, V. V. Kapnist and P. S. Kaisarov, followed his lead in making translations and paraphrases.[69]

No less than in the case of the *Night Thoughts*, the gloomy Ossianic atmosphere provided a local color nicely suited to the lachrymose heroes and heroines of the Russian eighteenth-century novel. The ready-made backgrounds of nature wild, penetrated with the vague intangible sadness of vanished glory, were ideal settings for these pale characters. In Galinkovski's *Hours of Pensiveness* the hero, like Ben Jonson's Stephan seeking a "stool to be melancholy upon," goes out on the balcony to view in the moonlight the sombre Olonetski woods. "And there," he chants, "I would sing in the wild gloomy oak forest pensive songs of sadness — songs of Ossian, pleasant to my spirit when it is burdened with sadness!" [70] The heroine of another novel "gives herself up to the pleasure of reading the *Poems of Ossian*," and preferably in the proper Ossianic background of dark, mist-filled forests. She admires these ancient people and regrets that she "does not live in their age and country." [71] In Klushin's *Unhappiness* and Stolypin's *Fragment,*[72] as in the tales of Karamzin mentioned above, the Ossianic landscape is regularly the setting; and Narezhny's *Slavic Evenings* was greeted by the reviewers as a patent imitation of Ossian.[73]

A more searching study of the sentimental novels of the period would doubtless produce many similar examples. Their heroes are often endowed with Fingal's magnanimity of soul, if not with his fierce spirit. And there existed a veritable penchant for hallowed settings of gnarled forests with the moon gliding in and out between the clouds, all steeped in the agreeable melancholy of the *Poems of Ossian*.

After the appearance of Kostrov's translation (1792), it is noticeable that Russian writers began to show a serious interest in their country's mediaeval period. Ossian had brought Europe closer to the Middle Ages, and the "Gothic" past now inspired both the creation of original literature and the recovery of ancient literary remains. As in England and Germany, this interest was closely associated with the growth of romanticism. Investigators began to burrow into the forgotten repositories of ancient manuscripts, seeking records of Slavic antiquity. Soon the famous *Tale of Igor's Raid* was brought to light and in an article Karamzin immediately compared it to the "beaux morceaux d'Ossian." [74] Scandinavian, German, and English ballads were read and several translations were made from Percy's *Reliques*.[75] And collectors began to search the unusually rich store of Russian folklore in an effort to find their country's past as honored in literature as Ossian's Scotland. Zhukovski in particular was to carry this pre-romantic interest in antiquities into the romantic period.

It would be too special a task to consider in detail the history of Ossian in Russia in the first two decades of the nineteenth century. The subject has been adequately handled by native scholars. According to one contemporary, Ossian

became so popular that selections were used as prize pieces
for recitation in the schools, "because of their elevation of
feeling and their novelty, but especially because of their
quality of beauty of form, thought, and expression." [76] Hor-
ace Walpole would have perhaps sneered at this measure of
devotion to Macpherson's poetical prose, and one can imagine
that Dr. Johnson would have been seriously tempted to
make good his threat of violence against the Scotchman.
Ossian even became a subject for drama. V. Ozerov wrote
a tragedy, *Fingal* (acted in 1805), with theme and choruses
in Ossianic settings, which is said to have won considerable
success on the stage. [77] And later writers, such as N. I.
Gnedich, M. N. Muravev, K. N. Batiushkov, Ryleev,
Kiukhelbeker, Pushkin, and Lermontov, in translations,
paraphrases, and original compositions owe more or less
to the *Poems of Ossian*.[78]

Zhukovski, perhaps, was the last great writer to reflect
the powerful influence of Ossian in the sentimental manner
of Karamzin and his followers. He was the connecting link
between the generations of pre-romantic and romantic
authors. He speaks of himself as the "poetical nurse of the
devils and witches of the Germans and English," [79] meaning
by this his inclination for romantic "Gothic" and folk literature. However, he was a sentimentalist before he was a
romantic, and, in fact, he never quite divested himself of
the sweetness and sadness which were his characteristic
poetical moods.

Zhukovski's interest in Thomson and Young has already
been mentioned. Gray likewise strongly attracted him and,
as with the English poet, melancholy became his most

faithful companion. In fact his fine translation of Gray's *Elegy* (1801)[80] gained him his first literary fame. Versions of the *Elegy*, as well as of other pieces of Gray, had appeared earlier, and soon the periodicals were strewn with doleful poems written in graveyards or about graveyards.[81] Gray, indeed, must be accorded an important place in the growth of Russian sentimentalism.

The influence of Ossian on Zhukovski is to be observed not so much in borrowed details as in the pervasive melancholy which shrouds so much of his original poetry. Sad regrets for things beyond the grave, the quiet yearning under the moon after the marvellous deeds of dead heroes, and the strange charm of the more mournful aspects of nature are the Ossianic leit-motives that run through Zhukovski's poetry. "His [Zhukovski's] marvellous wears the special character of Young's *Night Thoughts* and Ossian," writes his biographer.[82]

The history of Ossian in Russia had more significance, of course, than merely to furnish an endless source of imagery and melancholy inspiration for the sentimental writers. To the extent to which these writers may be considered forerunners of the Romantic Movement, they found in Ossian a form and substance which had a definite bearing on the future history of that movement in Russia. A native scholar stresses the importance of this contribution of Ossian, and in a less degree his words might be applied to Thomson and Young:

Such a close contact with Ossian did not remain, of course, without intimate influence on the growth of our poetry. All these translations and imitations strengthened still more the inclination in our literature towards a national poetry, enriched our poetic, creative power with new and fresh forms and manners foreign to the pseudo-classical muse, and thus provided material for a new, that is to say, romantic *poetics*.[83]

At the risk of violating the fixed categories of literature, I have reserved Sterne for detailed consideration in this chapter rather than in the previous one on the novel. Some justification for the procedure has already been advanced; more can now be added with the background of the present chapter in mind. No one but a determined purist in the matter of literary forms would deny Sterne the title of novelist on the basis of *Tristram Shandy*, although even eclectic historians have often been puzzled as to the precise type to which this unique book belongs. With the *Sentimental Journey* we are not on such solid ground. But if it is not a novel, then in what category are we to place it? It is easy to beg the question, of course, and decide that the work created a category all its own. One critic dismisses the issue by classifying it as "the confession of a soul," which, unhappily, so far as type is concerned, makes of the book neither literary flesh nor fish. At any rate, it was the *Sentimental Journey* rather than *Tristram Shandy* that won for Sterne the unrivalled admiration of the Russian reading public. And to some extent this fact, for my immediate purpose, takes Sterne out of the class of novelists.

Sterne was quickly accepted in France and Germany, but for reasons quite different from those that obtained in England. His countrymen were amused by his eccentric humor, yet it would never have occurred to them to consider him a profound thinker and a great genius. On the Continent, however, he was hailed as a philosopher, as in the case of Young.

Many, like Goethe, believed that there was something free and beautiful in his soul, and the philosophy of Sterne, as one critic remarks, was the most brilliant invention of eighteenth-century Anglomania. And the medium for expressing this philosophy is sensibility or sentimentality. In short, we have again a writer who preaches a philosophy of tears, and it is this aspect of Sterne's works that his French and German readers most admired.

It was likewise as a sentimentalist that Sterne was received and exalted in Russia. A leading Russian student of his influence makes this point clear. "He captivated us not as a humorist. His talent in this respect was all too little noticed by his Russian devotees." Sterne interested Russians chiefly "as a representative of the sentimental current," in which current was especially emphasized the "human spirit of Sterne, his constant appeal to the sensibilities in which he saw the most powerful means for improving human relations." [84] And it may be emphatically stated now that of all the foreign authors mentioned here Sterne filled the key position in the Russian Sentimental Movement. To quote once more from his Russian investigator:

Following the fashion of the West, Russian literature at the end of the eighteenth century began to pay attention to Sterne. From this time on his name is frequently met with in the pages of our press, translations of Sterne's works appear in Russian; many read these works with interest, use citations for epigrams, translate articles about Sterne from foreign journals, include his name in the programs for reading in general knowledge; interest themselves in Western imitators of Sterne, translate their works into Russian, and finally, while borrowing from Sterne forms and ideas, they themselves try to create original productions in the spirit of the English writer.[85]

But this amazing popularity served mainly to buttress the sentimental tendencies of such writers as Karamzin and his followers. Sterne, so to speak, synthesized the several phases of sentimentality emanating from Thomson, Young, and Ossian, and it is for this reason primarily that I have ventured to include him in a chapter with these other English authors. Although the sentimentality of these writers differed in kind, it combined the quality of subjectivity, which in the Russian literature of the time was to carry over into the Romantic Movement.

There were fragmentary periodical translations from the *Sentimental Journey* as early as 1779,[86] but it did not come out in complete form until 1793. But even before this date the famous *Letters to Eliza* (1789)[87] had been translated, and their supposedly autobiographical character and their sentimentality sufficiently explain the comparatively early interest in them. On the other hand, it was not until 1804–07 that *Tristram Shandy* appeared, and although there was only one edition of this, the *Sentimental Journey* went into three.[88] Sterne perhaps reached the height of his fame in Russia in 1801 with a translation of *The Beauties of Sterne, or a Collection of his Best and Pathetic Tales and Most Distinctive Observations on Life.*

Among the early popularizers of Sterne in Russia Karamzin again takes the place of chief importance. It should now be doubly apparent that this author, like Rousseau in France, was the distributing centre for Russian interest in English literature throughout the period. Over Sterne, writes an historian of the early Russian novel, Karamzin "positively raved!" [89] In his effort to escape the harsh realities of life

Karamzin found a refuge in the imaginary world of tears and refined sensibilities created by Sterne. The broad love of humanity and the minute psychological self-analysis that fill the pages of the *Sentimental Journey* were features which Karamzin sought to incorporate in his own works. "The original, inimitable, sensitive, kind, clever, beloved Sterne"[90] is Karamzin's description of the English author. "Incomparable Sterne! In what university," he asks, "wast thou taught to feel so tenderly? What rhetoric revealed to thee the secret of agitating with a word the finest cords of our hearts? What musician commands so skilfully by the sounds of his strings as thou commandest by our feelings?" [91]

Like Sterne, Karamzin revelled in the analysis of his own heart. In life, feeling was to take the place of reason, which, according to him, had lost its force and application. Such a doctrine, or illusion, will be immediately recognized as all-important in Sterne's scheme of things. The *Sentimental Journey*, in fact, was the brilliant model for Karamzin's most characteristic work, *Letters of a Russian Traveller*. Ostensibly written to a friend, the letters were the outgrowth of Karamzin's travels abroad.[92] They take a journal form after the fashion of eighteenth-century letter-writers who wrote with their eye on publication. The influence of many foreign authors is patent — Thomson, Young, Ossian, Sterne, Rousseau, Klopstock, Gessner, Haller, and others. But none is mentioned so often as Sterne, and there can be no doubt that Karamzin was attempting to imitate him.[93] To be sure, the individuality of both writers is different, and their reactions to things observed and to adventures experienced on the road differ accordingly. Sterne is concerned mainly with the sentiments of the heart. He likes to dally with his imagination and to create illusions wherein he finds happiness. Karamzin does this also, but he is often concerned with the arts, politics, and literature of the countries which he visits, things that never concern Sterne. Despite this difference, however, there are numerous occasions in the *Letters* when Karamzin tries to imitate the typical sentimental delirium of Sterne, or his brilliant humor, or his fine cynicism; and certain scenes, witticisms, and apothegms reappear in Karamzin's work with little or no change.

Thus the author and his friends meet on the road a pretty Frenchwoman clad in mourning. Their sympathy aroused, they invite her to dine with them. She agrees, and after the meal they ask for her story. In the course of narrating her sad experiences Karamzin notes that "she wiped away a tear which rolled from an honest eye, as Yorick would have said." [94]   In truth, this is precisely what Yorick might have said, and the whole incident has a typically Sternian flavor.

On another occasion the traveller finds a beautiful maiden in his coach. She suits admirably the sentimental atmosphere, for she is reading the *Vicar of Wakefield*. The maiden falls asleep over her book, slumbering peacefully on the author's shoulder. He steals shy glances at her fresh young face, marvels at her beauty, but remains motionless for fear of waking her. Then, struck with his own sense of virtue, just as Sterne might have been under such circumstances, he compares himself to a "chaste knight, fearful of offending by one immodest glance the bashfulness of innocence entrusted to me.   Rare are such examples at the present time, my friend, rare!" [95] This is a pure Sternian touch. It would be easy to accumulate such adventures recalling the *Sentimental Journey*, and many direct borrowings could be pointed out [96] which pretty much justify the title of "Russian Sterne" which the critics of St. Petersburg and Moscow employed to characterize Karamzin.

There is a good deal of matter in the *Letters* that appeals more to the mind than to the heart, and in these instances Karamzin is original or indebted to writers other than Sterne. Nor is he ever quite so preoccupied as Sterne with his own ego. Nevertheless, the general sentimental impression made by the *Letters* upon his contemporaries was at once ascribed to the influence of Sterne, and it served more than anything else to identify him as one of the leaders of the Sentimental Movement. "Children, do not forget Sterne, Sterne and Karamzin!" [97] exclaims a character in a contemporary tale, and the association of the two authors was a natural one in the minds of Russian readers.

The form of the *Letters*, however, owes very little to that of the *Sentimental Journey*, but it was the form of Sterne's work especially that influenced one of the most notable productions of the period, *A Journey from Petersburg to Moscow* (1790).[98] This book was written by A. N. Radishchev (1749–1802). In his studies abroad Radishchev came under the sway of French and German liberal thought, and he returned to Russia with a mind prepared to object to the political and social abuses of his country. *A Journey from Petersburg to Moscow* is a bitter attack on these abuses, particularly the enslavement of the peasants. The book caused a great

stir and was quickly banned by the government. The author
was exiled.

It is very possible that Radishchev read the *Sentimental
Journey* in a German translation as early as 1769, during his
student days at Leipzig.[99] We know that later he learned
English and read Shakspere and Milton in the original,[100] and
it is likely that he also read Sterne's work at this time in
English. On his way to Siberia he ironically recalls the *Sentimental Journey*, numbering himself among the travellers by
necessity: "Relégué dans la classe que Sterne appelle des
voyageurs par nécessité, l'utilité n'est pas le but de mon
voyage."[101]

The narrative of *A Journey from Petersburg to Moscow* consists of the observations of a traveller on the life and social
customs of the people in the various way-stations between
the two great Russian cities. The traveller intersperses
little stories or incidents of human interest that occur on the
road. The form of the work was directly suggested by the
Sentimental Journey. There is no essential connection between the varied adventures and meditations of the traveller,
nor is there any particular order in the chapters. That is,
the book does not represent the growth of a single complete
subject, and what unity it possesses derives from the central
figure of the traveller himself. This method is the one employed by Sterne.

The most characteristic feature of Radishchev's style —
his unusual emotionalism, charged with sentiment and feeling
— is a product of the literature of sentimentality. But
Radishchev's sentimentality, although often inspired by
the same subjects and feelings as Sterne's, is in essence quite

different from that of the English author. Radishchev's
pathos and sentimentalized indignation over political op-
pression and social abuses have little in common with the
sentimentality of Sterne, which was concerned primarily
with his own ego.

Nevertheless, Radishchev is obligated to the *Sentimental
Journey* for several incidents, treated in a manner very like
that of the master. In his chapter "Edrovo" the author
relates how he meets a peasant girl, Anuta. She tells her
story and he sympathizes with her unhappy lot and offers
to aid her. Then he kisses Anuta and philosophizes about
the incident in very sentimental language. The situation
and some of the details were no doubt suggested by Sterne's
chapter, "The Fille de Chambre — Paris."

Further Radishchev relates the tale of an old blind beggar to whom he gives a rouble.[102] The old man refuses to
accept the money for fear that it may be stolen from him and
thus provoke a crime. The blind beggar has much in common with the "pauvre honteux" in Sterne's chapter, "Mon-
triul." Sterne, it may be remembered, thought that the
beggar thanked him most of all because of the tears he shed
over his gift.

Other parallels could be pointed out,[103] but enough has
been said to indicate the extent of Radishchev's debt to
Sterne. It was not merely a matter of initial inspiration. A
more tangible debt exists in the fact that the form and
certain incidents of the *Sentimental Journey* were used by
Radishchev in writing his famous book.

After Radishchev's unhappy fate no one dared to imitate
his work, but Karamzin's *Letters* was quickly followed by a

host of imitations. "Sentimental Journeys" or "Letters" were turned out in abundance by various writers who posed as pure-souled travellers. It would take much more space than is available to study them in detail.[104] Practically all of these imitators were inspired in their travels by the same incidents and feelings that had stirred Karamzin. However varied the verses may be, sentimentality is the common burden of their song. Sterne is often mentioned, and the travellers, like Karamzin, display an ecstatic love of nature, affect a sweet melancholy, and pour forth tears for no good reason. In fact, the wide influence of the *Letters of a Russian Traveller* unquestionably served to crystallize as a literary movement the sentimentality that had entered Russian literature more than a decade earlier in translations of *La Nouvelle Héloïse*, *Werther*, *Pamela*, and *Clarissa*.

The tendency, as I have already observed, strongly affected the novel of the period. *Tristram Shandy* seemed to be too formidable a model for full-length imitation, but in this and the *Sentimental Journey* Russian novelists found an endless source of inspiration in the matter of details and characterization. Thus in the *Voyage of my Friend* the author shows his comprehension of Sternian humanitarianism when he has a character, from whom a dog is begging a morsel of food, exclaim: "I wager — on what thou desirest — that if Sterne were in my place under the tent, then, in truth, he would this minute have thrown thee his own food." [105] Love at first sight puzzles the author of another tale and he turns to Sterne for help: "O beloved Sterne! sensitive philosopher, thou art able to solve such enigmas! Thou art the master who penetrates into the secret recesses of the heart; thou dost know the reason for Sophia's tears!" [106] Similar quotations from novels and short stories could easily be multiplied.[107]

Sterne continued to influence Russian writers, although with diminishing significance, well into the nineteenth century. To mention only the more famous names, such authors as S. Glinka, Zhukovski, Marlinski, Griboedov, Pushkin, Lermontov, and Gogol are in a large or small measure indebted to Sterne. Zhukovski, however, was the only one among these writers to reflect the Sternian sentimentality that Karamzin had popularized.[108] With much more sincerity than the English author, Zhukovski possessed a tender feeling and sympathy for man and beast, and he was equally capable in the art of weeping in literature. Nevertheless, as I have already indicated, Zhukovski's sentimentality was more closely related to the sad melancholy of Young and Ossian and their German imitators. He is essentially a singer of sorrows, the poetic recorder in beautiful elegiac language of humanity's eternal sadness.

Pushkin valued Sterne highly and all his works were found in the poet's library.[109] "All of *Lalla Rookh*," Pushkin wrote to an admirer of Moore, "is not worth ten little lines of *Tristram Shandy*." [110] And he listed Sterne, along with Richardson and Fielding, as an exponent of the best prose.[111] Some students insist that the poet's digressive habit in *Eugene Onegin* was a device he caught from his reading of Sterne.[112]

Strangely enough, Pushkin himself seems to have been the first authority for the notion that Gogol was influenced by Sterne. Concerning Gogol he wrote: "He will be the Rus-

sian Sterne; . . . he sees all, he is able to laugh, but besides
this he is sad and obliged to cry." [113] There is, indeed, much
of the Sternian "smile mingled with tears" in the works of
the great Russian novelist, but Gogol was so characteristically Russian that it is always hazardous to predicate foreign
influence without conclusive proof.[114]

It would lead us too far afield, however, to go into the rami-
fications of Sterne's influence, slight enough in most cases,
on all these writers. An adequate study of the subject has
already been made by a native scholar.[115] Nor can I devote much space to the recently investigated problem of the
relations of Sterne to certain literary members of the Decembrist conspiracy against Nicholas I in 1825.[116] In the case of
the romantic Marlinski-Bestuzhev (1795–1837), certainly,
the influence was of considerable importance to Russian
literature. Marlinski, who, on his own admission, "never
separated from Sterne,"[117] was much under the sway of the
Sentimental Journey. And the personality of this revolu-
tionist was in many respects colored by the feeling and atti-
tudinizing of Sterne.

In the first decade of the nineteenth century we begin to perceive in Russia a conscious reaction against the Sentimental
Movement. From its very nature the fashion laid itself open
to ridicule, and satire was not long held in abeyance. Perhaps the most telling blow was delivered in a comedy, *The
New Sterne*,[118] by Prince A. Shakhovskoi, acted with great
success in 1805. The hero, Count Pronskoi, is so devoted to
sentimentality that he refuses to enter military service or to
marry "without passion." To escape his importunate
father he sets out on a journey with the intention, in Sternian

fashion, of writing a journal. In the presence of nature and simple peasant life the hero exclaims: "O Nature! O Sterne! I am silent and my silence alone is worthy of you!" (scene III, 1822 edition). The country folk, of course, find him incomprehensible, and after listening in dumb amazement to his sentimental raptures, they conclude that he is mad. In a soliloquy in the fourth scene he cries out, à la Sterne: "Here I lost a friend, sincere, fine, frugal. O Lady, Lady! you are no more!" Lady, it turns out, is his English dog which has been run over. Then the hero finds "true passion" in his love for a peasant girl, Malana. He appeals to her in grandiose language and Malana giggles, thinking he is speaking in German. Finally, the father sends a friend to entice his son home. Ipat, Pronskoi's servant, puzzled at his master's mania, asks the friend whence comes "this sentimental devilry?" And the friend replies: "It was formed in England, rehashed in France, exaggerated in Germany, and came to us in a sorry state" (scene IX). The dénouement is cleverly worked up. Pronskoi intends to marry Malana, become a simple tiller of the soil, and read "Cicero, Sterne, and Young" (scene XII). However, urged on by the friend, Ipat decides to marry Malana's sister and settle down with his master in bucolic felicity. But the possibility of having his servant as a brother-in-law shakes Pronskoi's determination, and after a little persuasion on the part of his father's friend, he returns home, cured of his sentimentality.[119]

The Sentimental Movement wasted away before such satire. Even Karamzin, in the latter part of his life, was inclined to turn his back on his youthful philosophy of feeling. Nevertheless, the movement had revealed new sources of sensibility, aided materially in bringing to an end the neo-classical literature of reason, and profoundly influenced the life and works of many of the foremost Russian writers. In this connection the works of Thomson, Young, Ossian, and Sterne played a most significant part. They contributed themes of nature, melancholy, and a reverence for the past to what I have described as pre-romantic literature. But more especially it was the undercurrent of sentimentality that runs through all these writers which most affected Russian readers and authors. And sentimentality, making for the inner contemplation of man's soul and his relation to the universe, was a state of mind highly characteristic of the next generation of romantic writers.

BIBLIOGRAPHY

BIBLIOGRAPHICAL STUDIES

V. Sopikov, *Ukazatel k opytu rossiskoi bibliografii* (sostavil V. Rogozhin), St. Petersburg, 1908. (For bibliographical details concerning all book translations of the works of English authors mentioned in this chapter.)

N. K. Piksanov, *Dva veka russkoi literatury*, Moskva, 1923. (See especially pp. 27–28, 38–39.)

Chapter V, Bibliography, pp. 131–133. (For bibliographical details concerning periodical translations of the works of English authors mentioned in this chapter.)

INVESTIGATIONS

Russian Sentimentalism

"Sentimentalizm" (*Entsiklopedicheski slovar*, vol. LVIII).

N. Kotlyarevski, *Mirovaya skorb v kontse proshlago i nachale nashego veka*, St. Petersburg, 1898.

A. N. Veselovski, *V. A. Zhukovski*, St. Petersburg, 1904. (See "Epokha chuvstvitelnosti," pp. 31–46.)

Thomson in Russian Literature

D. I. Dimitrevski, *Chetyre vremeni goda*, Moskva, 1798. (See predislovie.)

N. S. Tikhonravov, *Sochineniya*, Moskva, 1898. (See I, 124; III, 287–288, 290, 292, 428, 445.)

V. V. Sipovski, *N. M. Karamzin*, St. Petersburg, 1899. (See pp. 64, 66, 132.)

Young in Russian Literature

N. S. Tikhonravov, *Sochineniya*, Moskva, 1898. (See III, 287, 290, 422, 427.)

V. V. Sipovski, *N. M. Karamzin*, St. Petersburg, 1899. (See pp. 61, 63–64, 92, 132.)

> *Ocherki iz istorii russkago romana*, St. Petersburg, 1909. (See I, 14, 18, 103; II, 459, 462, 463, 465, 470, 474, 490, 556, 557, 574, 578, 623, 646, 778, 779.)

A. N. Veselovski, *V. A. Zhukovski*, St. Petersburg, 1904. (See pp. 36, 40, 45, 440.)

I. I. Zamotin, *Romantizm dvadtsatykh godov XIX stoletiya v russkoi literature*, St. Petersburg, 1911–13. (See I, 34, 175, 356; II, 12, 90, 94.)

Ossian in Russian Literature

N. K. Piksanov, "Etiud o vliyanii ossianovskoi poezii v russkoi literature" (*Sochineniya Pushkina*, red. S. Vengerova, St. Petersburg, 1907, I, 108–114).

E. Balovanova, "Pushkin i Ossian" (*Sochineniya Pushkina*, I, 98–108).

D. N. Vvedenski, *Etiud o vliyanii ossianovskoi poezii v russkoi literature*, Nezhin, 1916.

V. I. Maslov, "K voprosu o pervykh perevodakh poem Ossiana-Makfersona" (*Sbornik Otdeleniya russkago yazyka i slovesnosti Akademii Nauk*, Leningrad, 1928, No. 3).

> "Ossian v Rossii, bibliografiya" (*Trudy Pushkinskogo Doma Akademii Nauk*, Leningrad, 1928, L, 9–57).

Ossianizm Karamzina, Priluki, 1928.

Sterne in Russian Literature

V. Vinogradov, "Siuzhet i kompozitsiya povesti Gogolya 'Nos'" (*Nachala*, 1921, No. 1, p. 83).

Sterne, *Sentimentalnoe puteshestvie po Frantsii i Italii*, per. D. V. Averkieva, Gos. Izd., 1922. (See predislovie P. Gubera.)

V. P. Semennikov, *Radishchev: ocherki i issledovaniya*, Moskva, 1923. (See pp. 254 ff.)

B. L. Modzalevski, "Pushkin i Sterne" (*Russki sovremennik*, 1924, No. 2, pp. 192–193).

V. I. Maslov, "Interes k Sternu v russkoi literature kontsa XVIII i nachala XIX veka" (*Istoriko-literaturny sbornik*, posvyashchenny V. I. Sreznevskomu, Leningrad, 1924, pp. 339–376).

M. K. Azadovski, "Sterne v vospriyatiyakh dekabristov" (*Bunt Dekabristov*, Leningrad, 1926, pp. 382–392).

CHAPTER VIII

The Early History of Shakspere in Russia

THERE is sufficient critical justification and not a little chronological necessity for considering Shakspere at this point in our study. The influence of the English authors already treated actually preceded the influence of Shakspere. An explanation of this relatively late appearance is easy to ascertain. As we have seen, Russia was largely indebted to France for its initial knowledge of English writers. But despite its Anglomania and the dubious sponsorship of Voltaire, neo-classical France had little stomach for the rule-defying genius of Shakspere. Throughout the eighteenth century he achieved little popularity, and the few French critics who admired him did so with many reservations. And this lack of enthusiasm in France was reflected in eighteenth-century Russia. Furthermore, the steady popularity of French neo-classical drama in the theatres of St. Petersburg and Moscow helped to prevent an early acceptance of Shakspere. However, in the first thirty years of the nineteenth century Russia learned to appreciate the plays of Shakspere, primarily through the efforts of the German critics connected with the Romantic Movement.

In its initial stages Russian drama underwent all the fluctuations and vicissitudes of the country's spasmodic cultural development. We have already observed that the first dramatic impetus was furnished by the German pastor, Gregori, in the reign of Tsar Aleksei in 1672.[1] Versions of English sixteenth-century plays were included in the German collections from which Gregori selected his repertoire, but Marlowe's *Tamburlaine* is the only Elizabethan play he is known to have staged. In the reactionary movement that followed, drama virtually came to a standstill until the time of Peter the Great. As part of his Europeanizing policy the tsar in 1702 imported a troupe of German players, who performed in a public theatre in Moscow. The plays of Molière predominated in their repertoire, although there is a tradition that a comedy of "Julius Caesar" was staged, and this may possibly have been a reworking of Shakspere's drama.[2] The tsar's favorite sister, Natalia, supported the movement by writing plays herself, and in 1705 the learned F. Prokopovich produced his own tragi-comedy, *Vladimir*. Peter was too much engrossed in practical affairs to devote much time to the drama, but in the reign of his sister Elizabeth (1741–61), the theatre took a new lease of life; and it was during this period that French influence became a deciding factor in the development of a native drama and that Shakspere got his first hearing.

A. Sumarokov (1718–77) gained the title of "father of Russian drama" by virtue of his series of original plays. He was both writer and director and under him the theatre, modelled strictly after the French neo-classical style, progressed rapidly. Technical features were improved and actors of talent, such as Volkov and Dmitrievski, were developed. Dmitrievski is reported to have gone to London to study with Garrick.

One of Sumarokov's first attempts was a curious version of *Hamlet*, printed in 1748 and acted in 1750. Few English post-Elizabethan travesties of Shakspere are comparable to it for complete detachment from the original. Amusingly enough, Sumarokov proudly denied any slavish adherence to his model. "My *Hamlet*," he wrote, "except for the monologue at the end of the third act and the praying of Claudius, hardly resembles the tragedy of Shakspere." [3] Nor does he understate the case. A voice in a dream explains to Hamlet the murder of his father and the complicity of Polonius. The prince is then torn between his love for Ophelia and his duty of killing her father and Claudius. Polonius, meanwhile, has formed a plan to get rid of both Hamlet and Gertrude in order to marry his daughter to the king. But Ophelia refuses and the stern father promptly condemns her to death. The action now speeds up. Hamlet rescues Ophelia at the opportune moment, the people revolt, Claudius is killed, and Polonius commits suicide. The play ends with Hamlet's receiving the acclaim of the people and Ophelia's performing the last rites for her villainous father.

Sumarokov's knowledge of *Hamlet* was derived from P. A. de la Place's translation (1746), but he makes the play over to suit the typical "love and duty" conception of neo-classical drama. And his further dependence on French rules is obvious in that the play is written in Alexandrine couplets and the unities are observed. The drama, of course, is utterly false to the spirit of Shakspere.

However, it would have been unique at this time if Sumarokov had exhibited anything of the Shaksperean manner, for practically all his plays are pale imitations of the French.

There is perhaps less of compliment and more of the implication of plagiarism in the sobriquet of "Russian Racine" with which his critics honored him. By his own example he helped to encourage the popularity of Corneille, Racine, Molière, and Voltaire, and some idea of the preponderance of French neo-classical drama throughout the whole period may be gained from the fact that up to 1787 there were one hundred and thirty-four translations from French plays, and only thirty from German and five from English.[4]

Sumarokov's garbled *Hamlet* had no immediate effect. It is recorded that Volkov and Dmitrievski translated and acted *Richard III* in the Winter Palace in 1759, but no trace of the manuscript has survived. The French continued to reign supreme. But the Anglomania which began to affect the country after 1770 brought with it an interest in Shakspere which was first manifested in the periodicals. Some French-inspired criticism appeared along with a few fragmentary translations from the plays.[5] It is very likely that Wieland's great translation of Shakspere's works (1762–66) and that of Letourneur (1773) helped to stimulate the new interest, although neither of them was turned into Russian. And no doubt the praise of Mercier in his *Essai sur l'art dramatique* (1778), which had little of Voltaire's neo-classical strictures, penetrated Russia and contributed to the improved opinion of Shakspere. Then in 1783 a translation of the *Life and Death of Richard III, King of England* was made.[6] Nevertheless, nothing of Shakspere's had actually been staged since Sumarokov's *Hamlet*. Now no less a person than Catherine the Great turned her attention to the English dramatist and the resulting products were curious, yet not unimportant, elements in the growth of Shakspere's popularity.

We have already observed Catherine's interest in English literature, especially her indebtedness to the *Spectator*.[7] Of all the products of her pen the plays of Catherine occupy a place second only to her famous correspondence. Among these dramas are: something that passes for a translation of *The Merry Wives of Windsor*, two historical plays that are classified as "imitations of Shakspere," and a fourth play that was inspired by *Timon of Athens*.

Catherine's interest in Shakspere can hardly be described as a matter of life-long devotion. Unlike Frederick the Great, she did not take her literary accomplishments very seriously, and in most of her attempts at *belles lettres* the spirit of the dilettante is everywhere apparent. She would run out an inspiration in breathless haste and then immediately turn to some new project. Catherine's four "Shaksperean plays," for example, were all written in about six months. Yet her natural enthusiasm partly compensated for her unwillingness to prune and polish.

Since Catherine did not know English, her interest in Shakspere dates pretty definitely from her reading of Eschenburg's translation,[8] which appeared in 1775–82. In 1786 she wrote to the critic Frédéric-Melchior Grimm: "Ces faiseurs de comédie font présentement des pièces historiques à l'imitation de Shakespeare,[9] que nous avons lu en allemand, traduit par Eschenburg; neuf tomes sont déjà gobés." [10]

Apparently she lost no time in putting her reading to some practical use, for in June of the same year her secretary wrote in his diary: "I compared the comedy, *The Basket*, with the original of Shakspere." [11] The reference is to Catherine's reworking of *The Merry Wives of Windsor*, to which she gave the curious title, "This is what it means to have a basket and linen," adding the explanation: "A free but weak adaptation of Shakspere." [12] The play was published and acted in 1786.

Catherine was careful not to use the word "translation" in describing her version of *The Merry Wives*. Yet her play might well be termed a "free rendering," for she departs radically from the original only when she has a purpose of her own to serve. In fact she displays considerable skill in making over Shakspere's comedy so that it may have a direct and contemporaneous appeal to her Russian audience. The scene is shifted from Windsor to St. Petersburg, and all the characters are given Russian names, many of them simple transliterations of the English. On the whole, she makes a definite attempt to retain the original characterizations, although in several instances, notably in the case of Falstaff, she deliberately transforms Shakspere's characters to fit a design of her own.

From the very opening of the play it becomes evident that Catherine is bent on turning *The Merry Wives* into a satire. Falstaff, in the person of Polkadov, becomes a Frenchified Russian coxcomb who has just returned from Paris. He has none of the inimitable humor or gorgeous language of the big-bellied knight, nor does he love like a soldier, but rather as the "lisping hawthorne buds." But by a kind of scissors-and-paste method she does succeed in fashioning an amusing satire against the Russian tendency to imitate everything French.

Catherine follows Shakspere's plot scene for scene, and for the most part she is faithful to the language of the original so long as it is easily comprehended. Her changes are always on the side of simplicity or in order to further her satirical purpose. Generally speaking, she seemed unable to fathom the language of that strange trio, Bardolph, Pistol, and Nym, which, indeed, is reproduced in Eschenburg's translation with no little success. Bardolph's comparatively normal speech is rendered with some faithfulness, but the "red-lattice phrases" of Pistol and the word-clipping of the enigmatic Nym were quite beyond Catherine. And unfortunately many of Falstaff's best speeches are cut, and it must be admitted that she missed what charm exists in the dialogue of the pseudo-fairies. Catherine was no poetess, and hence the airy playful atmosphere Shakspere created in the latter part of his play is quite lacking in the Russian.

Although much of the humor and poetry of *The Merry Wives* escaped her, Catherine deserves commendation for the skilful manner in which she transformed her original into a vehicle for satire against the prevailing Gallomania.[13] And she has the further merit of presenting to a Russian public the first play that actually bore on its title page the name of Shakspere.

Catherine's *Spendthrift*,[14] the last act of which was left unfinished, is a reworking of *Timon of Athens*. Once again she sets out to write a play which shall be more or less an imitation of Shakspere's up to a point consistent with a new design she has formed. This time, instead of satirist, she turns moralist, and where she diverges from the original it is

usually with the intention of bringing out the moral purport
of her drama.

Catherine rejects entirely the Athenian localization of
Timon of Athens and she also discards the historical significance connected with the names of Shakspere's characters,
substituting purely Russian names. For example, Timon
becomes Tratov (in Russian, "Spendthrift"). But with a
few minor exceptions all of Shakspere's characters are retained and the action of the original is followed rather
closely. As in her previous attempt, however, long speeches
are often shortened and several of the scenes are telescoped.
She softens Timon's insane hatred of humanity, for she
definitely entertains the idea of reforming him. In fact, her
obvious intention in the unfinished last act was to have the
misanthropic Tratov marry and regain his place in society, a
happy but a wiser man.

This may seem like a lame and impotent conclusion when
compared with Shakspere's. However, it must be remembered that the dramatic but bitter end of Timon, who dies
cursing all mankind, was not in keeping with the highly
moral tone of Russian literature at this time. And, as in the
case of *The Merry Wives of Windsor*, Catherine had an axe
of her own to grind. She was determined to make an actable
play which should contain a moral and provide an ending
suited to her audience.[15]

Catherine described each of her two historical plays, *The
Life of Rurik* and *The Beginning of the Rule of Oleg*, as "an
imitation of Shakspere without observing the usual rules of
the theatre." [16] Attempts had been made to write historical
plays in Russia before Catherine tried her hand at it. The

best known are those of Sumarokov, cast in the neo-classical mold, but, as one critic remarks, "there is nothing historical about them except the titles." [17]   The new and significant fact is that Catherine's plays were written with the broad sweep of Shakspere's historical dramas and with something of his scorn for the three unities. In the letter to Grimm already mentioned, she pays her respects to neo-classical rules by way of commenting on her historical plays: "Or, ces imitations de Shakespeare sont très commodes, parceque n'étant ni comédies, ni tragédies, et n'ayant d'autres règles que celles du tact du supportable pour les spectateurs, je les crois susceptibles du tout." [18]   At a time when the Russian theatre was still dominated by French formalism, Catherine's determination to defy the traditional rules was a step in the direction of a better understanding of Shakspere. Logically she put the question: If twenty-four hours can be represented by an hour and a half, why could not the action of two years be compressed within the same length of time? [19]

Although Catherine called her two historical dramas "imitations of Shakspere," they have little of the manner and none of the poetry of the master. After having read the chronicle plays in Eschenburg's translation, Catherine was inspired to present to her subjects certain of the great events of Russian history. But beyond the initial inspiration, which was important enough, and the general matter of form, there is little other Shaksperean influence to be observed. She retells historical events with little attempt to inform them with dramatic feeling. Her characters, for the most part, are mere mouthpieces for her own moral aphorisms; or she uses them to retail the dry facts which she had

culled from history books. Here and there one can find
borrowed incidents, a character molded on one of Shakspere's, or a whole scene suggested by one of his,[20] but the
significance of such parallels must not be pressed too far.

I have dwelt at some length on the part Catherine played
in bringing Shakspere before the Russian public, yet one
must be careful not to overemphasize her efforts. Her "Shaksperean" dramas are neither great literature nor exception-
ally fine acting plays. Nor did they inspire any imitations.
People continued to see and read French plays, and Russian
dramatists did not cease to copy them. Nevertheless,
Catherine's "Shaksperean" dramas did arouse much com-
ment, if not because of their intrinsic merit, then because the
empress had written them.[21] Her particular achievement
was to stimulate an interest in Shakspere by introducing
him to the Russian public in a new light. This interest soon
bore fruit, for in 1787, just a year after Catherine's productions, Karamzin published his translation of *Julius Caesar*,
the first competent translation of Shakspere to appear in
Russia.

As a matter of fact, Karamzin's concern with Shakspere
may possibly have antedated that of Catherine, for as early
as 1785 we hear that he had already begun to read the plays.[22]
Shakspere, indeed, was to take a prominent place in Karamzin's interest in English literature. In his *Poesy* he hails the
dramatist:

> O Shakspere, nature's friend! who hath portrayed
> Better than thou the hearts of men? Whose brush
> Hath limned them with such art? In the soul's depth
> Thou hast the key to life's great secret found,
> And with the light of thine immortal spirit
> Hast like the sun made bright men's darker ways.[23]

Since Karamzin knew English, there is no reason to doubt his statement that he translated *Julius Caesar* from the original,[24] although it is very likely that he received some assistance from Letourneur's version. His prose is not very inspired and he fails utterly to assimilate the Shaksperean manner. But he does labor after exactness, unlike so many of the contemporary French translators, and his mistakes in understanding or in interpreting the text are comparatively few. Of much greater value, at this particular time, than the translation was his critical introduction. In this Karamzin not only professes a profound admiration for Shakspere, but he makes bold to take issue with his French detractors, such as Voltaire, — a critical independence which Russian writers had rarely permitted themselves heretofore. After insisting upon Shakspere's unquestioned position and influence in English literature, Karamzin goes on to praise his genius. "All his magnificent scenes," he writes, "imitate nature directly; all the nuances of these scenes astonish those who examine them attentively, and each class of men, each age, each passion, and each character speaks in its own proper language. For each thought he finds an image, for each sensation an expression, for each impulse of the soul the best turn of phrase. His picture is strong and his colors are brilliant when he wishes to show the splendor of virtue; his brush is very beguiling when he represents the soft emotions of the most tender passions; but this same brush becomes gigantic when he describes the cruel emotions of the soul." [25] Then he summarizes Voltaire's objections and pointedly remarks: "I esteem it superfluous now to refute at length these ideas, which have as their ob-

ject to minimize the glory of Shakspere." Karamzin ab-
solves Shakspere for failing to comply with the neo-classical
rules of the drama, because of "his ardent imagination,
which cannot be bound by any prescriptions." And he concludes with the declaration that Shakspere's drama, "as the
incommensurable theatre of nature, is filled with variety;
but everything is brought together to compose a perfect
whole which defies the management of contemporary dramatic writers." [26]

"Tell me how many European critics judged so truth-
fully about Shakspere at this time?" [27] asks one of Karamzin's biographers apropos of the introduction to the translation of *Julius Caesar*. And if we omit the German critics,
there is little exaggeration in this challenge. At any rate,
Karamzin's introduction is the first adequate critical presentation of Shakspere in Russia. More than this, it marks the
real turning point in the influence of French neo-classical
drama. Karamzin refused to submit to the rules of neo-
classicism, and his devotion to English and German sentimentalists made him a precursor of the subsequent Romantic Movement. In this respect it is interesting to note that
he used Shakspere as an argument for breaking with the
French literary traditions.

Karamzin may have been indebted to Letourneur for
some of the critical ideas in his introduction, but we
find him repeating and amplifying in later works the conviction that Shakspere was a much greater dramatist than
Corneille or Racine. In the *Letters of a Russian Traveller*, which is rich in references to Shakspere, he declares that
French dramatists seem to him noble and majestic, but that

they do not "touch or fire my heart like the muse of Shakspere and some of the Germans (fewer in number)." [28]   And
he challenges the critics to find in Corneille or Racine anything comparable to certain scenes in *Lear*. To appreciate
the unique value of such criticism at this time (1790), one
must be conversant with the general flavor of Russian dramatic opinion as it was expressed in the various literary
periodicals. For example, one critic, as late as 1802, after
exalting the French stage, remarks: "The English stage is
entirely of another kind, but I do not understand why people,
unacquainted with the theatre as a whole, and not possessing
sufficient talent for judging Corneille and Racine, prefer the
English Melpomene to the French." [29]   Then he continues
with praise for Corneille and condemnation for Shakspere
and his sensationalism.

When he was in London Karamzin attended a performance
of *Hamlet* at the Haymarket.[30]   His account of the experience
has some value for students of the eighteenth-century English theatre and is perhaps worth quoting in full:

I saw Shakspeare's *Hamlet* for the first time — and it would
have been better if I had not seen it! The actors speak but do not
act; they are badly clothed, and the decorations are poor. Hamlet
was in a black French kaftan with a hugh headdress and a blue ribbon; the queen wore a rounded robe and the king a Spanish mantle.
Lackeys in livery brought the decorations on the scene, bearing
them on their shoulders — and this takes place while the performance is going on! How different from the Paris theatre! I was
angry with the actors, not for myself, but for Shakspere, and I was
surprised at the spectators, who sat quietly and listened with
great attention; from time to time they even applauded. Guess
what scene the public reacted to more than any? That where they
dig Ophelia's grave and where the workers, playing on words, say

that the first nobleman was Adam, "the first that ever bore arms,"
and so on. Ophelia herself interested me; a beautiful actress,[31]
excellently costumed, and touching in the mad scene; she reminded
me of Dugazon in Nina; and she sings very agreeably.[32]

After this disappointing performance, and regretting that
Mrs. Siddons was not then in town, he goes to an opera,
"which they did not play very well, but much better than
Hamlet." [33]

It was Karamzin's misfortune, apparently, to attend one
of the poorer representations of *Hamlet*, although his general comments on the London theatre of the time have some
justification. He also takes to task the contemporary writers
of tragedy, who "have Shakspere's bombast but not his
genius." [34] He likewise condemns *The Fair Penitent* and *Jane
Shore*, which he very likely witnessed, "because they make
their effect more by their contents and scenes than by their
feeling and the power of the author's talent." [35]   And,
mirabile dictu for a Russian critic in the eighteenth century,
he disparages *Cato* for its "insupportable love scenes,"
though he allows the play other merits.[36]

On the whole, Karamzin comes to the conclusion that "in
dramatic poetry the English have nothing excellent apart
from the creations of one author; but this author is Shakspere, and England's treasure!" [37]   He compares the critics
who laugh at Shakspere to "wild boys who surround a
strangely dressed man in the street and cry, 'How funny!
how queer!'"   "Every author," he continues, "bears the
impress of his own country.   Shakspere wished to please his
contemporaries;   he knew their taste and catered to it. . . .
But every sincere talent, while paying tribute to the age,

creates also for eternity. Temporal beauties fade, but the universal ones, based on the human heart and on the nature of things, preserve their own power, as in Homer and in Shakspere." [38]

I have been endeavoring to elucidate Karamzin's appreciation of Shakspere by quotations from his frequent passages in praise of him. Excerpts from his well-reasoned arguments and acute criticisms of the plays themselves, of which there is much, might have been more convincing. However, I have probably strained the privilege of quoting already, though in this instance there are extenuating circumstances. Karamzin was no doubt influenced by certain of the German devotees of Shakspere, but there can be no question as to the sincerity of his appreciation. And in this respect he stood quite alone in Russia at this time, or for that matter, for some time to come. He seemed to know the plays with thoroughness, and various characters, situations, and lines entered into the substance of his own works.[39]

Nevertheless, Karamzin's understanding of Shakspere's plays was somewhat conditioned by the peculiar quality of his own genius. He gave a grudging sanction to the Shaksperean heresy of mingling comedy and tragedy, but for English comedy itself he had little use. Indeed, he preferred the French. "English comedy for the most part," he writes, "is boresome, coarse, indecent, and offensive to every refined taste." [40] Such a critical attitude, right or wrong, is a bad one with which to approach Shakspere's plays, for it implies a lack of sympathy with a highly important characteristic of English dramatic genius. It soon becomes evident, in studying Karamzin's interest in Shakspere, that he ad-

mired him most of all for his understanding of the human
heart and for his melancholy passages. In Shakspere, as
in Thomson, Young, Ossian, and Sterne, Karamzin sought
for the feeling and sadness so peculiarly suitable to his sentimental nature. He quotes the famous passage in *The Tempest*
(IV, 1) — "The cloud-capp'd towers, the gorgeous palaces,"
etc. — and exclaims: "What sacred melancholy inspired in
him these verses?" [41] And on leaving his native country, he
remarks: "I should like to have wept my heart out, as Shakspere says." [42] Speaking of his friend Lenz, he writes: "Profound sentimentality, without which Klopstock would not
have been Klopstock nor Shakspere Shakspere, destroyed
him." [43] And in his criticism of the plays his mind is always
searching for the moral and his eye for the sweet melancholy
of the more philosophical lines.

Notwithstanding this one-sided approach, Karamzin deserves full credit for having been the first Russian to perceive and declare the real genius of Shakspere. In a smaller
way, though with nothing of the same success, he performed
for Shakspere in Russia the service Lessing rendered him in
Germany.

No one appeared in the remainder of the eighteenth century to carry on Karamzin's enthusiasm and critical judgment of Shakspere. Fragmentary translations in the journals
noticeably increase along with criticism of a poor quality.
In 1795 a translation of Mercier's rendering of *Romeo and
Juliet* was published in Moscow, but apparently it attracted
little notice. The century closed with Shakspere's works
more appreciated but still not widely known among the general reading public. However, although French drama held

the boards, the example of Shakspere's plays, and perhaps of Catherine's imitations plus the critical opinions of Karamzin, was gradually turning the tide against the neo-classical tradition.

The first twenty years of the nineteenth century witnessed a further growth in the popularity of Shakspere; yet it cannot be said that the plays were any better understood than in the two previous decades. In truth, there were few critics in this period who brought to the plays the keen, if sometimes circumscribed, critical taste of Karamzin. The theatre itself was making vigorous strides forward in acting, staging, and repertoire, and the increased frequency of production testified to a greater public interest in the drama. But the two prevailing literary tendencies, sentimentality and neo-classicism, fused to produce a most lugubrious type of play, and it was Shakspere's misfortune to run counter to this mongrel standard of dramatic taste.

At the beginning of the century partial translations of the plays continued to appear in the periodicals [44] and some favorable criticism was published, most significantly a rendering of the German treatise of K. Meiner in which Corneille was vehemently condemned and Shakspere deified.[45] But it was not until 1806 that anything of Shakspere's was staged. This was Velyaminov's translation of *Othello*, which was played in St. Petersburg with the famous actor Yakovlev filling the title rôle.

As in the case of Sumarokov's *Hamlet*, however, it is only by a generous extension of courtesy that we can consider this performance a play of Shakspere's. The translation was based upon the French version of *Othello* by Ducis. The ex-

traordinary concoctions which Ducis made of Shakspere's
plays are well known. He took unforgivable liberties, and
although he was translating in the last ten years of the eighteenth century, he still felt it necessary to confine the plays
within the neo-classical straitjacket. The unities were enforced, the themes of love and duty were exaggerated or
even introduced where they did not exist, and everything
that might offend "good taste" was banished. Yet these
Shaksperean versions of Ducis are important for our purpose, for during this period they invariably served as the
source of Russian representations.

Velyaminov, however, was not wholly satisfied with
Ducis's rendering, and it appears that he had recourse to the
original. For not only does he restore some of the names of
characters changed by Ducis, but the wickedness of Iago,
dispensed with as too shocking by the Frenchman, reappears
in the Russian. Velyaminov also displays a fondness for
elaborating the more gruesome aspects of *Othello*, and the
passages of grief and remorse are invariably extended. In
brief, the sentimental, the pathetic situations which call
forth tears, were obviously considered the high points in the
play. Its success was great and for more than twenty years
it held the stage. Shakspere, regularized and sentimentalized, was the only form in which he appeared in the Russian
theatre for some time.

Velyaminov, an infantry general, had few designs on literature, but the next adapter of Shakspere was the young
Nikolai Gnedich, who later won fame as a poet. His version
of *Lear*, the first in Russian, was produced in St. Petersburg
in 1807 and printed the next year. As in *Othello*, Ducis's

translation is the immediate source, but Gnedich does not hesitate to depart from it to suit his own purposes, and in so doing he occasionally makes use of the original. The resulting *réchauffé* is a curious performance, twice removed from Shakspere. Pathetic situations are pyramided and every care is taken to wring tears from the spectators. A good sentimental ending is provided in which Lear and Cordelia throw themselves into each other's arms, and the wicked sisters are punished and the country regained for the old king.

Both *Othello* and *Lear* are in prose, but the *Hamlet* of S. Viskovatov, which was produced in St. Petersburg in 1810, is in verse. It is perhaps less of a translation of Ducis than the other two plays, for Viskovatov infused into his *Hamlet* more than a moiety of the sentimental feeling which by now was definitely going out of fashion. Hamlet, king of Denmark, is torn between his love for Ophelia, who is represented as the daughter of Claudius, a prince of the blood, and the duty of revenging himself on the latter as the murderer of his father. Eventually Claudius kills Gertrude, and the action concludes with Hamlet's stabbing Claudius.

It is interesting to observe the misdirected ingenuity with which Viskovatov transforms Hamlet into a sepulchral philosopher of the *Night Thoughts* variety. The sadness and melancholy of the hero are described as his birthright, not as a state of mind induced by the unfortunate circumstances of his life. He thoroughly enjoys roaming about graveyards at midnight, and, sitting on a tomb, he nurses thoughts of revenge while calling up horrific images of earthly corruption. His soliloquies on these occasions abound with echoes of Young,

Gray, and Mrs. Radcliffe. No opportunity is missed to play upon the sensibilities, and even Gertrude and Ophelia take on the aspect of a sentimental queen and heroine. This curious hodge-podge of melodrama and sentimentality gives one the impression that the author must have been steeped in *The London Merchant* of Lillo, which, incidentally, had been translated into Russian. Nevertheless, the play had great success and was the vehicle for the triumphs of renowned actors in the first quarter of the nineteenth century.

In 1817 *Romeo and Juliet* was staged in the form of an opera, and in the same year fragments of *Macbeth*,[46] translated from the version of Ducis, appeared in a periodical. In 1821 the satirist of sentimentality, Prince A. Shakhovskoi, put on for the first time in Russia a version of *The Tempest*. This is not altogether lacking in charm,[47] but the comic scenes are hopelessly exaggerated and melodrama is gratuitously interpolated.

It must not be supposed that these garbled performances did not encounter the opposition of certain critics who still favored the neo-classical traditions or argued for a strictly national repertoire. But on the whole there was little protest on the score of their remoteness from the originals, and only a few discerning critics of the time advocated a Shakspere undefiled. The theatre, for the most part, continued to feature the drama of Paris, and it was not until the Romantic Movement that the example of the Germans was followed and Shakspere was brought upon the Russian stage in anything like a pure form.

In the early years of the movement, from 1815 to 1825, the young Russian romantics regarded Shakspere as a symbol of universal genius, a writer whose mind comprehended all phases of humanity, and who dared to treat the unreal and the supernatural as well as the actions of real men and women. The very features for which he had been condemned by adherents of neo-classical drama were now acclaimed. They praised him for disregarding the unities, for mingling comedy and tragedy, and for including in his plays the romantic elements of ghosts, witches, and fairies. Even his characteristically English comedy, which previously had been a stumbling block to his admirers, was now appreciated, though not always with much understanding. At first this new and profounder insight into the plays was primarily expressed in critical works, but Shakspere also began to influence the original productions of the young Russian romantics.

Macbeth quickly became a favorite. In his youth A. I. Turgenev had begun a translation of the play and wrote enthusiastically about his work to Zhukovski.[48] The latter could not wholly approve of *Macbeth*, but, reflecting the new tastes, he praised the scenes of horror, — the witches, the murder of Duncan, and the sleep-walking scene.[49] P. Pletnev contributed his *Thoughts on Macbeth*,[50] in which he vigorously defends the scene with the Porter. Indeed, Shakspere's attraction for Pletnev was so compelling that he thought of renouncing all other literature in order to spend the rest of his life studying the plays.

In 1825 V. Kiukhelbeker wrote a dramatic farce in two acts, *Ghosts of Shakspere*,[51] in which Oberon, Titania, Puck, Ariel, and Caliban confront a poet who is given to dreaming about these creatures of Shakspere's imagination. The sequel is amusing, and despite the rather crude burlesque the farce contains some clever fantasy. In the same year the versatile Prince Shakhovskoi produced a comedy in one act, *Falstaff*, which is based mainly upon the second part of *Henry IV*.[52] It is a mere cento of humorous episodes built about the fat knight and his mirth-provoking rout, notable in that more than a vague suggestion of English humor was retained and was apparently enjoyed by the Russian audience. Shakhovskoi was a writer of catholic tastes and a devout partisan of Shakspere. S. T. Aksakov tells an interesting story about him and the novelist Zagoskin, who was himself indebted to English literature. Zagoskin called the author of *The Merry Wives of Windsor* a "beast," and Aksakov relates how Shakhovskoi rebuked him, saying that "one does not talk about Shakspere with the young and the weak-minded; that all Russian literature compared with English is not worth a groat, and that it is necessary for such a backward people as the Russians to live a long time in order to understand and value Shakspere." [53] Although the two disputants were great friends, Zagoskin resented the snub and attacked Shakhovskoi with his fists.

The famous dramatist Griboedov had for Shakspere an admiration quite free from much of the idolatry so common among the romantic writers of the period. He seriously endeavored to encourage the staging of his plays by making overtures to one of the famous actors of the day.[54] Griboedov had little patience with contemporary translators who mutilated the dramas, or with the adapters who produced mere monstrosities, and he insisted that Shakspere be read in the original, for like every great poet "he is untranslatable because he is national." [55] His own dramatic fragment, *A Georgian Night* [56] (1828), was powerfully influenced by *Macbeth*. The witch scenes in particular he closely imitated.

In the great poet Pushkin the plays of Shakspere had at once an unusually acute and sympathetic critic and an imitator whose efforts had so completely assimilated the spirit of the originals that they were Shaksperean without being mere imitations. His acquaintance with the plays began rather early in his literary career, for in 1824 we find him writing in a characteristic vein to Vyazemski: "Reading Shakspere and the Bible. The Holy Spirit is sometimes in my heart but I prefer Goethe and Shakspere." [57] *The Rape of Lucrece*, however, strikes him as a rather weak poem and he jocularly demands what would have happened if the harassed damsel had thought to give Tarquin a buffet. "Perhaps that would have cooled his venturesome nature and in shame he would have felt constrained to be on his way." [58] Indeed, he could not resist the temptation to parody the story, and in "two mornings" he produced his extremely amusing *Count Nulin*.[59]

Meanwhile Pushkin was occupied with the idea of his historical drama, *Boris Godunov*, and by way of preparation he read Shakspere hard and studied the laws of the theatre in Schlegel's *Dramaturgie*. The results of these labors were soon announced to his friends. He writes to Raevski: "La vraisemblance des situations et la vérité du dialogue, voilà la véritable règle de la tragédie. Je n'ai pas lu Calderon, ni Véga, mais quel homme que ce Shakespeare!" [60] In fact he will have nothing to do with neo-classical restrictions, and Shakspere and his own critical sense bear him out.

"On a tâché d'en baser les loix [the laws of the drama] sur la vraisemblance, et c'est justement elle qu'exclut la nature du drame; sans parler déjà du tems, des lieux, etc., quel diable de vraisemblance y a-t-il dans une salle coupée en deux dont l'une est occupée par 2000 personnes, sensés n'être pas vues par celles qui sont sur les planches." [61] As in the case of Catherine the Great, the unities failed to recommend themselves to him on the basis of common sense.

He was now ready to write *Boris Godunov* (1825). The theme is based upon one of the great events of Russian history, — the overthrow of Godunov by the False Dmitri. He makes no secret of his inspiration and model. "A l'exemple de Scheks. [Shakspere]," he writes again to Raevski, "je me suis borné à développer une époque et des personnages historiques sans rechercher les effets théatrals, le pathétique Romanesque, etc. . . . le style en est mélangé. Il est trivial et bas, là où j'ai été obligé de faire intervenir des personnages vulgaires et grossiers." [62]

In short, Pushkin has conceived the historical drama quite in the manner of Shakspere, and the complete freedom it allowed suited his genius. The form of *Boris Godunov* is blank verse, interlarded with occasional prose passages, a method unquestionably derived from Shakspere; and certain scenes in lyric stanzas must have had their form suggested by a similar usage in the banquet scene in *Romeo and Juliet*. His characters are vivid and natural, not conforming to types and the exigencies of plot. He ridiculed dramatists who so portrayed their kings and conspirators that every little action had to be in character. "Un consp. [conspirator] dit," he writes, "'Donnez-moi à boire en conspirateur,

— ce n'est que ridicule.'" Then he adds: "Lisez Sc. [Shak-spere], il ne craint jamais de compromettre son personnage, il le fait parler avec tout l'abandon de la vie, car il est sûr en tems et lieu de lui faire trouver la langue de son carac-tère." [63] There is a distinct resemblance between Godunov and Henry IV in their ambition, fate, and remorse, and in particular in their instructions to their sons. There are also specific borrowings from *Henry V*, *Richard III*, *Macbeth*, and *Hamlet*.[64]

Despite its national appeal, *Boris Godunov* did not prove a popular success when it was staged in 1831. The critics, curiously enough, disliked its objectivity and the sober way in which Pushkin had treated Russian history. Yet of its kind nothing greater had been done previously, and after Pushkin only the famous historical trilogy of A. Tolstoi may be compared with *Boris Godunov*.

Pushkin, however, did not cease to be inspired by Shak-spere. His *Dramatic Scenes*, written about 1830, contains more than an echo of the plays, especially in *The Stone Guest* and *The Avaricious Knight*.[65] In the former, the scene be-tween Don Juan and Dona Anna was very likely suggested by the scene between Lady Anne and Richard III,[66] both in situation and details. Of *The Avaricious Knight* [67] the critic Belinski wrote: "In its well-sustained characters (the miser, his son, the Duke, and the Jew), its skilful arrangement, the fearful force of its pathos, its wonderful poetry, its complete-ness, and its ending, — in short, in everything, — this drama is a very great production, worthy of the genius of Shakspere himself." [68] This is rather high praise and was no doubt prompted by the obvious reminiscences of Shakspere in the

play. In an unfinished article on *Shylock, Angelo, and Falstaff*
unusually discerning in its appreciation of these characters,
Pushkin compares Shylock to the miser in Molière's *L'avare*.
He points out that Molière's character is "only a miser," a
type of a single passion or a single vice. Shylock, too, he
observes, is a miser, but he is also "quick-witted, vindictive,
devoted to his daughter," a character filled with many passions and vices, a living human being.[69] Pushkin had learned
something from Shakspere's portrayal, for Solomon in *The
Avaricious Knight* bears a resemblance to Shylock that goes
much deeper than the fact that he is both a Jew and a money-
lender. His love for gold is a reasoned love, and, like Shylock,
he can defend his profession and his actions with wisdom and
trenchant sarcasm. In his words there lurks Shylock's
scorn for his Christian victims, and the whole scene between
Solomon and Albert recalls the scene in which Antonio requests a loan from Shylock.[70] Then, fugitive as the suggestion
may be, there persists a Shaksperean flavor in Solomon's
description of Toby, the little old man and apothecary, who
"compounds drops magnificently." [71] Their efficacy is no
less than the poison which the apothecary gives to Romeo.[72]

But Pushkin's indebtedness consists in more than the
delineation of character. The Shaksperean quality of his
blank verse is a notable feature of *The Avaricious Knight*.
The free swing of the lines, the frequent feminine endings,
and the clever and consistent use of enjambement are all in
the good Shaksperean tradition. The Baron's famous monologue in the second scene, for example, constantly reminds
one of Shakspere's style in its splendid poetry and opulent
imagery.[73] And further than this, one critic has pointed out

that in a few instances Pushkin has actually borrowed whole lines from the English dramatist.[74]

Pushkin's final noteworthy tribute to Shakspere found expression in his admiration for *Measure for Measure*. In 1833 he undertook a translation of this play in blank verse. But after finishing the first scene he abandoned the idea in favor of a narrative poem which retains, more or less, the story of the play as a framework. Despite the free treatment, he leans heavily upon the original and renders a large number of Shakspere's lines.

Pushkin learned a great deal from Shakspere in dramatic structure, in the portrayal of character, and in the writing of blank verse. His approach to the English dramatist was little tinctured by the excessive romantic enthusiasm of his contemporaries. It was not so much the over-praised "romantic elements" in the plays that aroused his admiration as the extraordinary objective art. This perception ranks Pushkin among the most understanding and appreciative Russian critics of Shakspere at this time.

From 1825 to 1830 Shakspere's fame was kept brightest in the periodicals, especially in the *Moscow Telegraph* of Polevoi and the *Moscow Messenger* of Pogodin.[75] In these numerous articles appeared, sometimes original but more often translated from French, German, and English, which praised and interpreted Shakspere in the romantic spirit. A question frequently raised was the proper method of translating the plays. It must be remembered that up to this time no version had appeared, with the possible exception of Karamzin's prose *Julius Caesar*, which could pretend to be a faithful rendering of the original. French and German translations were invariably the models, and no hesitancy was evinced in cutting or in adding material. The idea of reproducing the spirit of the original by subscribing to a policy of exact translation was entirely lacking. Apparently as an answer to the demand of periodical contributors for a literal rendering, M. Vronchenko published his verse translation of *Hamlet* in 1828. He was able to make the proud boast that he had translated line for line, and where the agreement of the two languages permitted, word for word.[76] Despite his conscientiousness, however, he was not above making concessions to the taste of his day, for expressions which he thought were indecent he toned down, altered, or omitted altogether. But these offenses were few and Vronchenko's *Hamlet* may be regarded as the first faithful translation of Shakspere into Russian in which a sincere attempt was made to reproduce the spirit of the original.

After this model rendering a number of partial translations of several of the plays appeared in periodicals,[77] likewise a long eulogistic biography of Shakspere which drew copiously upon Schlegel.[78] By 1830 Shakspere had won a wide popularity with the reading public; and in view of this it might be expected that the plays would receive a more adequate presentation on the Russian stage than had been accorded them hitherto. However, throughout all this period the far-fetched adaptations of Velyaminov, Gnedich, and Viskovatov remained popular, and no effort was made to produce the plays as they were written. Naturally a correct conception of Shakspere, as well as a true understanding of his essentially dramatic genius, was difficult without some opportunity of seeing his plays staged in their original form.

This lack was remedied in the course of the next ten years, and it is during this period that Shakspere attained the height of his fame in Russia.

In the first years of the 1830's Polevoi continued his critical articles in the *Moscow Telegraph*, in which he hailed Shakspere as the perfect representative of romanticism. But a greater critic, V. Belinski, now appeared, who did not hesitate to rank Shakspere above the ancient dramatists of Greece as well as above the French and the much-worshipped Germans. For him he was the "great Shakspere who understood hell, earth, and heaven," the king of nature whose every drama is a world in miniature, who has not, like Schiller, borrowed his ideas and his favorite heroes, but has represented life with impartiality.[79]

Meanwhile biographies and translations multiplied, the latter following closely the principles set down by Vronchenko. In 1833 V. Yakimov rendered *Lear* and *The Merchant of Venice*, and in the same year *Richard III* was translated for a benefit performance for the actor Ya. Bryanski.[80] It was at this time that two great actors, P. Mochalov and V. Karatygin, appear, who, by their powerful and wholly natural interpretations and their use of faithful texts and proper scenic effects, won for Shakspere a hitherto unexampled popularity in the Russian theatre.

No less a person than the Shaksperean enthusiast, Polevoi, provided the translation of *Hamlet* for Mochalov. More than this, he attended the rehearsals and impressed upon the actors the exact meaning of various difficult passages. The first performance took place on January 22, 1837, in Moscow. It was a complete triumph for Mochalov, and ten performances were given within the next few months, — an extraordinary success for a Shaksperean play in Russia at this time.

At this distance it is difficult to credit the reported impression made by Mochalov's *Hamlet*. The actor must certainly have been the equal of a Garrick or a Kean (his devotees thought he was better than Garrick). The Russian audience, however, is unusually susceptible to fine acting, and this fact may in some measure account for its frenzy on this particular occasion. Belinski, who attended eight of the ten performances (a significant bit of testimony in itself), has left a report of the effect the tragedy had on the audience. He describes the setting of the play within the play and the fearful effectiveness of Mochalov's rendering of Hamlet's comments as the dumb-show is in progress. "As under the compulsion of a nightmare," he writes, "all this breathed such hidden but feeling power that the blood froze in the veins of the spectators, and all these people, different in condition, character, inclination, education, taste, age, and sex, were molded into one enormous mass, animated by a single thought, a single sentiment, its face strained, its attention fascinated, holding its breath, while watching this little man with his black hair and his face as pale as death carelessly sprawled on the bench. Thunderous applause began and then ceased several times; hands were raised to applaud and then fell, powerless; a strange hand held a strange hand; and a stranger prevented the expression of rapture by another stranger, and yet this did not seem strange to anyone." [81]

In October of the same year Karatygin played *Hamlet* at

St. Petersburg with a success apparently no less than that of his rival.[82] More than any previous productions these performances brought home to the Russian public the universality of Shakspere's appeal, and for the first time criticism unanimously comprehended the purely objective nature of his art. Opposition ceased, justification no longer appeared, and romantic as well as neo-classical strictures were dropped. Shakspere had finally come into his own.

For the remainder of the 1830's and into the 1840's translations accumulated, and one full-length biography appeared.[83] English critics of Shakspere were also given a hearing. The opinions of Pope and Johnson were quoted and the preface of Hazlitt's *Characters of Shakespeare's Plays* was reproduced in one of the periodicals.[84] Mrs. Jameson's studies of Juliet and Ophelia were translated [85] and were hailed with enthusiasm by Belinski.[86]

Apart from Pushkin's *Boris Godunov*, however, no noteworthy Russian plays appeared which were written directly under the influence of Shakspere. But this is little to be wondered at, since the theatre at this time boasted few dramatists who were equal to the task. Nevertheless, with the passing of another generation such dramatists as Ostrovski, Chaev, and Aleksei Tolstoi became his worthy disciples, and in the 50's and 60's Annenkov, Botkin, A. Grigorev, Fet, and Ivan Turgenev were much influenced by the plays. But in this age Shakspere in Russia, as in nearly all the countries of Europe, had become a household word.

BIBLIOGRAPHY

Bibliographical Studies

A. Lirondelle, *Shakespeare en Russie, 1748–1840*, Paris, 1910. (For a full bibliography of translations of Shakspere from 1748–1840, see pp. 229–234.)

Investigations

Anonymous, "Shekspir v perevode russkikh pisatelei" (*Otechestvennyya zapiski*, 1865, I, 500–512).

V. Lebedev, "Znakomstvo s Shekspirom v Rossii do 1812 goda" (*Russki vestnik*, Moskva, 1875, No. 12, 755–798).
   "Shekspir v Anglii, Frantsii i Rossii" (*Filologicheskiya zapiski*, 1878, III, 73–91).

C. Ziolecki, "Shakespeare in Poland, Russia and other Slavonic Countries" (*Transactions of the New Shakespeare Society*, 1880–85, pp. 431–441).

P. Gnedich, "Hamlet, ego postanovka i perevody" (*Russki vestnik*, Moskva, 1882, CLVIII, No. 4).

S. Timofeev, *Vliyanie Shekspira na russkuiu dramu*, Moskva, 1887.

P. Morozov, *Ocherki iz istorii russkoi dramy XVII–XVIII stoleti*, St. Petersburg, 1888.
   Istoriya russkago teatra, St. Petersburg, 1889.

N. Dole, "Shakespeare and the Russian Drama" (*Poet-Lore*, Philadelphia, 1889–90, I, No. 11, pp. 497–507; II, No. 3, pp. 113–125).

N. Storozhenko, "Shekspir i Belinski" (*Mir bozhi*, 1897, No. 3, pp. 126–140).

M. Pokrovski, "Puschkin und Shakespeare" (*Jahrbuch der deutschen Shakespeare Gesellschaft*, Berlin, 1907, XLIII, 169–209).

A. Lirondelle, *Shakespeare en Russie*, 1748–1840, Paris, 1912. (This book is easily the most comprehensive study of the subject.)

M. Pokrovski, "Shekspirizm Pushkina" (*Sochineniya Pushkina*, red. S. Vengerova, St. Petersburg, 1912, IV, 1–20).

N. Bakhmin, "Shekspir v russkoi literature" (*Sochineniya Shekspira*, red. S. Vengerova, St. Petersburg, 1913, V, 558–597).

J. A., "Shekspir v Rossii" (*Biblioteka*, St. Petersburg, 1914, No. 4, pp. 3–21).

E. Friedricks, "Shakespeare in Russland" (*Englische Studien*, 1916, pp. 106–136).

Ch. Vetrinski, "Shekspir v Rossii" (*Russkaya mysl*, 1916, pp. 50–79).

O. Kartoschinsky, "Shakespeare in Russia" (*The Russian Review*, 1916, No. 3, pp. 141–146).

N. Kotlyarevski, "Shekspir i staraya Rossiya" (*Vestnik Evropy*, 1916, V, 23–31).

C. Herford, *A Russian Shakespearean*, Oxford, 1925.

E. Simmons, "Catherine the Great and Shakespeare" (*P.M.L.A.*, XLVII, 1932, No. 3, pp. 790–806).
   "A. S. Pushkin, *The Avaricious Knight*" (Harvard Studies and Notes in Philology and Literature, 1933, XV, 329–344).

CHAPTER IX

WALTER SCOTT AND THE RUSSIAN ROMANTIC MOVEMENT

THE Romantic Movement in the last years of the eighteenth and the beginning of the nineteenth century made its way into Russia with much less difficulty than earlier literary influences from the West. The effect on the development of the national literature was more widespread and the resulting productions of much greater significance. No doubt the swift dissemination was facilitated by the earlier pre-romantic efforts of such writers as Karamzin and Zhukovski. Sentimentalism, an interest in national antiquities, and a growing admiration for the poetry of nature helped to win a ready acceptance of the new literature. Then, too, the *rapprochement* between Russia and the West was now more intimate and mutually beneficial than ever before. Politically and economically the two broad divisions of the Continent were drawn closer together, and the West could no longer afford to regard Russia as a helpless giant unaware of its own strength. Under Alexander I (1801–25) the country, as the most formidable enemy of Napoleon, became an inspiring force in European affairs. And as the leading spirit in the Holy Alliance (1815) Russia gained a respected and feared position among the nations of Europe.

Culturally, also, the country had come of age. It had finished its long apprenticeship, and in the romantic period

(1820–40) critics, poets, and novelists appeared who could claim an honorable place beside the best writers of Western Europe. They did not cease to learn from their more advanced neighbors. But they assimilated what they learned, and with Belinski in criticism, Pushkin in poetry, and Gogol in the novel all the former truckling to foreign models eventually ended, and a literature grew up that had its roots in the soil and whose chief aim was to reflect the life and idealism of the Russian people.

The long reign of neo-classicism was at an end. Throughout the romantic period, to be sure, members of the older generation, devotees of the literature of rule-and-line, did not fail to protest against the changing fashion· but their protests went unheeded in the enthusiasm for the new poetry. Russian writers variously interpreted the nature and substance of the fresh movement. For some it meant simply an emancipation from neo-classical restrictions; others conceived of romanticism as a literature of fairy tales, legends, ghosts, and witches; a few critics declared that it marked a revival of the Middle Ages. Nor was the identification of romanticism with the national past lacking in Russia. Both poets and novelists strove to glorify their country's antiquity and traditions, paying particular attention, as they had never done before, to local color and native traits and characters. The conflict of man with nature and of the individual with society or organized government, features so closely associated with the movement in the West, likewise became vital questions in Russian life and literature. The romantic libertarian impulse which swept over Europe after the French Revolution affected young Russian lovers of freedom and was echoed in song and story, and in a more positive way in the Decembrist Revolt of 1825.

Some critics have argued that the Russian genius was temperamentally ill-suited to Western romanticism. But such generalizations are treacherous, and doubly so when applied to the Russian. Although by nature he may be sober and essentially realistic, he is too cosmopolitan to be forced into any hard and fast categories. Certainly nothing could be more genuinely romantic than Pushkin's Southern poems, Marlinski's tales, or Lermontov's life. Yet it is true that a strain of sound sense and an abiding scepticism saved these writers from the worst excesses of romanticism. Thus the movement never obtained complete allegiance but rather encouraged Russian authors to win a final victory over foreign literary dominance.

Apart from the early romantic tendencies communicated by the works of Thomson, Young, Gray, Ossian, and Radcliffe, Russian literary historians usually credit the German *Sturm und Drang* group with the introduction of romanticism. In the first decade of the nineteenth century Zhukovski, in a number of translations, made the works of the German writers famous. Goethe, Schiller, the Schlegels, Herder, and Bürger ultimately came to be regarded as the prophets and exemplars of the movement. And the popularity of Hegel's philosophy of idealism, which in the realm of pure thought supplemented these authors, established the supremacy of the Germans as the tutelary deities of Russian romanticism. Later the influence of Alfred de Vigny, Alfred de Musset, and Victor Hugo cast the Germans somewhat in the shade. However, if we search about for commanding figures in the welter of foreign influence, for authors who appealed to the Russians as embodying the very incarnation of the romantic spirit, the choice unhesitatingly falls upon Shakspere, Scott, and Byron. All three of these writers profoundly influenced literary production, and both Scott and Byron were worshipped by the young Russian romantics as popular heroes of the day. Shakspere has already been considered; Scott will be studied in the present chapter, and Byron in the next.

In the speedy and intelligent reception of Scott and Byron one can discern a more enlightened attitude towards English literature and culture than had existed in the eighteenth century. For that matter, Russia's new position of critical independence had brought about a better understanding of Western Europe in general. The Anglomania that had flourished in Catherine's time had in no sense diminished. Rather it had ceased to be a mere fashion and had become a sincere and profitable understanding of English institutions and culture. Discredited neo-classicism and the hatred engendered by the invasion of Napoleon had effectually terminated the long period of subservience to the French. This fact in itself helped to strengthen the regard for England, Russia's ally in her war against Napoleon. All the people of consequence were members of the "English Club" in Moscow,[1] which appears to have been modelled after the London coffeehouse. English manufactured goods flooded the country. Onegin equipped his house with English furnishings, ate "roast beef," and dressed in the "latest fashion as a London dandy."[2] Indeed, when Pushkin's famous hero is out of sorts, he is described as afflicted with "English spleen."[3]

English liberalism affected the growing demand of the young Russian intellectuals for a constitutional form of government and in the first quarter of the nineteenth century they studied English jurisprudence, political science, and educational methods in a serious manner. The results were everywhere noticeable. Russian officials now turned to English life and models in their various projects of reform. When a revision of the legislative functions of the realm was contemplated, advice was sought from the English expert Sir James Mackintosh, and especially from Jeremy Bentham.[4] Bentham spent several years in Russia (1785–88) on a visit to his brother, who was an engineer in Catherine's navy. Many of the liberals were impressed by his doctrine of the greatest good for the greatest number, a theory which has gained a more practical application under the Soviets than in the time of Alexander I. Even the ladies, Pushkin tells us in his *Eugene Onegin*, discussed the ideas of Bentham.[5]

As a disciple of Adam Smith, Bentham may have had something to do with the introduction of his master's economic speculations. Although *The Wealth of Nations* was not translated until 1802–06, the fame of its author and the importance of the work were known somewhat earlier.[6] When once translated the book became popular. The Anglophile and adviser of the emperor, Admiral Mordvinov,[7] did much to acquaint the liberals with Adam Smith, and his own projects for economic reform were largely inspired by *The Wealth of Nations*. The dramatist Griboedov became seriously interested in the new economics, and Pushkin tells how in 1818 in the St. Petersburg social world people meditated deeply on the new teaching. "Severity ruled then," he remarks, "and political economy was in fashion; now the French quadrille is substituted for Adam Smith." [8] And with a discerning eye for contemporary characteristics, he describes the youthful Onegin as a "profound economist" who "read Adam Smith." [9]

The question of popular education, which had lapsed since the time of Catherine II, was revived under Alexander I, largely owing to the interest stimulated by the Lancastrian system of mutual instruction. Four scholars were sent to England to investigate the method, and it was subsequently given a trial in Russia. In the army and factories it met with considerable success and for a time it became the chief topic of discussion in educational circles.[10]

All this practical interest in England facilitated the prompt acceptance of English romantic literature. A knowledge of the language, hitherto rare in Russia, made much headway and many of the writers of the period could read English works in the original. English poets and novelists were freely discussed, quoted, and translated with an awareness that indicated an appreciation and understanding never achieved in the eighteenth century. There was nothing of dilettantism, for example, about Pushkin's knowledge. One has merely to glance through the catalogue of his splendid library,[11] which contained a large number of authors extending from the Elizabethans to his own time, to realize that his interest was not simply a passing attraction. Nor were these volumes mere library adornments, for they were read with care and contain the poet's annotations. Zhukovski's knowledge of English literature was scarcely less broad than that of Pushkin. Among his translations we find an unusual variety of poems from Dryden, Pope, Thomson, Gray, Goldsmith, Scott, Byron, Southey, and Moore. Other Russian writers of the period who show a knowledge of English literature are the Turgenev brothers, Vyazemski, Polevoi, Marlinski, Raevski, Kozlov, and Belinski.

After all, however, a literature is never really comprehended until it is studied historically, that is to say with some conception of growth, movements, and artistic relations among separate authors. With the possible exception of Karamzin, such a knowledge had been conspicuously lacking before the romantic period. Now studies began to appear in which the literature of England was considered with something of historical perspective. In 1822, for example, Professor A. F. Merzlyakov, in his work on European literature, gave a large place to England.[12] In the section on drama there is, besides Shakspere, a treatment of such figures as Jonson, Beaumont and Fletcher, Massinger, and Dryden. And S. P. Shevyrev, in his *History of Poetry*,[13] goes into the then comparatively esoteric subject of the development of the English language, paying special attention to Chaucer and Spenser, virtually unnoticed previously.

As in the eighteenth century, however, the periodicals were the chief agencies for popularizing a knowledge of English literature, and especially of the romantic writers. Such well-known publications as the *Moscow Telegraph*, the *Moscow Messenger*, the *Messenger of Europe, Native Records, Son of the Fatherland*, and the *Northern Archive* [14] contain many reviews, criticisms, and translations of English works. The leading periodicals of the time were, in most respects, imitations of the *Edinburgh Review* or its followers. Thus

Polevoi's *Moscow Telegraph* (1825–34), one of the finest of the lot and the leading organ of romantic writers, is closely patterned after the *Edinburgh Review*. We find the same division of articles into sections on politics, economics, and *belles lettres*, and a similar critical approach in reviewing books. Often, indeed, the very material of the *Moscow Telegraph*, and of certain of the other periodicals, is drawn directly from the *Edinburgh Review*, the *Quarterly Review*, *Blackwood's Magazine*, and the *New Monthly Magazine*.[15] Polevoi made no secret of his indebtedness. "Neither the French nor the German journals," he writes, "could have been such excellent sources for the Russian journalists as the English reviews. . . . At present Anglomania appears everywhere. Indeed, do we not limit ourselves solely to English fashions, and do we deny ourselves the advantage which a passion for everything English may obtain for us? Englishmen steeped in learning can bring to our readers treasures which we do not find in either Germany or France." [16]

Scott and Byron were carried into Russia on this wave of interest in English literature. They soon attained an unrivalled place in the esteem of romantic writers. Vyazemski, one of the leading literary figures of the day, summed up the sentiment of his contemporaries when he wrote: "In our age it seems impossible for a poet not to echo Byron or for a novelist not to reflect Walter Scott." [17]

The poetry of Scott had some vogue in Russia before his novels came along to eclipse it. It is a curious fact that both Scott and Zhukovski won their spurs in the field of romantic poetry by translations of Bürger's *Leonore*. The Russian poet was partial to the ballad form, and in 1821 he published a free version of Scott's *Eve of St. John*. On its initial appearance before the censor, that benighted and heartless slayer of Russian literary aspirations, Zhukovski's translation was condemned because of its irreligious title and the lack of any "moral purpose." [18] And it was only after changing the title[19] and several of the verses that permission was granted to publish the ballad. Some years later, in 1832, Zhukovski issued a spirited version of the second canto of *Marmion*.

There is plenty of evidence that Pushkin was a great admirer of Scott's poetry. His library contained English editions of *The Lay of the Last Minstrel*, *The Lady of the Lake*, *The Lord of the Isles*, and *Rokeby*.[20] In a letter to his brother in 1824 he acclaims Scott's poems as "food for the soul." [21] In two instances, at least, a clear case may be made out for the influence of *The Lady of the Lake* on Pushkin. On the appearance of *Boris Godunov* Bulgarin pointed out that the scene in which the False Dmitri mourns over his dying horse[22] was suggested by a similar passage in Scott.[23] That Pushkin read *The Lady of the Lake*, at least the first canto, has been conclusively proved by a recent investigator who has studied the striking parallels between certain of the stanzas and Pushkin's draft of an unfinished poem, *The Soughing Bush*.[24] The theme of the poem, along with several of the lines, was unquestionably borrowed from Scott. And Pushkin certainly knew *The Minstrelsy of the Scottish Border* in a French translation, for his perfect little poem, *A Scottish Song*,[25] is a close paraphrase of *The Twa Corbies*.

Marlinski also read Scott's poems, some of them no doubt in the original. He describes the hero of one of his tales as

particularly fond of the works of several writers, among them
"the strophes of Byron, the melodies of Moore, and the
verses of Walter Scott in *The Lady of the Lake* and *The Lay
of the Last Minstrel.*" [26]

The blind poet, Kozlov, was a warm admirer of Scott and
boasted that he knew all his poems by heart. He made a
free rendering of a ballad from one of the novels [27] and the
conclusion of his popular verse tale, *The Monk*, was written
in imitation of *Marmion*. Like Zhukovski he adopted the
ballad form, and he learned a good deal from Scott concerning
this type of poetry. Byron was to have many eulogists in
Russian verse, but Kozlov is quite alone in his long poetic
tribute, *To Walter Scott*.[28] He greets him as "Scotland's
bard, singer beloved," and he dwells with sincerity upon the
pleasure he derived from reading *Marmion*.

Lermontov appeared a little too late in the romantic
period to come under the influence of the initial popularity
of Scott's poetry. According to the testimony of one of his
contemporaries, however, he read the poems: "Mishel
[Lermontov] began to study the English language in Byron,
and after several months he was able to understand him
freely; he read Moore and the poetical works of Walter
Scott." [29] Briefs have been made for the influence of *The
Field of Waterloo* [30] and parts of *Marmion* on Lermontov's
famous poem, *The Demon*, but the evidence is rather con-
jectural.[31]

As in England, the appearance of *Childe Harold* and
Byron's Eastern tales quickly overshadowed Scott's poetry.
But Scott's historical romances soon came along to increase
his fame, and the Russian reading public, no less than the

French and German, was completely conquered by the "Wizard of the North."

The appearance of *Waverley* was recorded in a Russian periodical in 1815,[32] less than a year after the publication of the novel. For the next five years the Russian journals took little notice of Scott's romances, although certain of them were unquestionably known and read in French translations. But from 1820 to 1830 his popularity reached an unprecedented height. During this period no less than thirty-nine separate translations were made, including nearly every title in the whole collection of historical romances.[33] So great was the interest in Scott that works apart from his verse and novels, such as the essay on *Romance, Letters on Demonology and Witchcraft*, and parts of the *Life of Napoleon*, were rendered into Russian.[34] In a critical way the periodicals devoted much space to Scott, and articles, both original and foreign, appeared in which various questions connected with the novelist and the new literary *genre* were discussed.[35] And the tremendous interest he excited in the historical romance was reflected in the large number of translations of his French, German, and Italian imitators.

The Waverley novels were the subject of conversation in the family circles of humble country landlords as well as in the literary salons of St. Petersburg and Moscow. The scene which Karamzin describes in a letter to a friend in 1825 could be frequently paralleled in the memoirs of the time. "At nine o'clock we drink tea in a circle about the table," he writes, "and from ten to half-past eleven we read, with my wife and two daughters, the romances of Walter Scott, but with such innocent food for the imagination and heart we regret that the evening is so short." [36]   Scott's heroes and heroines were discussed as though they were real persons, and boys were given the novels, along with other classical productions, to improve their minds.[37] "I rejoice," writes Prince A. A. Shakhovskoi to a young friend, "that you are fond of reading, and it is particularly pleasant to me that you, so it seems, are much attached to W. Scott; this Scottish animal [38] is not like our animals who have at times occupied you. . . . I very much wish you to read *The Antiquary*." [39] Vyazemski, who appears to have contemplated translating some of Scott, grew lyrical over his works: "The poetry of the Scottish bard, the light of our century, penetrates imperceptibly as the light of day, or still better, inscrutably penetrates there where the immediate effect of its rays is not at once apparent." [40]

From the rank of a widely read novelist Scott was raised to the position of a popular hero. His Russian readers became intensely interested in his personality, his domestic affairs, and his daily occupations; and in periodical articles there was an endeavor to satisfy this public curiosity. In one, his study is minutely described; another discusses his relations with Washington Irving; a third considers the unfortunate bankruptcy of his partner, Ballantyne.[41] The aging Karamzin, whose "soul was refreshed by reading the romances," [42] dreamed of erecting a monument to Scott in his garden, and "Walter Scott cloaks" became the fashion in Moscow and St. Petersburg.[43] Even the names of his characters achieved a kind of vogue and we find them cropping up in the literature of the time.[44] Nor was the Emperor Nicholas I untouched by the prevailing enthusiasm. When

Pushkin's play, *Boris Godunov*, was submitted to him for censoring, he ordered Count Benkendorf to tell the poet that he should have been better pleased if the subject had been worked up in the form of an historical romance after the fashion of Walter Scott's novels.[45]

Russian travellers made pilgrimages to Abbotsford. In 1827 A. I. Turgenev paid a visit to Southey and wrote to his brother: "I spent more than an hour with him in conversation about literature and showed him Zhukovski's book with his verses; but the two pieces printed under his name in Russian are not his. I spoke to him of Zhukovski's translation, *Starushka*,[46] and he then encouraged me to go straight to W. Scott, saying that he loved foreign visitors who were interested in literature." [47] Turgenev maintained his interest in Scott for years, as his correspondence proves.[48] Pushkin's close friend, D. Davydov, wrote several letters to Scott and Scott sent him his portrait.[49] Several of the most popular romances were turned into plays by that literary Jack-of-all-trades, Shakhovskoi. He served up *Ivanhoe* to the Russian theatre-goers under a title which would have delighted Thackeray: "Ivanhoe, or the return of Richard the Lion-hearted. A romantic comedy in five acts in the English fashion with a great spectacle, hippodrome, battlefields, divertissement, songs, ballads, and choruses." [50]

Studies and controversies about Scott's novels filled the periodicals, memoirs, and correspondence of the period. Vyazemski testifies to the "fever of curiosity, yearning, avidity, and enthusiasm" aroused by Scott, "perhaps the most excellent writer of all peoples in any age." [51] Belinski raised his powerful voice against detractors of the new literary form: "Walter Scott has created, invented, discovered, or, still better, has divined the epic of our time, — the historical novel. Many persons bearing the impress of great talent or even genius have followed in his train; yet he has remained a genius of a unique kind." [52]

Of course Scott profoundly influenced Russian novel-writing in this period. He aroused the interest of Russians in their historical past, and "Russian nationalism" became a pronounced phase of the Romantic Movement. Native writers turned their attention to the national past for material, and soon a whole series of Russian historical romances appeared, all more or less in imitation of Scott.

Translations of English, French, and German sentimental novels carried over into the first years of the nineteenth century and for a time constituted the chief reading matter in this form. Of the English authors Richardson, Sterne, and Goldsmith were still read, and Mrs. Radcliffe's tales of terror gained a wide popularity. But even before Scott's works became generally known, novels were written in Russia which embodied, although quite unsuccessfully, certain features of the historical romance. In a few of the novels of F. Emin and M. Kheraskov we may discern a weak and confused attempt to bring in historical events. Also several of the tales of Karamzin and certain novels of Narezhny, Batiushkov, and Kaisarov employ an historical treatment which is vaguely similar to that of Scott before his historical romances had become familiar in Russia.[53]

All these productions, however, palely reflected the national past, and the course of historical events was often sacrificed to the interests of the plot. But after 1820, when

Scott's novels had become generally known, their influence was soon made manifest in a series of historical tales published by Marlinski from 1823 to 1825. He followed these up with more pretentious works [54] which were rather well received, although the critic, Belinski, complained that they violate historical truth.[55] Marlinski's unquestioned genius was better suited to the short story than to the novel, and he was primarily interested in the purely romantic elements rather than in historical veracity.[56]

In 1829 appeared *Iuri Miloslavski, or the Russians in 1612*, and its author, M. Zagoskin (1789–1852), was at once hailed as the "Russian Walter Scott." The book was immediately recognized as a masterpiece and its popularity has lasted to the present day. Zagoskin achieved the manner of Scott and wrote an historical romance which fully answered the literary and social demands of Russian romanticism.

Early in his career Zagoskin had applied himself to the drama, and in this endeavor he became interested in themes drawn from Russian history. The period 1820–25 coincided with the beginning of Scott's popularity, and this fact appears to have turned Zagoskin's literary aspirations towards the field of the historical romance. Just what novels of Scott he read is not known, but his biographer provides evidence that *Waverley* was one of them.[57] At any rate, it was under the direct inspiration of Scott's works that Zagoskin began to write *Iuri Miloslavski*.

The story is placed in 1612, a year which marked the climax of The Times of Trouble, when Michael Fedorovich, after a long period of bitter civil war, finally gained the throne. Against this warlike background most of the action takes place. Iuri, the hero, falls in love with a beautiful noblewoman, who is already contracted to another. After many adventures in which Kirsha, a stout bodyguard of the hero, performs prodigies of valor, Iuri wins his fair damsel and they live happily ever after. Native investigators have pointed out the unusually close resemblance between the plot and that of Scott's *Legend of Montrose*.[58] In fact, the principal events and some of the details of both narratives may be drawn up in parallel columns, and the persistent similarities leave one with the conviction that Scott's novel suggested the theme and development of *Iuri Miloslavski*.[59]

But in a fuller sense Zagoskin appropriated the whole literary manner which Scott employed in his historical romances. He was by no means the equal of Scott as a student of archaeology. Nevertheless, he was careful about the historical background of his tale, although he did not investigate the original sources. Contemporary interest in Russian antiquities and the great history of Karamzin provided him with all the necessary details of seventeenth-century life. Zagoskin's method of utilizing this material to create historical verisimilitude closely resembles that of Scott. Costumes and setting are precisely described, and the popular speech of the period is imitated, even to the extent of sprinkling the dialogue with archaisms. And in the manner of Scott, Zagoskin likewise imparts a popular air to his narrative by putting folk songs of the period in the mouths of his characters. He does not always assimilate his historical material so well as Scott, but on the whole his attempt to make vivid and real a past age succeeds admirably, and it is little wonder that his efforts were pronounced unique in

Russian literature and that *Iuri Miloslavski* was at once accorded the position of a classic.

Contemporary critics were prompt, without intending any slight, to point out Zagoskin's dependence on Scott. S. T. Aksakov wrote: "Obviously, reading the historical romances of Walter Scott inspired the author with the idea of writing a Russian historical romance; and it is also obvious that he borrowed the form and even certain effects from the renowned Scotchman." [60] Even the foreign reviews, which had begun to take some notice of Russian literature during the romantic period, praised *Iuri Miloslavski* and commented on its indebtedness to Scott.[61] One German critic went so far as to maintain that "Zagoskin has every perfection of Walter Scott without his defects. The Briton does not surpass the Russian either in the correct delineation of character or in the fascinating painting of details." [62] English reviews were favorable, though they resented the occasional elevation of Zagoskin above Scott. Thus one English critic, referring to the German reviewer just quoted, declares: "One of them indeed has even gone so far as to assert that it [*Iuri Miloslavski*] possesses all the excellencies of Sir Walter Scott, without his defects; an eulogium to which, however gratified we have been with it, we cannot possibly subscribe." [63]

Iuri Miloslavski went through eight editions in a few years and was translated into several European languages, including English. It is said that the governess in a well-known Russian family translated the novel into English and sent it to Scott, to whom she dedicated her work.[64] It would be interesting to know what Scott thought of his disciple's production. At any rate, it is certain that he had corresponded with Zagoskin. S. T. Aksakov informs us that he saw at Zagoskin's "many letters from various European literary notables, letters filled with flattering testimonials; there were even one or two letters from Walter Scott, but these (like many others) since that time have disappeared from the papers of the deceased." [65]

Zagoskin followed *Iuri Miloslavski* with other historical romances, the best of which are *Roslavlev, or the Russians in 1812* and *Askold's Grave*.[66] Neither of these, however, added to his fame. Zagoskin gave a powerful impetus to the writing of historical novels, and in him romantic nationalism found its chief expression in Russia. What he had borrowed from Scott was handed on to his successors. He followed Scott in the selection of his subjects and in the assorting and grouping of the composite parts of his tale. But his chief debt is reflected in his use of local color, in the manner in which he worked into the fabric of his story those elements which recreated the national life and spirit of old Russia.

A host of historical romances appeared after *Iuri Miloslavski*, the most successful of which were written by Bulgarin, Polevoi, Lazhechnikov, Masalski, Kukolnik, Pushkin, and Gogol.[67] Certain of these authors were influenced by Zagoskin, others turned directly to Scott for inspiration. Pushkin and Gogol, because of their great eminence in the literary development of the period, have a special claim upon our attention.

Pushkin's indebtedness to Scott's poetry has already been pointed out; the influence of his novels was much more extensive. Russian scholars have exhaustively studied this influence. In his own day it was noted by Vyazemski, and since that time every phase of the relationship has been investigated.[68]

It is an interesting fact that Scott first began to attract Pushkin at the time when Byron's influence on him had begun to decline. After 1825, when Pushkin shows a tendency to be sharply critical of Byron's works, Scott's poetry begins to gain his favorable attention. In the next ten years his laudatory references to Scott increase in number and the influence of the novels on his prose works, such as the *History of the Village of Goriukhino* (1830) and the *Tales of Bélkin* (1830), is noticeable. This influence culminates in a significant manner in his historical romance, *The Captain's Daughter* (1836). Indeed, one critic goes so far as to divide Pushkin's literary development into two periods, the "Byron Period" and the "Scott Period," [69] holding that in the former he submitted to a subjective romantic influence and in the latter to an objective romantic influence. With certain reservations, it would be difficult to quarrel with this apt generalization.

Pushkin no doubt began to read the novels in French translations in the 1820's. Always alive to the fashionable tastes of the day, he describes his heroes as devoted to Scott. The flippant Count Nulin lies abed with the latest romances of Scott,[70] and Onegin reads him in his country retreat.[71] But Sasha in the *Fragments from a Romance in Letters* finds too many "unnecessary pages" in the novels,[72] and the hero of the *Autobiographical Sketch* gratefully comforts himself with a bottle of champagne in lieu of the romances of Walter Scott.[73]

Even before the publication of *Iuri Miloslavski* Pushkin had become interested, in a critical way, in the literary *genre* of the historical romance, and his views were largely influenced by his reading of Scott, whose novels, both in the original and in French translations, were among the books in his library.[74] He jotted down for his own use the following notes:

> The principal charm of the novels of W[alter] S[cott] consists in that we are made familiar with the past times not with the *enflure* of the Fr[ench] tragedies — not with the primness of the sentimental novels — not with the *dignité* of History, but in a contemporary, homely way — Ce qui me dégoûte c'est ce que — Here, on the contrary, ce qui nous charme dans le roman historique — c'est ce qui est historique est absolument ce que nous voyons — Sch[iller] Goethe W[alter] S[cott] have not the servile passion for Kings and Heroes — They — do not resemble (like the Fr[ench] heroes) servants mimicking la dignité et la noblesse — ils sont familiers dans les circonstances solennelles — car les grandes circonstances leur sont familières.
>
> On voit que W[alter] S[cott] est de la petite société des Rois d'Angleterre.[75]

This was written in 1825 and the remarks here made about characterization have especial point, for it was at this time that Pushkin was preoccupied with his historical drama, *Boris Godunov*. At this very time he was also learning much about characterization from Shakspere. Five years later, in his criticism of Polevoi's *History of the Russian People*, he writes in somewhat the same strain:

> The effect of W. Scott is clearly reflected in all branches of contemporary literature. The new school of French historians was formed under the influence of the Scottish romancer. He revealed to them entirely new sources, hitherto unsuspected, despite the existence of the historical drama created by Shakspere and Goethe.[76]

Certainly by the time Zagoskin's great novel appeared (1829) Pushkin was thoroughly read in Scott's works and in those of his followers, and he had developed a well-defined critical attitude toward the historical romance. In 1830 he prefaced his review of *Iuri Miloslavski* with a statement which clearly shows his admiration for Scott: "Walter Scott has drawn after him a whole crowd of imitators. But how far removed are they all from the Scottish wizard!" [77] And the review itself, while in general quite appreciative of Zagoskin's efforts, indicates by its critical strictures that Pushkin had read Scott's romances with care and understanding.

The very next year Pushkin published his *Tales of Belkin*,[78] which marks the first decisive instance of Scott's influence on his prose. The elaborate mystification with which Scott surrounded the authorship of the *Tales of My Landlord* attracted Pushkin. It will be remembered that the several novels of the series were represented as the work of a certain Peter Pattieson, assistant to the schoolmaster, Jedediah Cleishbotham, who sold them to a publisher. And in order to connect the various novels Scott employs the "literary-frame" device. In the *Tales of Belkin* Pushkin adopts the same scheme, borrowing many of the details directly from Scott's introduction. Thus in his own introduction Pushkin endeavors to create the illusion of reality by concocting a plausible account of the manuscript and of the life of the supposed author, much in the manner of Scott.[79] He clung to this method of literary mystification in other works,[80] and, no doubt through Pushkin, it affected contemporary writers, notably Gogol.[81]

The compositional scheme, however, was not the only contribution of Scott to the *Tales of Belkin*. In one of the tales, *The Lady-Rustic*,[82] Pushkin uses the general theme of *The Bride of Lammermoor* — romantic love between the son and daughter of two estranged fathers. And the hunting scene in Scott's novel (chapter IX), where the two enemies are inadvertently brought together, suggested a similar scene in *The Lady-Rustic*, where Muromski and Berestov meet while on a hunt.[83] In still another tale in the collection, *The Coffin-Maker*,[84] Pushkin is again indebted to *The Bride of Lammermoor* for certain hints drawn from the conversation between Ravenswood and the gravedigger (chapter XXIV). In fact, Pushkin actually mentions Scott in this narrative. "The enlightened reader," he writes, "is aware that both Shakspere and Walter Scott have represented their gravediggers as lively, jocular people, no doubt in order to affect our imagination more powerfully."[85] Indeed, on the basis of the rather numerous similarities, the principal investigator of the matter comes to the conclusion that "when writing the *Tales of Belkin* at Boldino, Pushkin recollected or had before him *The Bride of Lammermoor*, and he took sharp notice of the theme and literary manner of the Scottish romancer."[86]

Meanwhile Pushkin was responding to the intense interest in the historical past which the novels of Scott had helped to stimulate in Russia. This interest had already been reflected in his *Boris Godunov*, and finally in 1836 appeared his historical romance, *The Captain's Daughter*.[87] This work, a tale based on the Pugachev rebellion in the reign of Catherine the Great, was instantly hailed by the critics as belonging to the school of Scott. Although it is in every sense an original and accomplished production, there can be no doubt of Pushkin's inspiration or of the fact that he directly laid the novels of Scott under contribution.

During the few years immediately preceding the writing of *The Captain's Daughter* it is noticeable that Pushkin in his letters refers to Scott frequently. "I read Scott and the Bible," he writes in 1834; in 1835: "I took with them Walter Scott and reread him;" and in another letter in the same year he writes: "I walk and ride and read the romances of W. Scott." [88] Clearly Pushkin was steeping himself in Scott while he was planning his own novel. And he borrowed considerably from his models. In particular he was influenced by *The Heart of Midlothian*. Pushkin's heroine, Marya Ivanovna, is cast in the image of Jeanie Deans; and several situations which concern these characters are too closely paralleled to be a matter of mere coincidence.[89] The resemblance between old Grinev and Davie Deans is also striking.[90] Finally, various small details which Pushkin obviously borrows leave little doubt that he was indebted to *The Heart of Midlothian*. The peasant-servant, Savelich, however, is unquestionably modelled after Caleb in *The Bride of Lammermoor*.

But these rather scattered similarities take on an added significance in the light of an influence at once more subtle and yet more concrete. Like Scott recreating the past of eighteenth-century Scotland in *The Heart of Midlothian*, Pushkin brings to life a period of eighteenth-century Russia by his genius for characterization and by the great care which he lavished on local color and historical details. In the manner of Scott, Pushkin introduces his chapters with quotations drawn from popular songs; and the speech of his characters is enlivened by archaisms and snatches from contemporary writers, all cleverly contrived to provide an historical background in keeping with the period and nature of the story. Even the prose of *The Captain's Daughter* has caught something of the flavor of Scott's. Although his influence on Pushkin was not so sweeping as Byron's, from one point of view it was of greater importance. For Pushkin gained from Scott a certain balance in artistic structure and a sense of realism which aided him along the path of his natural literary development.

Gogol (1809–52) had little of Pushkin's literary cosmopolitanism, and his place among the "Westernizers" during the Romantic Movement was a small one. Conservative by temperament and rather limited in education, Gogol's intensely subjective nature precluded any great sympathy with writers in or outside of Russia. Except for Italian, he had no solid knowledge of any foreign language, and in his youth he was not above poking fun at German, French, and English productions, though later this attitude of mind was considerably readjusted. His early works were somewhat indebted to Voss and E. T. A. Hoffmann, and in the *Revizor* he laid Molière under contribution, but of English influence there is little trace.

Pushkin called Gogol the "Russian Sterne," [91] because in *Dead Souls* he showed that he could both laugh and weep at the everlasting comedy of life. But in reality the art and the artistic purpose of Gogol and Sterne are poles apart. A brief has been made for the influence of Maturin's *Melmoth the Wanderer* on *Dead Souls,*[92] but here again the evidence is very thin. However, it is quite certain that Maturin's novel, which had already been translated into Russian, did influence Gogol's short story, *The Portrait*; and there is no doubt of Gogol's obligation to De Quincey's *Confessions of an English Opium Eater* (translated in 1834) in his famous tale, *The Nevski Prospect.*[93]

Scott was among the foreign authors whom Pushkin advised the future novelist to read. But Gogol, if we can believe his friend, P. Annenkov, had a strong partiality for the great romancer. "Of all foreign writers," Annenkov maintains, "there was only one name he knew not by hearsay and by rumor only — the name of Walter Scott."[94] In fact, there is evidence that he read the novels of Scott "with great enthusiasm, beginning in his youth."[95] Indeed, Gogol himself writes from abroad in 1836, while seeking inspiration for continuing *Dead Souls*: "I am undertaking to read again all of Walter Scott, and that may start my pen."[96]

Whether it was because of his fondness for Scott's novels or from mere intellectual curiosity it is hard to say, but early in his career Gogol plunged into the study of history. In 1834 he actually occupied the chair of history at the University of St. Petersburg, and at this time he gathered material for an unfinished tragedy on King Alfred.[97] Besides *Taras Bulba*, he left behind him the fragment of another historical romance, *The Hetman*, along with an outline for a history of the Little Russian Cossacks and several articles on historical themes.

Scott's influence on *Taras Bulba* (1835), the most effective, if not the best, historical romance of the period, has been generally recognized by Russian critics, but the matter of indebtedness must be evaluated with caution. It is a brilliant picture of Cossack life in the sixteenth century and has a good deal of the simplicity and elemental character of a folk epic. Pushkin thought that the beginning was "worthy of Walter Scott." [98]   *Taras Bulba*, however, gives one the impression of an historical period recreated by some process of divination rather than by a careful selection of material from original sources. In this respect it is quite unlike the novels of Scott or Pushkin's *Captain's Daughter*. Perhaps the rhetorical character and the extraordinary swiftness of Gogol's style contribute to the impression that the historical background is neglected. Scenes rush past in a bewildering fashion, and there is none of the studied lingering over details which in Scott serves to give the illusion of historical reality. Nevertheless, it is certain that in the matter of external features and in the complete subordination of the love element in *Taras Bulba* Gogol learned much from Scott's novels.

In *Dead Souls* (1842) Gogol abandoned the romantic themes of his youth and revealed the realistic and satirical bent of his natural talent. Then it was that the realism of Dickens found favor in his eyes. And, generally speaking, after the publication of Gogol's masterpiece the popularity of the historical romance waned, and writers turned to the realistic novel, in which the literary genius of Russia has found its most enduring expression. To be sure, Lermontov, the last of the great romantics and himself the descendant of an old Scottish family that had settled in Russia in the seventeenth century,[99] was influenced by Scott, but by his poetry more than by his novels. Lermontov certainly knew the novels, and it is significant, perhaps, that he represents Pechorin in the *Hero of Our Times* as reading *Old Mortality* before the duel. "At first I read with effort," says Pechorin, "but soon forgot everything else, entranced by the charming fiction." [100] One critic credits Scott with a general influence on the narrative art of Lermontov: "Comme tous ses contemporains en Russie, Lermontov a appris à son école l'art du récit, le développement d'une action. Ses nouvelles en prose procèdent, vraisemblablement, pour une large part, de W. Scott." [101] However, a close examination of the prose tales hardly supports this judgment, and one is inclined to believe in the sincerity of the remark Lermontov made to Belinski concerning the novels: "I do not love Walter Scott; there is little poetry in him. He is dry." [102] On the same occasion he made known his preference for Cooper over Scott.

Despite the diminishing interest in the novels themselves after 1830, Scott and the historical romance still continued to be favorite subjects for critical debates. The well-known journalist, O. I. Senkovski, while admitting Scott's genius, severely censured him for inventing a false form of art and for perverting literary taste by introducing all manner of bizarre effects and horrors.[103] Senkovski's protest was like a ghostly echo from the long dead spirit of neo-classicism, though some of his strictures recall those of Scott's English critics. He contended that the historical novel is simply a forgery of history, and, as such, a bastard form of art at best. Belinski, however, rose to the defense. He accused Senkovski of not knowing what historical truth is. Belinski maintained that it consists not so much in statements of fact as in a true presentation of the development of the human spirit in any particular epoch. He insisted that Scott never failed to catch and express the spirit of the period which he set out to describe, and that in this respect he was an historian in the full sense of the word. As a final refutation of Senkovski, he called to his support the people's verdict, which is less fallible than that of the critics. "Walter Scott," he writes, "has long since been crowned with poetical glory by the people, by peoples and mankind; it remains for the ages and posterity to confirm the verdict of contemporaries — and this posterity will do." [104]

The question, to be sure, is an old one, as old as Shakspere's historical plays; and perhaps both Senkovski and Belinski were beating against an unlocked door. History is a legitimate subject for artistic treatment, and Scott's handling of it is no less genuine or correct than that of Shakspere. He simply availed himself of the artist's privilege to falsify the facts in small things, should the occasion demand, provided he does not outrage the historical sense of his readers. All that mattered was the correctness of the general impression and the unity of his artistic purpose.

Belinski's admiration for Scott continued to the end of his life. In his later years, curiously enough, a disciple of Scott was to vie with him for supremacy in Belinski's mind. This was James Fenimore Cooper, whose works were much translated and read in Russia from 1830 on. In 1840 Belinski writes to K. S. Aksakov: "Now about Gogol. He is a great artist — of that there is no question. And I will not say now that he is inferior to Walter Scott and Cooper, but I do not

think it impossible that his later works have not demon-
strated that he is above them." [105] Belinski was obviously
dwelling upon the relative merits of both novelists at about
this time, for in the same year we find him remarking in a
letter to Botkin that he was reading again *The Fair Maid of
Perth* and *The Fortunes of Nigel* and liking them as much as
ever. "But," he declares, "you do not know Cooper, who,
if he is not the equal of Walter Scott, is certainly superior to
him as an artist." [106] He was immensely pleased when Lermontov agreed with his preference: "I was beside myself
with joy when he told me that Cooper was greater than
Walter Scott, that in his romances there is more depth and
more artistic unity. I have thought so for a long time, but
he is the first man I have met who agreed with me." [107] The
popularity of Cooper in Europe at this time is well known,
and perhaps Belinski was simply catering to an established
vogue. Cooper had the good fortune to bring to the historical novel a different setting and a new type of character.
Besides, the European has never failed to respond to the lure
of the American Indian.

Despite this competition, however, Belinski did not desert
Scott. As late as 1846, in reviewing the third volume of a
new translation of Scott's complete works, he returns to his
favorite with undiminished zeal and praise: "Walter Scott
does not belong to the number of those writers who are read
once and then ever after forgotten. More than once in a lifetime can a man renew the inexpressible charm gained from
reading the romances of Walter Scott. He is not simply a
writer familiar to you: he is the constant friend of your whole
life, whose charming conversation will always comfort and de-

light you." [108]   Even when Dickens appeared, whose works Belinski disliked at first but later extolled, he praised him because he was so English and "hence so close to Walter Scott." [109]

In truth, despite the trend toward the realistic novel and the popularity of later English writers, such as Marryat, Dickens, and Bulwer-Lytton, the reading public in Russia never quite lost its affection for Scott. Eventually, of course, his historical novels suffered the same fate as in England; that is, a sophisticated modern age considered them merely as entertaining reading for children.

Yet Russian critics have never ceased to accord Scott a place beside Byron as one of the most significant factors in their Romantic Movement. He gave an impetus to the Russian romantic interest in the past and his works served as models and inspiration for the literary treatment of historical themes. In 1841, Professor S. P. Shevyrev, a pioneer in the historical and comparative study of the national literature, clearly recognized this debt of Russia and the rest of Europe to both Scott and Byron:

Neither of these great literary phenomena of the present century could have existed without each other. In them, not England alone, but the whole of Europe has manifested itself. The stormy spirit of Byron has found a reflection in the public life of the peoples and in the private life of men; it has been counteracted by W. Scott's tendency to preserve the past and to consecrate every nationality.[110]

BIBLIOGRAPHY

Bibliographical Studies

A. Smirdin, *Rospis rossiskim knigam*, St. Petersburg, 1898, I–IV (For a list of translations from Scott see items, 6717, 6783, 6787, 6789, 6792, 8467, 8522, 8574, 8594, 8636, 8689, 8847, 8905, 8906, 8992, 9035, 9048, 9174, 9175, 9472, 9473, 9563, 9576.)

S. Vesin, *Ocherki russkoi zhurnalistiki dvadtsatykh i tridtsatykh godov*, St. Petersburg, 1881.   (Contains a descriptive bibliography of periodical articles on Scott.)

Investigations

O. I. Senkovski, "Istoricheski roman," 1834 (*Sobranie sochineni*, St. Petersburg, 1859, VIII, 29–59).

A. Galakhov, "O podrazhatelnosti nashikh pervoklassnykh poetov" (*Russkaya starina*, 1887, LVII, 17–30).

A. Veselovski, *Zapadnoe vliyanie v novoi russkoi literature*, Moskva, 1896, 5th ed. (see pp. 149, 155–156, 159, 174, 176, 180, 193, 202).

"Pushkin i evropeiskaya poeziya" (*Etiudy i kharakteristiki*, Moskva, 1903, 3rd ed., pp. 629–647).

N. K. Kozmin, *Ocherki iz istorii russkago romantizma*, St. Petersburg, 1903, pp. 1–67.

N. Kotlyarevski, *Dekabristy A. A. Bestuzhev i kn. A. I. Odoevski*, St. Petersburg, 1907.

E. Duchesne, *Michel Iouriévitch Lermontov*, Paris, 1910, pp. 292–294.

M. Hofman, "Kapitanskaya dochka" (*Pushkin*, red. Vengerova, St. Petersburg, 1910, IV, 353–378).

I. I. Zamotin, *Romantizm dvadtsatykh godov XIX stoletiya v russkoi literature*, St. Petersburg, 1911–13, I–II.   (See II, 283–379.)

N. P. Dashkevich, *Stati po novoi russkoi literature* (*Sbornik otdeleniya russkago yazyka i slovosnosti Imperatorskoi Akademii Nauk*, Petrograd, 1914, XCII).   (See pp. 272–274, 341, 357, 378, 440, 483, 511.)

V. V. Sipovski, "Pushkin i romantizm" (*Pushkin i ego sovremenniki*, Petrograd, 1916, XXIII–XXIV, 223–280).   (See pp. 277–279.)

Iu. Oksman, "Siuzhety Pushkina" (*Pushkinski sbornik pamyati profes-sora S. A. Vengerova*, Moskva, 1923, pp. 27–34).

D. Yakubovich, "Predislovie k *Povestyam Belkina* i povestvovatelnye priemy Valter Skotta" (*Pushkin v mirovoi literature*, Leningrad, 1926, pp. 160–187).
"Reministsentsii iz Valter Skotta v *Povestyakh Belkina*" (*Pushkin i ego sovremenniki*, Leningrad, 1928, XXXVII, 100–118).
"Iz zametok o Pushkine i Valter Skotte" (*Pushkin i ego sovremenniki*, Leningrad, 1930, XXXVIII–XXXIX, 122 140).

P. Struve, "Walter Scott and Russia" (*The Slavonic Review*, London, 1933, XI, No. 32, pp. 397–410).

CHAPTER X

BYRON IN RUSSIA

IN *Don Juan* Byron pays Catherine the Great a typically double-edged compliment[1] and then hints, with unconscious prophesy, that his verses may one day reach her far-off land:

> But oh, thou grand legitimate Alexander!
>   Her son's son, let not this last phrase offend
> Thine ear, if it should reach — and now rhymes wander
>   Almost as far as Petersburgh, and lend
> A dreadful impulse to each loud meander
>   Of murmuring Liberty's wide waves, which blend
> Their roar even with the Baltic's — so you be
> Your father's son, 't is quite enough for me.[2]

Byron's poetry did reach Russia, even before his death, and it received a welcome greater than he had any reason to expect. Furthermore, his verses actually lent an impulse to "murmuring Liberty's wide waves" in a manner that troubled both the "legitimate Alexander" and his successor. In truth, of all the countries that came under the spell of Byron's pen and pageantry in the first half of the nineteenth century, none was more deeply entranced than Russia. Literary historians in general do not appear to be aware of this fact, but Russian scholars have emphasized it often.[3] Certainly there was hardly a Russian poet in the romantic period who was not directly or indirectly influenced by Byron's life and verse. His name became synonymous with "romantic," and he was regarded as the "leading mind" of the age. Of contemporary figures only Goethe could compete with him in renown, and certain liberty-loving Russians ranked the Englishman above the great German.

The first notice of Byron's works which I have found in Russia is an account of *The Corsair* which appeared in a periodical in 1815, about a year after the publication of the poem.[4] "Lord Byron is one of the greatest of living English poets," says this reviewer; and he then goes on to discuss his earlier productions. He quotes a number of lines from *The Corsair* and renders them into prose. This is perhaps the earliest translation in Russian. Three years later (in 1818) appeared a short article on Byron in another periodical,[5] and henceforth his name and works achieved the widest publicity.

Among the initial enthusiasts were the romantics, Zhukovski, Vyazemski, and A. I. Turgenev. No doubt they first learned of the poems through French translations, but they quickly appreciated the necessity of going to the originals. In 1819 Turgenev wrote to Vyazemski that a copy of *Mazeppa* had been sent to Zhukovski from London.[6] Vyazemski replied from Warsaw, where there already existed a Byron cult: "I read and reread Lord Byron, naturally in the pale French extracts. . . . Do you know his *Pilgrim*, four cantos? But why does not Zhukovski, who understands the English language, and the still more difficult language of Byron, — why does he not turn it to his gain? . . . Who in Russia reads English and writes Russian? Give him to me here! I would weep out my life for each verse of Byron!"[7]

The periodicals of the 1820's devoted much space to the poet, discussing at length the manifold interests of his private life and evaluating his literary productions.[8] Many of the articles were translated from French, German, and English reviews, but not a few were original. In a large measure they helped to satisfy an ever-growing curiosity about Byron's absorbing personality.

Hard on the heels of the periodical articles came a myriad of translations and imitations. A Russian authority lists one hundred and forty-three separate renderings or paraphrases, covering the years 1819 to 1830.[9] French versions were often the immediate source, but many in both prose and verse were translated from the originals. At first the shorter poems, such as *Darkness* and selections from the *Hebrew Melodies*, proved most popular. But these quickly gave place to what were described as the "lyrical epic" poems — *The Prisoner of Chillon*, *The Siege of Corinth*, *The Giaour*, *The Corsair*, *Lara*, *Mazeppa*, *Parisina*, and *The Bride of Abydos*. These works, particularly the Eastern poems, "turned everybody's head," as Marlinski recorded.[10] Some were translated a number of times, and critics were not slow to discover in them a new type of poetry.

It is a curious fact that certain of the most important works were not translated until later, and then not always completely. Thus *Manfred* did not appear until 1828, and *Childe Harold's Pilgrimage* and *Don Juan* were never fully rendered in the romantic period. Yet these poems were well known in their entirety by the chief Russian writers of the time, who did not fail to rank them among Byron's greatest productions; and it is noticeable, as we shall presently see, that *Childe Harold* and *Don Juan* exercised a powerful influence on the Russian romantic poets.

Through these frequent translations Byron achieved a wide popularity in the 1820's, the extent of which may be gauged by the countless and enthusiastic references to him in diaries, correspondence, and memoirs. As in the case of Scott, he became a kind of fashionable hero among the reading public. A. D. Chertkov reported that the young countesses in his wife's family, the well-known Chernyshovi, hung the portrait of Lord Byron over their beds instead of an icon.[11] In truth one gets the impression that romantically-minded youths, like Onegin, felt that such a portrait was an indispensable adornment of the bedroom.[12]

Among the young men who agitated for Russian political freedom in the first quarter of the nineteenth century Byron exercised a tremendous influence. His verse and personal endeavors gained the fervid admiration of these idealizing revolutionists. Byron's influence in this respect was particularly important among the group known as the "Decembrists," some of whom were authors of genius. Their plot was a sad failure. Ryleev, who was hanged, carried a volume of Byron's poetry with him to the scaffold, and Marlinski, Kiukhelbeker, and Yakushkin found consolation in reading his works in exile. Through the medium of the Decembrists Byron's political influence spread to society in general.

The strong feeling expressed in Western European literary circles on Byron's death was echoed in Russia with no less sympathy and often with more sincerity. "Have you heard the news?" Odoevski wrote to Kiukhelbeker. "One horrible thing perhaps you have heard — Lord Byron is dead!" [13] In the same strain Vyazemski wrote to A. I. Turgenev: "The day before yesterday was for me a day of most powerful

impressions. I heard in the English Club of the death of
Byron. . . . What a poetic death was that of Byron! . . .
I know the singers who are worthy to chant his end. Here is
a chance for Zhukovski! If he does not make use of it, then
his business is ended. . . . Ancient Greece, the Greece of
our day, and Byron a sacrifice, — this is an ocean of
poetry!"[14]

But Zhukovski did not heed the call. Many Russian writers, however, took up the pen to honor the dead poet. Kozlov, Ryleev, Kiukhelbeker, Venevitinov, Fedorov, Bestiu-
zhev-Riumin, Vyazemski, and others eulogized his genius and
paid tribute to his service in the cause of Greek freedom.[15]
Editors of periodicals dedicated panegyrics to the deceased
poet. Bulgarin declared that "Greece had lost its protector,
England a man of genius, and the world a hero!" [16] Grech
in *The Son of the Fatherland* and Polevoi in *The Moscow
Telegraph* published laudatory pieces.[17]

In a positive way Byron's influence is clearly traceable in
the works of the foremost poets, and it was a determining
factor in shaping the romantic literature of the time. Zhukovski, as we have seen, was one of the first to respond to
the new influence. In the words of A. I. Turgenev, "he
raved" about Byron,[18] and his diary records his reading of
the poems and testifies to his keen interest in any foreign
gossip concerning Byron's life.[19] Included in his plans for
translation was a promise to render both *The Giaour* and
Manfred, but neither work was performed. In 1821, however, while travelling in Switzerland, Zhukovski visited the
castle of Chillon, and with sudden inspiration he translated
the famous poem from the English text. This rendering of

The Prisoner of Chillon, published in 1822, was received with high praise. Pushkin exclaimed: "Zhukovski's translation is a *tour de force*. The villain! There is uncommon power displayed in the struggle with the difficulties. One must be a Byron to express with such passionate sincerity the initial indications of madness, but Zhukovski repeatedly conveys this." [20] It is one of the best Russian versions of any of Byron's poems. Although he handles the original rather freely, softening the prisoner's complaint a good deal, it must be admitted that his changes are an improvement.

Zhukovski had a kind of spiritual kinship with the theme of *The Prisoner of Chillon*. But despite the urgings of his friends, especially Vyazemski he translated nothing else from Byron with the single exception of *Stanzas for Music*, [21] a poem which is again on a theme congenial to his sad and sentimental nature. He much preferred to render, often beautifully, the paler verses of Moore, such as *The Death of the Peri* and *Lalla Rookh*, a fact which excessively irritated Pushkin, for whom Moore was "an affected imitator with a vile Eastern imagination." [22] As a matter of fact, after the first flush of discovery Zhukovski grew cool towards Byron's poetry. The truth of the matter, as Vyazemski expressed it, is that Zhukovski was afraid of the Byronic "poison." [23] In a letter to Kozlov, apropos of *The Prisoner of Chillon*, Zhukovski reveals his real attitude: "Many of its pages are eternal, but in it there is a most terrible, a most depressed spirit. It does not belong to a poet solaced by life." [24] That is, the hate for society, which runs through so much of Byron's poetry, struck a discordant note in Zhukovski, whose character and genius were quite different. He disliked politics and hence refused to strike the revolutionary lyre of Byron. What influence Byron had on him was the result of a passing sympathy for the general enthusiasm which the new type of poetry aroused.[25] In a sense Zhukovski typified a distrust which was sporadically voiced by conservatives throughout the whole period, but which was never powerful enough to hinder materially the growing popularity of Byron.[26]

K. N. Batiushkov (1787–1855), the Russian Tibullus, was likewise early attracted by Byron's poetry. When in Italy in 1820 he obtained a French version of the fourth canto of *Childe Harold* and made an excellent translation of the two famous stanzas — "There is a pleasure in the pathless woods" and "Roll on, thou deep and dark blue Ocean, roll!"[27] Batiushkov was still quite young when his mind became clouded, and in his madness he wrote a letter to the dead Byron in which he expressed the wish that he could read his poetry in the original.[28] But even in his more lucid years he had little natural sympathy with the Byronic spirit. Like Zhukovski he merely went along with the crowd, and at any rate his deep devotion to the classics would have prevented any lasting affection for Byron.

In I. I. Kozlov (1779–1840), however, we have a poet who takes an important place among the early Russian Byronists.[29] Byron was "the poet of his heart," [30] in whose sadness and disillusion he found a faithful reflection of the unhappy circumstances of his own life. His first acquaintance with him was in 1819 when he read *Childe Harold* with Zhukovski.[31] According to the testimony of Zhukovski, Kozlov "knew all of Byron by heart," [32] a boast similar to that which

Kozlov made in the case of Scott's works. And Polevoi lends some slight support to this extraordinary statement: "With surprise," he writes, "I heard him [Kozlov] recite to me from memory many of Byron's verses." [33] It is of a piece with Kozlov's prodigious feats of memory that he is reported to have learned the English language in three months in order to read his favorite poet in the original.[34] In his diary Kozlov pays Byron an unusual tribute:

> I have read Byron a great deal. Nothing can be compared with him. The *chef d'œuvre* of poetry, the gloomy greatness, the tragedy, the energy, the inimitable force, the enthusiasm, the striving towards a kind of delirium, the grace, flame, feeling, the thrilling poetry — I am enraptured by him. . . . But he is already something of a misanthrope; I should only wish that he had more religious ideas, for they are necessary for happiness. But what a soul, what a poet, what a delightful genius! It is simply magic![35]

In this otherwise enthusiastic praise, however, Kozlov betrays a side of his poetic nature which always prevented him from accepting Byron unequivocally.

His initial interest resulted in a long series of translations. Between 1820 and 1838 he published a rendering of *The Bride of Abydos*, selections from *Childe Harold, The Giaour, The Corsair, The Siege of Corinth, Lara, Manfred, Don Juan,* and a number of the shorter poems.[36] The influence of Byron's poetry soon made itself apparent in Kozlov's original productions. The most important instance is his popular verse tale, *The Monk*,[37] which is essentially a reworking of the second part of *The Giaour*. The form is the same as Byron's and the central motif, the confession of a monk who has been involved in a disastrous love affair, closely resembles the Giaour's confession. For the general conception of

the monk and for several important circumstances connected
with his life Kozlov was indebted to Byron. The hero's
dark, morose appearance and his gloomy brow recall the
Giaour, and he reacts in a similar way to the tragic experience of the loss of his beloved one. The total impression,
nevertheless, is different from that made by the titanic,
thunderous Giaour. For Kozlov allows the un-Byronic element of repentance to creep into the nature of his monk,
who ultimately submits to the will of God and hopes for
absolution for his sins.[38]

Kozlov's other two narrative poems, *Natalya Borisovna
Dolgorukaya* and *The Mad Girl*,[39] likewise show traces of
Byron's influence, especially in the portrayal of the heroines
and in the descriptions of nature.[40] But here again the characters are somewhat sentimentalized in their humility and
submissiveness to fate. *The Monk* is by far his finest Byronic
poem. It won great popularity and inspired a number of
imitations, many of which retained the striking similarities
to *The Giaour*.[41]

On the whole, despite his enthusiasm, Kozlov's softer
poetic nature did not harmonize very well with the rebellious
spirit of Byron. He was more at home with Burns, Scott,
Wordsworth, and Moore, from all of whom he translated.
For the fierce gloom, the pessimism, and the social protest
of Byron he had little sympathy. But in the matter of form
and in the themes of suffering and sadness Kozlov's literary
development was much influenced by Byron.

The hardness and pessimism which Kozlov lacked were
dominant traits in E. A. Baratynski (1800–44), whose
temperament made him an ideal follower of Byron. For him

man obeyed only one law, and that the law of destruction. Against a background of profound melancholy he wrote poems memorable at once for their romantic sentiment and a keen, psychological insight into human motives and behavior. But a hopeless pessimism prevails in most of his work. Such a poem as *The Skull*,[42] for example, is furnished forth with more than Byronic scorn and pessimism. Baratynski, however, was a singularly independent spirit who preferred to travel his own poetic road, and one predicates cases of influence with some hesitancy. His melancholy and pessimism certainly echo Byron's, and if anything they go much deeper. It is possible to class him with these disciples in the first quarter of the nineteenth century, not so much because he borrowed directly from the master, as because he typified powerfully one phase of the Byronic state of mind.

Opposed to Zhukovski, Kozlov, and Baratynski, there existed a group of writers which was essentially interested in Byron's poetry of opposition to the existing social order. Most of them played an important part in the ill-fated Decembrist revolt. In Byron they saw a genius who in beautiful, compelling verse and in glorious deeds struggled against the forces of reaction and raised the battle cry of freedom.

Thus V. Kiukhelbeker (1797–1846), filled with the radical fervor of the contemporary French political publications, suddenly discovered in Byron the ultimate expression of his own revolutionary ideals. He deplored his subjectivity, but as a champion of liberty he placed him beside Milton. His diary,[43] written while in exile in Siberia, bears testimony to his lively interest in Byron, and in prison and banishment he projected lyrical effusions in the spirit of *Childe Harold*.

The hate and satire of *Don Juan* disturbed him, but Byron's biography made a deep impression and he copied into his diary various striking aphorisms of Byron. In his *Death of Byron*,[44] one of the best of the eulogies, Kiukhelbeker lamented the passing of the poet with genuine feeling, lauding him especially as the protector of liberty. He was perhaps more significant as a critic than a poet, but Byron's influence on his verse is well marked, particularly in the important work, *Izhorski*,[45] which he described, after the fashion of *Cain* and *Heaven and Earth*, "A Mystery." *Childe Harold*, *Lara*, and *Manfred* all contribute characteristics to the typically Byronic hero who bears a mysteriously sad countenance, is forever wandering from place to place, and is given to swift transitions from riotous living to gloomy isolation. *Izhorski* is an unequal performance, however, only fitfully illuminated by passages of real pathos. The best that Belinski could say for *Izhorski* was to describe it as "the thousand-and-first parody of *Childe Harold*." [46]

K. F. Ryleev (1795–1826), one of the most brilliant and unfortunate of the Decembrists, was likewise one of the most independent of them in his literary endeavors. For a time, however, he succumbed to the popular craze for Byron, whom he admired as a revolutionary poet and social satirist. *Don Juan* was his particular favorite in which he found the "loftiest vices and highest virtues." [47] In his chief work, *Voinarovski* (1824), a narrative poem, we can discern a Byronic coloring, and in certain details the influence of *The Prisoner of Chillon* and *Mazeppa*. For the themes of several of his unfinished poems Ryleev was also indebted to Byron.[48]

Of all the Decembrist group who produced literature of consequence Marlinski (1797–1837)[49] was perhaps the most powerfully affected by Byron. He was well versed in English, and his interest in Sterne and Scott has already been pointed out.[50] Marlinski was banished to Siberia and later transferred to the Caucasus, where he led a soldier's life. He liked to compare his wandering existence to that of Childe Harold, and he sought solace in exile by reading, among other things, the poems of Byron. There were months, he says, when he "held nothing in his hand except Byron." [51] His life of daring action would have delighted the English poet, and his death in battle, though perhaps in a less noble cause, was certainly more glorious from a romantic point of view than that of his inspirer in the malarial flats of Missolonghi. Marlinski's passionate nature was of the Byronic stamp, and it is noticeable that the heroes of his tales, who are more or less conceived in his own image, show a fondness for Byron.[52] It is in the romantic prose tale, rather than in verse, that Marlinski was influenced. There are several striking parallels between two of his best-known stories, *Ammalat Bek* and *The Red Veil*,[53] and *Childe Harold*.[54] The pronounced romantic individualism of the heroes, and their love of nature and scorn for society clearly place them in the Byronic category.[55]

There was also a rather large group of lesser Byronists who wrote many poems in direct imitation of their model or inspired by the works of their more famous contemporaries who were influenced by Byron.[56] Among these writers those worthy of mention are N. A. Markevich, O. M. Somov, A. I. Polezhaev, and D. V. Venevitinov. Markevich was a zealous but untalented translator of Byron. He rendered selections from the *Hebrew Melodies, Parisina*, and *Don Juan*, and he brought out his imitation, *Ukrainian Melodies*, in 1831. Somov translated *Darkness, To Moore*, and other small pieces. Polezhaev, who was implicated in the Decembrist conspiracy, steeped himself in the poetry of Byron, translating *The Vision of Belshazzar* and *Oscar of Alva*. Just before his own death he hailed Byron in a poem as "the divine voice that thundered under the misty heavens of England." [57] The melancholy and disillusion in his personal life taught him to sympathize with Byron, and his verses echo with Byronic themes, especially his *Demon of Inspiration*,[58] which was influenced by *Manfred*. Venevitinov called himself a "bold student of Byron." But he died young (at the age of twenty-two) and his few literary remains scarcely give any correct indication of the importance of this early influence of Byron. His promise was great and what lyrics he has left are filled with Byronic reflections.

I have left for final and more detailed consideration the extremely important part that Byron played in the lives and works of the two greatest poets of the period, Pushkin and Lermontov. It is a fact now generally recognized by native critics that Russian Byronism owes perhaps more to the influence of Pushkin than to that of Byron himself. For many writers found their inspiration in the Byronic poems of Pushkin without ever going directly to the English originals which he used. And in the case of Lermontov we have one of the greatest disciples of Byron in all European literature.

It is no reflection on Pushkin's originality to call him, as is often done, the most cosmopolitan of Russian poets. He was an eager student of French, English, German, Italian, and Polish literature. Like Shakspere he borrowed where he pleased, but the final product was always stamped with the indelible quality of his own genius, which was convincingly Russian in expression and thought. In his early youth he was much under the influence of French writers and his first productions were largely imitations of them. But in 1822 we find him writing in a letter: "English literature is beginning to have an influence on Russian. I think it will be a more useful influence than that of the timid and affected French poetry." [59] He is speaking here for his own particular generation, and accordingly he does not understate the case, although he ignores the generation before him, which had already experienced this influence. In reality his judgment in favor of English literature was no doubt prompted by the fact that at this time he was deep in Byron.

The circumstances of Pushkin's life between the years 1820 and 1824, which may be described as his "Byronic Period," curiously predisposed his mind and temperament to an intense sympathy for Byron and his works. In his contact with fresh scenes and exotic nature the period corresponds to Byron's first journey abroad, and in the fact of real exile it resembles Byron's voluntary exile in 1816. For in 1820 Pushkin was banished to the Caucasus for offending the government. He was considered a dangerous element to society and thus, like Byron, though for a different reason, he felt himself ostracized. Indeed, without forcing the facts, one can point to further similarities between the two poets which are interesting in the light of Byron's influence, though they prove nothing. Like Byron, Pushkin was naïvely proud of his aristocratic ancestry; both were early attracted to the great French writers of the Revolution; they both loved and expressed freedom in their poetry; while in exile both sought solace in pleasure and love; both were haughty and opposed themselves to the crowd; both were given to melancholy and addicted to suffering, though Pushkin much less so than Byron; and both died young. However, there were very positive differences in their natures and artistic ideals, and these differences soon lessened and eventually ended Byron's influence.

Although he had undoubtedly heard of Byron earlier, Pushkin first came in contact with his poetry in the original in 1820 at the home of the Raevskis, a family that did much to brighten the first years of his exile. Just how much English Pushkin knew at this time is difficult to ascertain. At the age of eight or nine he is supposed to have received some instruction in the language from his governess, but his efforts then, and for some time afterwards, were desultory and inconclusive. The Raevski sons and daughters, however, were students of English literature, and with their help Pushkin made considerable progress. By 1828, at the latest, he was able to read English with ease.[60]

With the Raevskis he assayed a translation of *The Giaour* into French, but the attempt ended unsuccessfully, and the fragment shows that their combined knowledge of English was as yet a little faulty.[61] But Pushkin continued to read Byron with sympathetic understanding, and like Childe Harold he fulminated against society, grew melancholy, reacted romantically to the luxuriant beauties of Crimean and Caucasian scenery, and compensated himself for the sorrows of exile by indulging in numerous love affairs. In 1823 he wrote to Vyazemski, begging him to come to Kishinev. And as a special inducement he offers to introduce him to "a girl who had been kissed by Byron." [62] Pushkin himself fell in love with this girl, who bore the fetching name of Calypso Polychrone. In *To a Greek Girl* [63] he dedicates a poem to Calypso in which he suggests that she may have been the inspiration for Leila in *The Giaour*.

It is unlikely, however, that Calypso Polychrone was the model for the unfortunate Leila,[64] but Pushkin's poem gives us some idea how thoroughly he was becoming immersed in the matter and spirit of Byron's works. Yet even earlier than this, in the very first poem that he wrote in his southern exile, the beautiful elegy *Vanished Is the Light of Day*,[65] we hear the unmistakable echoes of Childe Harold bidding farewell to his native land.[66] But in these few verses the essential difference between the two poets is already noticeable. The setting is the same, and Pushkin's melancholy at parting and his anticipation of new scenes recall the similar feelings of Byron's hero. However, there is nothing of pessimism or scorn in Pushkin's heart as he bids his native land farewell. He is filled with regrets for the friends, the loves, and the youthful pleasures that he leaves behind. This is a note that Byron sternly avoids. On the whole, Pushkin's mood is much more realistic and objective.

Between 1820 and 1824 Pushkin published his so-called "Southern poems," — *The Prisoner of the Caucasus, The Robber Brothers, The Bakhchisaraiski Fountain,* and *The Gypsies* [67] — narratives in verse which were immediately inspired by Byron's Eastern tales and which mark the high point of his influence.

In the precise matter of the form of these poems Pushkin was directly indebted to Byron. He appropriated the tetrameter line, which was new in verse narrative in Russia, and his use popularized the form. In narrative structure also Pushkin's tales bear a close resemblance to those of Byron. He employs the usual Byronic scheme of three characters, — the hero, the beloved, and the villain; and the plot unfolds in the manner of the Eastern poems. Pushkin's heroes, like Byron's, are not great princes and knights. The settings, too, are similar, — the Mussulman East, the robbers' den, the gypsy camp, and the sultan's harem provide the field of action. Finally, the usual Byronic theme runs through Pushkin's tales also — the tragic story of a European who comes in contact with an Eastern or exotic civilization and falls in love with a native woman. In smaller details Pushkin likewise lays the Eastern poems under contribution. Thus he borrows the "break" or "interruption" in order to indicate a different point of view or a change from simple narrative to dramatic; the Byronic manner of lyrical narrative with its questions, repetitions, and abrupt transitions; and the introduction of the story by a kind of descriptive overture.

Pushkin sometimes goes direct to the Eastern poems for precise situations and characters. There is a close thematic resemblance between *The Prisoner of the Caucasus*, *The Robber Brothers*, and *The Corsair*. Zarem in *The Bakhchisaraiski Fountain* is closely modelled on Gulnare in *The Corsair*, and Aleko in *The Gypsies* has much of Hassan in *The Giaour*.

Various passages in the Southern poems bear all the ear-marks of having been suggested by or taken directly from Byron's tales.[68]

Yet Pushkin was by no means content to follow his models slavishly, and the difference in his art from Byron's is strik-ing. It is particularly apparent in the portrayal of the chief characters. Byron's heroes are powerfully, almost heavily drawn. They are Satanic and in each case the hero dominates the story. With Pushkin, on the contrary, the leading char-acters are portrayed with swift, light strokes, and they are not allowed to monopolize the center of the stage. The hero-ines are no less important in his eyes than the heroes, and the spiritual world of both receives, if anything, more atten-tion than their external appearance, which is always em-phasized by Byron. Pushkin's method makes for a general softening in the demonic type of hero which Byron invariably portrayed, but it preserves him from falling into a tiresome sameness in characterization and the interest in the narrative element gains.

In the Southern poems Pushkin shows that he has learned much from the structure, theme, and narrative manner of Byron's verse tales, but throughout this period one observes a gradual strengthening of his own artistic talent. In the last of the group, *The Gypsies*, Pushkin is obviously follow-ing rather than imitating. And although his *Poltava* of a still later date (1828), was suggested by *Mazeppa*, Pushkin treats the theme in an independent fashion. Here he writes in the traditional romantic form a kind of epic poem which is based on a careful historical study of the sources, a work quite different from *Mazeppa*. This is a method never em-

ployed by Byron.[69] The Southern poems were of the utmost importance in the growth of Russian romanticism.
They inspired a long series of imitations by lesser poets, who
were content to go to Pushkin for their models rather than
to Byron. There soon sprang up whole groups of "Caucasian
Prisoner," "Robber Brothers," and "Gypsy" verse tales.[70]

During his period of exile Pushkin's lyric poetry was also
somewhat affected by Byron's influence. This is to be
observed not so much in form or expression — he was a
neater and more successful lyric poet than Byron — as in
his themes of sadness and pessimism. He was particularly
moved by Byron's poetry of revolt and in several lyrics he
pleaded the cause of political freedom and Greek liberty.[71]
But he soon lost all faith in the Greek cause. Pushkin was
altogether too knowing not to experience a sense of disgust
at the mercenary motives of the various parties concerned
in the struggle for Greek emancipation.[72]

It should be remembered that Pushkin was only twenty-
one when he first came under the powerful sway of Byron's
genius. The influence extended his literary horizon, strengthened his romantic tastes, and inspired him to write a series
of poems which enormously increased his popularity. The
circumstances of his life at this time, as I have said, made him
peculiarly sympathetic to the Byronic spirit. But in reality
Byron's pessimism, disillusion, and romantic posing were
essentially uncongenial to Pushkin's nature. In the first
blush of youthful enthusiasm he accepted these romantic
trappings because they suited his own misfortunes and his
disordered state of mind. But he soon cast them aside. In
fact, by the end of the Southern period in 1824 he was al-

ready beginning to regard Byron in quite a different light. During the four years of influence his own genius had matured and his critical sense had been extraordinarily sharpened. He now examined the Eastern poems with a cool, discerning intellect, nor did he except his own imitations from a similar treatment. His changed attitude is at once apparent in a letter written to Vyazemski in 1824, in which he refuses the latter's request to celebrate Byron's death by writing a fifth canto for *Childe Harold*:

> Thou art sad about Byron, but I am quite happy in his death as a glorious termination of his poetry. Byron's genius faded from his youth. In his tragedies, not even excluding *Cain*, he is not the flaming Demon who created *The Giaour* and *Childe Harold*. The first two cantos of *Don Juan* are superior to the succeeding ones. His poetry obviously changed. He had always created in a wrong manner. There was no gradation; he suddenly ripened and matured, sang and then grew silent, and his first melodies never returned to him. After the fourth canto of *Childe Harold* we did not hear Byron but rather some other poet who wrote with a lofty, human talent. Your idea of celebrating his death in a fifth canto of his Hero is charming — but it is not in my power.[73]

Like Zhukovski, Pushkin rejected this request, and several others [74] of the sympathetic Vyazemski, to eulogize the dead poet. But he carefully noted the date of Byron's death on the cover of his copybook, and in the same year he paid him his own modest tribute on a theme that the English poet loved well:

> He was, O Sea, thy singer.
> Thy form was not unknown to him,
> By thine own spirit was he wrought:
> As thee, a force, profound and grim,
> As thee, subdued by naught.[75]

On the anniversary of Byron's death a year later Pushkin ordered a candle to be lighted at supper "for the peace of his soul." [76]

Pushkin had definitely put behind him the period of his youthful Southern poems. He now turned from the purely romantic to the realistic and satirical. This development in his art was not unlike that of Byron after the fourth canto of *Childe Harold*, when he turned to such themes as *Beppo* and *Don Juan*. In fact, Pushkin himself had by now transferred his admiration to the later satirical works of Byron, and it is very possible that these poems suggested to him a new field of literary endeavor. Certainly *Eugene Onegin*, the greatest poem in this new phase of Pushkin's development, was directly inspired by *Don Juan*.

In a letter to Vyazemski in 1823 Pushkin remarks that he is writing a romance in verse "in the manner of *Don Juan*." [77] He had already begun his masterpiece, which, however, was not to be finished until 1831. In 1825 we again find him writing to Vyazemski: "What a miracle is D. J. [*Don Juan*]! I know only the first five cantos; after reading the first two I said at once to Raevski that this is the *chef d'œuvre* of Byron, and I rejoiced to see that W. Scott is of my opinion."[78]

On Pushkin's own testimony, then, it is very likely that the inspiration for *Eugene Onegin* came from *Don Juan*. The reviewers apparently thought so, for on its appearance it was at once compared with Byron's work. Pushkin was indignant at the comparison and he protested to Marlinski that in Don Juan "there is nothing at all in common with Onegin."[79] It is quite true that Pushkin did not slavishly imitate *Don Juan*. Everything he borrowed was made to serve his own artistic purpose. But the fact remains that he was much indebted to Byron for various features of *Eugene Onegin.*

He begins his poem with the form of *Don Juan* in mind and appropriates certain of Byron's narrative features, such as the digression, the address to the reader, the mingled witty and sad observations on life, the quick transitions from light, mocking subjects to serious thought or to beautiful descriptive passages, and the polemical tirades. As he got farther into the poem, however, Pushkin's purpose was modified. On a Byronic plan he proceeded to construct a social romance with a well-defined plot which would allow him to satirize the vices and foibles of his day.

In his original conception of his hero, Pushkin was obligated to the characterizations of both Childe Harold and Don Juan.

> Onegin in Childe Harold's manner
> Was sunk in thoughtful indolence.[80]

And again:

> He showed himself in drawing rooms,
> Morose and languid, like Childe Harold.[81]

But in his youth Onegin shows not a little of Don Juan's demonism. He has a "hard, cold mind"; he is scornful, and a "caustic disputant." [82] At first he regards Tatyana with a cool indifference and affects a bored and satiated attitude towards life in general. But these features are the more obvious Byronic traits of Onegin. What there is of the Satanic in his nature seems more like a pose which he forgets as his character matures. Indeed, as Pushkin develops the character of Onegin, he finds himself attempting to portray a type of man not at all uncommon in the society of his own

time. His approach, however, is entirely objective. Pushkin
is not Onegin in the sense that Byron is Childe Harold or
Don Juan.

Pushkin was perhaps a little too sweeping in his claim that
there is nothing in common between Onegin and Don
Juan, although his hero certainly stands as a great and original creation. There is also much else about *Eugene Onegin*
that is original — the plot, the minor characters, the splendid descriptive passages, and the immortal Tatyana. Yet
Pushkin's debt to Byron was not a small one. He drew upon
Don Juan for the form and for various narrative devices in
Eugene Onegin, and upon *Beppo* for his brilliant descriptions
of St. Petersburg life.

After his Southern period, however, Pushkin was inclined
to regard Byron with that fine critical judgment which he
eventually applied to all Western European writers. Convinced now of his own powers, he disliked being thought of
as a "Russian Byron," a title which the reviewers were not
slow to give him. In 1825 the patriotically-minded Ryleev
had abjured him: "Thou mayest be our Byron, but for
God's sake, for Christ's sake, for thy beloved Mahomet's
sake, do not imitate him!" [83] There may have been some
reason for such a warning in 1825, but the subsequent course
of Pushkin's development took him quite outside and beyond the sphere of Byronism. In these later years, however,
he did not forget the English poet. Byron's name occurs
frequently in his correspondence and Pushkin's keen interest in anything connected with Byron never lapsed. In the
considerable amount of formal and informal criticism from
Pushkin's pen Byron is often discussed. He objects vigor-

ously to his characterization in both the verse tales and the dramas, asserting that he never conceived a single original character. "Les femmes," he writes, "n'ont pas de caractère, elles ont des passions dans leur jeunesse"; and Byron's heroes merely possess "tel et tel trait de son caractère; son orgueil à l'un; sa haine à l'autre, sa mélancolie au troisième." [84] In a critical fragment on Byron in 1827 in which he reviews his works with insight, Pushkin expresses opinions which critics today, with the advantage of greater perspective and detachment, can wholly approve. Of the Eastern tales he singles out *The Corsair* and *Parisina* for high praise, reiterates his belief in the supremacy of *Don Juan*, and condemns the plays in which Byron "merely imitates himself." "Byron," he remarks, "cared little about the planning of his productions or did not even think about it at all. Rather scenes, weakly joined together, sufficiently served him for deep thought, feelings, and characterization." [85]

In another article on Byron, written in 1835, Pushkin gives his opinion on the poet's character, the chief traits of which were "bitterness and irritability," and the virtues "daring enterprise and noble feeling." He likewise censures him for his "unbridled passions, his caprice, and his arrogant scorn for popular opinion." [86] On this score one hears the authentic note of understanding in a letter to Vyazemski: "Why do you regret the loss of Byron's memoirs? [87] To the devil with them! He confessed in his verses involuntarily, with the captivating charm of poetry. In cold prose he would have lied and deceived, trying to show off his sincerity while smearing his enemies. . . . We know enough about Byron." [88]

Apart from the fact that he had reached literary maturity, Pushkin's changed attitude towards Byron was no doubt partly brought about by his wider knowledge of English literature. By 1825 Shakspere and Scott had given Pushkin a clearer notion of artistic objectivity, realism, and characterization.[89] The poetry of Moore he could not abide. Byron at his worst was infinitely preferable. "Do you know why I do not like Moore?" he explains to a friend. "Because he has gone to extremes in things Eastern. He imitates the puerile and the monstrous — the puerilities and monstrosities of Saadi, Hafiz, and Mahomet. The European, drunk with Eastern magnificence, must preserve the taste and point of view of the European. That is why Byron is so charming in *The Giaour* and *The Bride of Abydos*." [90] No critic now would be disposed to quarrel with Pushkin on these grounds, although in his own day such a judgment was unique, for Moore was highly thought of by the Russian romantics. Only for his *Life of Byron* does Pushkin concede Moore a modicum of praise, and then it is an oblique kind of compliment that he pays him: "This performance," he writes, "is better than his *Lalla Rookh*." [91]

Pushkin's acquaintance with the Lake Poets gave him a new outlook on English literature and increased his distrust of the extreme romanticism of Byron. His own account shows that he was aware of the general artistic purpose of this group:

In mature literature the time has come when, much wearied with the monotonous productions of art restricted to a language formed for the conventional and elect, people are attracted to fresh, native originality, and to strange, popular speech. As in

French society people were once ravished by the muse of Vadé, so now Wordsworth and Coleridge have gained the attention of many. But Vadé had neither imagination nor poetic feeling: his clever works breathe a certain jollity, expressed in the vulgar language of the tradesman and porter. The productions of the English poets, on the other hand, are filled with profound feeling and poetic thought, expressed in the language of honest, simple people.[92]

Whether Pushkin was actually in sympathy with some of the more radical literary ideas of Wordsworth, it is hard to say. At all events, he admired him sufficiently to translate two of his sonnets.[93] Strangely enough, he likewise seized upon *The Excursion* as material for translation. But after rendering thirty-five lines taken from the opening of Book I, he wisely abandoned the task.[94]

Coleridge's poetry of the supernatural unquestionably appealed to Pushkin, and his own compositions in this *genre* indicate that he must have derived considerable pleasure from reading the works of Coleridge. We have his own word for it that he read him,[95] and it has been conjectured that the mixed prose and verse form of Pushkin's well-known *Egyptian Nights* was suggested by *The Improvisatore.*[96]

Pushkin's first reference to Southey is hardly complimentary. Commenting to a friend upon a projected translation of Zhukovski, he writes: "Once he spoke to me about a poem, the *Roderick* of Southey. Beg him for me to let it rest in peace, notwithstanding the request of a certain young lady." [97] And in an article in 1830 Pushkin was more outspoken: "They all advise me to write an epic poem. . . . Indeed, have we not the poems of Southey? He has a *Joan d'Arc* and *The Curse of Kehama*, and may God bring as many curses on *The Last of the Goths*!" [98] But he does not utterly

condemn these poems, as Byron did, for in the same article
he expresses the belief that they are better than the Russian
epics. Considering the Russian epics he had in mind, however, one could easily construe this praise as sarcasm. By
1833 Pushkin's opinion of Southey appears to have improved,
for in that year he made a rather free rendering of the condemned *Roderick, the Last of the Goths.*[99]

I have thought it necessary to notice this broadening of
Pushkin's interest in English literature, for it helped to
give him a truer perspective of Byron's poetic accomplishment. Furthermore, the period of his interest in other English and Continental authors coincides with the years in
which his devotion to Byron declined. In short, after he
began *Eugene Onegin* the influence of Byron virtually ceased.
Pushkin's indebtedness, which was considerable, was confined to the period of the Southern poems. He understood the
significance of the Byronic revolt better than any of his contemporaries, and it was this clear comprehension that made
him realize how very little he had in common with Byron.
Once he had returned from his exile and settled down in
married life, the youthful spiritual and emotional bond that
had joined him to Byron when he was in the South was
severed. In the last analysis the temperaments of the two
poets were radically different. Pushkin was incapable of the
typical Byronic demonism or of the posing and unrelieved
pessimism and hate for society which pursued Byron all
through his life. His nature was healthier and his search for
truth was more elevated and sustained. The essentially objective character of his art saved him from chronic Byronism
and the worst excesses of the romantic school. At best, the

Byronic disillusion, melancholy, and scorn were but a pass-ing, though powerful, influence. He did more than any of his contemporaries to popularize Byron during the period of Russian romanticism, and if he refused to be the "Russian Byron," he showed the way for Lermontov, who had a more natural right to the title.

M. de Vogüé has summed up the difference in the debt of Pushkin and Lermontov to Byron: "Le créateur d'Oniéguine n'avait pris à celui de *Childe Harold* que sa poétique: Ler-montov lui a pris son âme." [100] While not suggesting the actual process, this statement aptly indicates the complete-ness with which Lermontov (1814–41) submitted to the let-ter and spirit of Byronism. Certainly there was hardly a figure in European literature at this time whose life, tempera-ment, nervous organization, and peculiar poetic ability more completely prepared him to play the Pollux to the Byronic Castor. A precocious childhood, family estrangements, and unhappy adolescent love affairs were his background by the time Lermontov reached the university and military school. Then came a period of over-indulgence in which a predilec-tion for evil and melancholy was fostered and a growing hate for the common herd encouraged. And finally in his man-hood social offenses, exile, revolt against injustice, poetic fame, warlike adventures, passionate love, frustration, deepening melancholy, duels, and sudden death all played their romantic and Byronic part.

As a boy Lermontov's English tutor taught him to read the language, and in his country home he wandered about in remote parts of the huge garden with volumes of Byron for his sole companions.[101] In a copybook which dates from his

thirteenth year we find translations from *The Giaour* and
Beppo, along with transcriptions of Pushkin's Byronic
Bakhchisaraiski Fountain and Zhukovski's rendering of *The
Prisoner of Chillon.* At the age of sixteen Moore's biography
fell into his hands, and at once Byron became something more
than a name and a poet. He became a vivid, living personality with whom this melancholy romantic youth immediately
identified himself. And Lermontov was quick to express the
discovery in verse:

> Youthful am I, yet sounds rage in my heart,
> And I would scale the heights of Byron's fame.
> We have one soul, and one and the same smart.
> Alas, if our two fates were but the same!
> Like him, forgetfulness and freedom crave,
> Like him, in childhood did my spirit soar,
> I loved to roam the mountains, breast the wave,
> The earth-born storms and heaven's fearful roar.
> Like him, I search for quietude in vain,
> Everywhere haunted by a single thought.
> I look behind me — and the past is pain,
> I look before me — of my soul there's naught.[102]

So forcibly does the resemblance strike him that he insists upon details with a childish eagerness. He is "amazed
at the similarity" of their methods of composing verse; and
he repeats the story of the old woman who predicted to
Byron's mother that he would be a great man and be married
twice, and then notes that an old woman in the Caucasus
had made a similar prophecy about him to his grandmother.
"May heaven ordain," he adds, "that this prediction about
me be fulfilled, in order that I may also be as unfortunate as
Byron." [103] Nor does he overlook the fact that the Scotland
of Byron's birth was the native land of his ancestors.[104] He

calls Scotland his mother country and burns with desire to hasten to Scotland, where Ossian is buried.[105]

Then, with the uncertainty of his shuttlecock state of mind during this youthful period, he suddenly swings to the other extreme, insisting, despite all these studied resemblances, upon the native character of his own genius:

> I am not Byron — yet I am
> One fore-elected, yet one more
> Unknown, world-hunted wanderer,
> A Russian in my mood and mind.
>
> Scant from my seed the corn was ripe,
> My mouth, while young, was early hushed;
> In depths of my own soul, the wreck
> Of hope lies, as in deep sea sunk.
>
> Who shall the counsels of the sea,
> Its awe sublime unloose? Who shall
> Read clear my spirit and my soul?
> Unless it be a Poet — no man! [106]

There is, no doubt, a good deal of insincerity and posing in all this, pardonable enough, perhaps, in a young man. Lermontov in these verses was not so much concerned with rejecting Byron as with describing his own poetic path. Pride was a dominant trait in his nature, and he could not admit, even to himself, that he was yielding to the superior genius of anyone. Although Lermontov rarely mentions Byron again, in reality his influence now becomes more decisive, making itself felt in the subject matter and structure of his original poetry.

At this very time Lermontov was reworking an earlier version of a poem which was to be his most famous, if not his best, production. This is *The Demon*, which Lermontov did

not actually complete until 1839. Against a background of
beautifully exotic descriptive passages, it tells the tale of a
demon's love for a mortal. The poem is filled with Byronic
Satanism, and it has been conjectured that the theme was
suggested by *Heaven and Earth*. For certain of the details
Cain may also have been drawn upon.[107]

In his succeeding lyrics, dramas, verse tales, and prose
works one continually hears echoes of Byron or encounters
themes, characters, and forms taken directly from the productions of Byron. There was so much in Byron that reflected his own actions and feelings that it seemed impossible
for Lermontov, even if he had so desired, to escape his influence. He read *The Dream* and immediately wrote a poem
in the same strain, *Night I*.[108] And the splendid *Darkness*
inspired a poem on a similar theme, *Night II*,[109] which, however, falls far short of the original. In the same year (1830)
Lermontov composed a free imitation of the *Epistle to a
Friend* [110], in which Byron, it will be remembered, recalls
with bitterness his love for Mary Chaworth. Lermontov
telescopes the piece and does not hesitate to distort the ending into lines of personal application.[111]

In fact, Lermontov translated many lines from Byron's
poetry, in which he often displayed a curious disregard for
the originals. Whenever the original could be twisted to
suit an experience in his own life, he deliberately changed
the poem accordingly. Such, for example, were his translations of *To a Lady* and *My Soul Is Dark*.[112] In the former he
reduces Byron's four stanzas to three and modifies the
thought considerably, and in the latter he is more or less
faithful until he reaches the last two lines:

> And now 't is doomed to know the worst,
>   And break at once — or yield to song.

which he renders with more than Byronic sentiment:

> Struck is the fateful hour — now it [the heart] is full,
> Just as the cup of death with poison filled.

Even the famous gladiator stanzas in *Childe Harold* [113] are translated with the utmost freedom, though in this case with some success. However, one can number among his more faithful renderings *Farewell! If Ever Fondest Prayer*, *Lines Written in an Album, at Malta*, a stanza from *Don Juan* (canto XVI, xl), and a fragment from the end of *Mazeppa*. And in many of the original lyrics of his youth one continually hears echoes of the characteristic Byronic themes of melancholy, disgust with life, bitterness, and defiance. Lermontov soon learned to regard the poetry of Byron as a kind of mirror in which he saw his own image faithfully and sharply reflected. In reading it he found ready made a psychological analysis of those dark and devious aspects of his nature which as yet he did not fully comprehend.

Pushkin, we have seen, was too objective an artist to allow himself to stand as the prototype of his poetical characters. But Lermontov, like Byron, continually cast his characters in the mold of his own personality. And in so far as he himself was Byronic, his creations naturally reflect this type. As if he were uncertain of the features, however, he often goes directly to Byron for inspiration and descriptive details. In two of his plays, *Menschen und Leidenschaften* and *A Strange Man*,[114] which are closely related in subject, Lermontov composed under the general influence of *Cain*. The hero of

Menschen und Leidenschaften revolts against God, and in words that closely recall those of Byron's Cain, he protests against the unhappy consequences of the divine will. In a similar strain Vladimir Arbenin, the hero of *A Strange Man*, cursed by his father and deceived in love, blames God for his misfortunes.

Like Pushkin, Lermontov wrote a series of Caucasian verse tales, and the heroes of them bear a striking resemblance to those of Byron's Eastern poems. At the age of fifteen he began to produce works in this *genre* with his *Prisoner of the Caucasus*,[115] a feeble imitation of Pushkin's Byronic poem of the same name. And in the same year (1828) he wrote *The Corsair*,[116] which is a rather poor imitation of Byron's poem. Lermontov's hero has all the external features of Conrad but little of his strength. His next attempt in this kind was *The Murderer*,[117] which represents a considerable gain in narrative power, though the execution is still weak. It is a story of vengeance, in which the young hero murders the slayer of his family and the slayer's daughter. The description of the avenger, gloomy, silent, awe-inspiring, and in revolt against his cruel destiny, is borrowed from *The Giaour*. *The Giaour* appears to have powerfully impressed Lermontov, for we find its influence recurring in several of his other tales. This is the case in *Izmail-Bei* (1832). The hero bears the legitimate stamp. Debauched and disillusioned by society, he returns to his native land. There he affects the familiar pose of the cold yet unresigned man, tortured by memories but scornful of death. *The Giaour* contributes to the characterization of both hero and heroine, and for some of the details Lermontov was indebted to

Lara. The hero of *Khadzhi Abrek* (1833–34) is again of the avenger type. He is the sad son of destiny, and the heroine, Leila, resembles the Leila of *The Giaour* in more than name.

The haunting influence of *The Giaour* likewise dominates three more verse tales of Lermontov, *The Confession*, *Boyarin Orsha*, and *The Novice*,[118] which in reality are three drafts of *The Giaour* theme. The story in each poem varies, but in a general way it concerns the fate of a youth who, out of love for a beautiful damsel, commits some deed which he confesses but insists on justifying The three heroes are close variations of the Giaour type. Like Byron's character, each is the victim of a fatal love but remains proud, fierce, and contemptuous of death.

In his prose tales Lermontov continues the Byronic tradition, but with a noticeable difference. For example, in *Vadim* (1832), the hero has all the lineaments of the type but is even more demonic. He has the customary gloomy brow and sombre bearing, and his soul is filled with bitterness. His comrades respect him yet fear him. He is a beautiful devil who would not torture men because he scorns them, and in order to scorn he must first hate. The theme likewise recalls Byron. Vadim's sensibilities are for the first time touched by the beautiful Olga who, it turns out, is his long lost sister, a fact which causes the hero to complain against destiny. But in analyzing the sentiments of Vadim, Lermontov displays a certain amount of psychological realism which is to reappear in a more highly developed form in the characterization of Pechorin, his greatest Byronic hero.

Pechorin in the novel, *A Hero of Our Times*,[119] has aroused much discussion. In the preface to the second edition Ler-

montov laughed at the critics who maintained that the hero
was a portrait of the author. Despite his denial, Pechorin is
cast in the image of Lermontov, or is rather an idealized
picture of him. And the general model is the Byronic hero,
a type which, as has often been conjectured, Byron himself may have secretly aspired to in real life.

Like Childe Harold, Pechorin has tasted all pleasures to
the point of satiety. He is bored with life, and nothing remains except travel. In appearance he resembles very closely
Conrad in *The Corsair*. He is of average height but powerful
frame, with an uncommon face which is particularly pleasing
to women. He has the characteristic pale and noble forehead, and his eyes do not laugh when he laughs, — a sign,
says Lermontov, of a wicked nature or of a profound and
constant sadness. This last trait immediately recalls Lara:

> That smile might reach his lips, but pass'd not by,
> None e'er could trace its laughter to his eye.[120]

Pechorin's nature is cold and haughty. He despises the
common herd, and though capable of noble deeds, he does
evil to escape from ennui. Women especially are his victims,
and he prefers the young and innocent girl, for in such cases
the seduction is all the sweeter because of the difficulties he
has to overcome. Above all, he must dominate, both man
and woman alike.

In all these features one easily recognizes the outlines of
his model. And with suggestive significance Byron's name
runs through the novel. A character remembers that a great
Moscow lady had assured him that Byron was a drunkard;
one of Dr. Werner's legs, "like Byron's," is shorter than the

other; and the clever daughter reads Byron in English. Finally, the trick of digression in narrative, which Lermontov favors in the novel, may well have been learned from Byron.

Pechorin, however, transcends the Byronic type. Lermontov develops the character so that at the end of the novel we perceive that there is much more to the hero than a mere pose. Pechorin is ultimately a positive and not a negative personality, and despite the will to destroy, he has a living force which Lermontov brings out by a searching psychological analysis quite foreign to Byron's genius

It would be a mistake to ignore or to minimize the influence of Byron on Lermontov's life and on the growth of his poetic nature, but there is also a danger in attributing too much to this influence, as has often been done. No one can deny that many of Lermontov's characters descend in a straight line from those of Byron; or that Byron's familiar note of pessimism and melancholy is reflected in Lermontov's lyrical poetry; or the fact that there are many striking analogies to Byron in form, subject matter, imagery, and actual phrasing. Finally, on his own testimony, Lermontov submitted to the moral and intellectual influence of Byron. On the other hand, this dependence is most noticeable in the poorer works of Lermontov, and certain phases of the similarity may in some measure be accounted for by their identical natures. Many of Lermontov's best works are comparatively free from Byronic influence, and in these he shows himself an original artist with a strong and unusual personality. Yet to his contemporaries he was always the "Russian Byron," and in the course of his short life no single factor played so significant a rôle as the life and works of Byron.

Byronism reached its height in Russia with Lermontov, and after his death (1841) it fell into a swift decline. Authors who were going through the apprenticeship stage in 1840–50, such as V. A. Sollogub, Ostrovski, Turgenev, Saltykov, Nekrasov, and A. Grigorev, were mildly influenced in their youthful productions. But with the end of the Golden Age of poetry and the rise of the great realistic novelists Byron vanished from the scene. Yet the part he played in the Russian Romantic Movement was a memorable one, and his influence on the two chief poets of the period, Pushkin and Lermontov, was of the utmost consequence.

After Byron no figure in English literature caught the popular imagination or won the devotion of Russian writers to the same extent. Influences continued, to be sure, but they were of a superficial and passing nature. Russia no longer had to go to school to Western Europe. No Karamzin or Vyazemski or Pushkin could now declare that Russia had no literature worthy of notice. Turgenev, Dostoevski, and Tolstoi were already beginning to write, and soon Russia in her turn was to be the benefactor of Western Europe. But throughout her long period of development, from the time of Ivan the Terrible through the reign of Nicholas I, Russia's contact with English culture and literature never ceased, and her obligations are profound and significant.

BIBLIOGRAPHY

Bibliographical Studies

V. I. Maslov, *Nachalny period baironizma v Rossii*, Kiev, 1915. (Contains a bibliography of Russian journal literature on Byron, 1818-30; see Prilozhenie I; a complete list of translations from Byron, 1819-30; see Prilozhenie II; and a selected list of the important investigations on Russian Byronism up to 1915; see pp. 33-36.)

N. K. Piksanov, *Dva veka russkoi literatury*, Moskva, 1923. (See pp. 105-106.)

Investigations

Russian Byronism

M. Zdziechowski, *Byron i jego wiek*, Krakowie, 1897. (See vol. II.)

N. K. Kozmin, *Ocherki iz istorii russkago romantizma*, St. Petersburg, 1903. (See *ukazatel* under "Bairon".)

A. Veselovski, "Etiudy o baironizme" (*Etiudy i kharakhteristiki*, Moskva, 1907, pp. 388-564).

I. I. Zamotin, *Romantizm dvadtsatykh godov XIX stoletiya v russkoi literature*, Moskva, 1911-13. (See *ukazatel* under "Bairon," vols. I-II.)

A. Veselovski, *Bairon*, Moskva, 1914.

N. M. Danilov, "I. I. Kozlov" (*Izvestiya otdeleniya russkago yazyka i slovesnosti Imperatorskoi Akademii Nauk*, Petrograd, 1914, XIX, 153-175).

V. I. Maslov, *Nachalny period baironizma v Rossii*, Kiev, 1915.

A. P. Grossman, "Russkie baironisty" (*Bairon*, sbornik statei, Moskva, 1924, pp. 61-76).

Pushkin and Byron

V. D. Spasovich, "Baironizm y Pushkina" (*Sochineniya*, St. Petersburg, 1889, II, 293-340).

V. V. Sipovski, "Pushkin, Bairon i Shatobrian" (*Pushkin, zhizn i tvorchestvo*, St. Petersburg, 1907, pp. 477 ff.).

N. P. Dashkevich, "Otgoloski uvlecheniya Baironom v poezii Pushkina" (*Sbornik otdeleniya russkago yazyka i solvesnosti Imperatorskoi Akademii Nauk*, Petrograd, 1914, XCII, 330-397).

M. Mindalev, "K voprosu o baironizme v tvorchestve Pushkina" (*Vestnik obrazovaniya i vospitaniya*, St. Petersburg, 1914, No. 12).

V. Zhirmunski, *Bairon i Pushkin*, Leningrad, 1924.

N. K. Kozmin "Pushkin o Bairone" (*Pushkin v mirovoi literature*, Leningrad, 1926, pp. 99–112).

E. J. Simmons, "Byron and a Greek Maid" (*Modern Language Review*, London, 1932, XXVII, No. 3, pp. 318–323).

Lermontov and Byron

V. D. Spasovich, "Baironizm u Lermontova" (*Sochineniya*, St. Petersburg, 1889, II, 343–406).

P. Viskovatov, "Biografiya Lermontova" (*Sochineniya Lermontova*, Moskva, 1891, vol. VI).

V. O. Kliuchevski, "Grust" (*Russkaya mysl*, 1891, No. 7, pp. 1–18).

E. Duchesne, *Michel Iouriévitch Lermontov*, Paris, 1910, pp. 244–288).

N. A. Kotlyarevski, *Lermontov*, 4-e izd., St. Petersburg, 1911.

N. P. Dashkevich, "Motivy mirovoi poezii v tvorchestve Lermontova" (*Sbornik otdeleniya russkago yazyka i slovesnosti Imperatorskoi Akademii Nauk*, Petrograd, 1914, XCII, 411–514).

M. N. Rozanov, "Baironicheskie motivy v tvorchestve Lermontova" (*Sbornik, Venok Lermontovu*, Moskva, 1914, pp. 313–384).

M. Breitman, "Lermontov, Bairon i Shendolle" (*Vestnik literatury*, 1922, Nos. 2–3).

NOTES

NOTES

CHAPTER I

1. E. Lodge, *Illustrations of British History, Biography, and Manners,* London, 1791 (1838 ed., II, 46).

2. Verse Epistle to Parker. Turberville's three verse epistles written from Russia are reprinted in Hakluyt's *Voyages,* London, 1927, II, 107.

3. Iu. Tolstoi, *Pervyya sorok let snoshenii mezhdu Rossieiu i Anglieiu,* St. Petersburg, 1875, p. 114, No. 28.

4. Cf. *The Travels of Sir Jerome Horsey (Russia at the Close of the Six-teenth Century,* ed. E. A. Bond, London, 1856, pp. 173–174). Horsey's narrative of his life in Russia, while extremely interesting, is filled with exaggerations, misstatements, and stupid authentications of mere rumors.

5. Cf. Tolstoi, *op. cit.,* p. xxxvi.

6. *Ibid.,* p. 30, No. 8.

CHAPTER II

1. Horsey, *op. cit.,* p. 217.

2. *Ibid.,* pp. 232–233.

3. Cf. *ibid.,* p. 228.

4. *Sbornik imperatorskago russkago istoricheskago obshchestva,* 1883, vol. XXXVIII (Donesenie Mikulina, p. 331).

5. *Ibid.,* p. 340.

6. *Ibid.*

7. *A voiag of ambasad,* 1618. (Cf. J. Hamel, *Tradescant der aeltere 1618 in Russland,* St. Petersburg, 1845.)

8. Bodleian Library, MS. James, 43. (Cf. F. E. Korsh, *Velikorusskiya pesni, zapisannyya v 1619–20 dlya Richarda Dzhemsa,* St. Petersburg, 1907.)

9. *A Newe enterlude, drawen out of the Holy Scripture, of godly Queene Hester, verye necessary:* newly made and imprinted MDLXI (reprinted 1863, ed. J. P. Collier).

10. Cf. N. Tikhonravov, *Russkiya dramaticheskiya proizvedeniya, 1672–1725 godov,* St. Petersburg, 1874, I, 204.

CHAPTER III

1. G. Oudard, *Peter the Great,* New York, 1929, p. 100.

2. John Cook, *Voyages and Travels Through the Russian Empire, Tatary, and Part of the Kingdom of Persia,* Hamilton, ed. 1778, pp. 56–57.

3. See the *Memoirs of Peter Henry Bruce*, London, 1782.

4. *Diplomaticheskaya perepiska angliskikh poslov i poslannikov pri russkom dvore, c 1704–1708 (Sbornik imperatorskago russkago istoricheskago obshchestva*, 1884, XXXIX, 263).

5. Cf. A. Veselovski, *Zapadnoe vliyanie v novoi russkoi literature*, Moskva, 1897 (5–e izd., 1916, p. 34).

6. Cf. *Sochineniya pisma i izbrannye perevody Knyazya Antiokha Dmitrievicha Kantemira*, red. P. A. Efremova, St. Petersburg, 1862, II, 99–100.

7. Cf. *ibid.*, I, 152 ff. For a parallel passage comparison see V. N. Aleksandrenko, *Russkie diplomaticheskie agenty v Londone v XVIII v.*, Varshava, 1897, I, 384, n. 1.

8. *Ibid.*, I, 385, n. 3.

CHAPTER IV

1. See particularly *Truten*, 1769–70; *Zhivopisets*, 1772–73; and *Koshelek*, 1774.

2. Often English and German periodicals satirizing French influence were the direct inspiration for these Russian articles.

3. *Chudaki*, II, 2.

4. *Neschastie ot karety*, I, 5.

5. *Brigadir*, III, 2.

6. One of the best studies on the subject is that of J. Texte, *Jean-Jacques Rousseau and the Cosmopolitan Spirit in Literature* (translated by J. Matthews), London, 1899.

7. *The Memoires of the Life of Edward Gibbon*, ed. G. Hill, London, 1900, p. 151.

8. Thus I. I. Shuvalov, fearful of the influence of the Encyclopedists on questions of religion and morals, writes to M. Vorontsov: "The English writers, even at the very time of changing their laws, tried to refute superstitions, yet they held the dogmas holy and in honor." (*Arkhiv Vorontsova*, Moskva, 1870–95, IV, 305.)

9. "Angliskaya progulka" (*Zhivopisets*, 1772, I, No. 13).

10. A good study of England's importance and influence in the development of Russian commerce in the eighteenth century is that of D. Gerhard, *England und der Aufstieg Russlands*, München und Berlin, 1933, chapter II.

11. Cf. *Lekartsvo ot skuki i zabot*, St. Petersburg, 1786, No. 2, pp. 35–36; *Magazin anglinskikh, frantsuzskikh i nemetskikh novykh mod*, St. Petersburg, 1791.

12. J. Carr, *A Northern Summer*, London, 1805, p. 293.

13. *Opyt trudov, Volnago rossiskago sobraniya*, Moskva, 1774, II, 106. Cf. also *Ippokrena, ili utekhi liubosloviya*, Moskva, 1799, I, 49–88; *Moskovski merkuri*, Moskva, 1803, I, 19–40.

14. See such journals as *Moskovskiya vedomosti*, Moskva, 1756, *et seq.*, *Sobranie novostei*, St. Petersburg, 1775; *Politicheski zhurnal*, Moskva, 1790–93.

15. Cf. *Satiricheski vestnik*, Moskva, 1790, I, 22, 79.

16. *Trudy, Volnago ekonomicheskago obshchestva*, St. Petersburg, 1765, p. 2.

17. For some illustrative articles on these themes see the following: *Ekonomicheskoi magazin*, Moskva, 1780, II, 196–203; *Akademicheskiya izvestiya*, St. Petersburg, 1780, IV, 529–548; *Ezhenedelnyya izvestiya, volnago ekonomicheskago obshchestva*, St. Petersburg, 1788, Nos. 53, 90, 94, 99, 105, 122, 124; 1789, Nos. 227, 243, 244; *Prodolzhenie trudov volnago ekonomicheskago obshchestva*, St. Petersburg, 1700, IX, No. XI.

18. "Baryshnya-krestyanka" (*Povesti Belkina*).

19. *Pisma imperatritsy Ekateriny II k Grimmu*, izd. Ya. Grota (*Sbornik imperatorskago russkago istoricheskago obshchestva*, St. Petersburg, 1878, t. XXIII. See 27 août, 1775).

20. *Diplomaticheskaya perepiska angliskikh poslov i poslannikov pri russkom dvore* (*Sbornik russkago istoricheskago obshchestva*, St. Petersburg, 1873, XII, 382). See *ibid.*, pp. 69, 87–88, 97; 1876, XIX, 3, 50, 123–124.

21. *Ibid.*, pp. 123–124.

22. *Ibid.*, pp. 475–477.

23. "Conversation de Sir Harris avec L'Impératrice de Russie, 1780" (P. Fauchille, *La diplomatie française et la ligue des neutres de 1780*, Paris, 1893, p. 588).

24. For an account of the considerable services rendered by the Scots in Catherine's reign, see A. Francis Steuart, *Scottish Influences in Russian History*, Glasgow, 1913, pp. 119–137.

25. K. Waliszewski, *Autour d'un trône*, Paris, 1894, p. 405.

26. Dymsdale's pamphlet, *The Present Method of Inoculating for Smallpox*, was translated into Russian in 1770.

27. Cf. *L'esprit des lois*, book XIX, chapter XXVII; book XX, chapter VIII.

28. *Pisma, op. cit.*, p. 52.

29. A. Radishchev, *Puteshestvie iz Peterburya v Moskvu*, 1790 (Podbereze).

30. See pp. 64, 69.

31. Cf. *Arkhiv Vorontsova*, IX, 145, 160–161.

32. V. Ikonnikov, *Gr. N. S. Mordvinov*, St. Petersburg, 1873, p. 75. For a consideration of English influence on Mordvinov, see *ibid.*, pp. 4 ff.

33. See p. 53.

34. "Je suis si pénétré de cette situation que, si je n'étais attaché à ma patrie par des liens aussi indissolubles, et ayant à choisir en même temps le pays auquel je devrais consacrer et ma vie et mes travaux, l'Angleterre serait sans aucun doute celui que je choisirais par affection autant que par conviction." (*Arkhiv Kurakina*, St. Petersburg, 1890–99, VI, 333.)

35. See pp. 60–61.

36. See pp. 69–70.

37. *Arkhiv Vorontsova*, XXXI, 439.

38. Cf. A. Pypin, *Obshchestvennoe dvizhenie v Rossii pri Alexandre I*, St. Petersburg, 1885, p. 89.

39. Cf. V. N. Aleksandrenko, *op. cit.*, II, 176 ff.

40. *Arkhiv Vorontsova*, IX, 99.

41. Collected in the *Arkhiv Vorontsova*.

42. *Ibid.*, X, 88.

43. Cf. *ibid.*, XV, 199.

CHAPTER V

1. *Ezhemesyachnyya sochineniya k polze i uveseleniiu sluzhashchiya*, 1757–62.

2. *Prazdnoe vremya v polzu upotreblennoe*, 1759–60.

3. *Trudoliubivaya pchela*, 1759.

4. *Poleznoe uveselenie*, 1760–62.

5. *Nevinnoe uprazhnenie*, 1763.

6. *Svobodnyya chasy*, 1763.

7. *Dobroe namerenie*, 1764.

8. *Zabavny filosof* (translator, L. Sichkarev), St. Petersburg, 1766, Introduction, p. 1. It is very likely that the book is a translation of a selected collection of English periodical essays.

9. Reprinted under the title of *Zritel mira*, St. Petersburg, 1784. More tales are added in the reprint (in all there are thirty-four tales and essays) along with a number of poems from the best Russian writers. The translated material is drawn from the *Tatler*, *Spectator*, *Guardian*, *World*, *Gentleman's Magazine*, *Rambler*, and the *Adventurer*.

10. Cf. "Dnevnik Petra Danilovicha Apostola" (*Kievskaya Starina*, 1895, L, 126).

11. Folio 138. Cf. P. Pekarski, *Istoriya Imperatorskoi Akademii Nauk*, St. Petersburg, 1870–73, II, 26.

12. Pismo ot 1-go Fevralya (cf. P. Pekarski, *op. cit.*, II, 26).

13. *Primechaniya v vedomostyakh.* There are at least eleven translations from the *Spectator* in this journal, extending from 1731 to 1735. For a full list of these and other translations from the *Spectator* mentioned in this chapter, see the bibliography at the end of the chapter.

14. *Vsyakaya vsyachina,* St. Petersburg, 1769.

15. *Ibid.,* pp. 123–124.

16. *Spectator,* No. 58.

17. *Vsyakaya vsyachina* (Ko chitateliu).

18. *Truten,* St. Petersburg, 1769, XX, No. 33.

19. V. Solntsev, "*Vsyakaya vsyachina* i *Spectator*" (*Zhurnal ministerstva narodnago prosveshcheniya,* Yanvar, 1892, pp. 132–148). Solntsev points out that it was a French translation of the *Spectator* that was used by the editors of *All Sorts and Sundries.* For a complete list of the translations from the *Spectator,* see the bibliography.

20. Solntsev, *op. cit.,* p. 148.

21. *Ibid.,* pp. 149–154.

22. *Ibid.,* p. 156.

23. The best known were *Poleznoe s priyatnym,* 1769, *I to i sio,* 1769, *Ni to ni sio,* 1769, *Podenshchina,* 1769, *Adskaya pochta,* 1769, *Truten,* 1769, *Pustomelya,* 1770, *Trudoliubivy muravei,* 1771, *Zhivopisets,* 1772, *Koshelek,* 1774.

24. A. Afanasev, *Russkie satiricheskie zhurnaly,* Kazan, 1871, p. 9. Cf. also P. Bulich, *Sumarokov i sovremennaya emu kritika,* St. Petersburg, 1854, p. 217.

25. V. Solntsev, *op. cit.,* p. 156.

26. *Truten,* St. Petersburg, 1769–70.

27. *Zhivopisets,* St. Petersburg, 1772–73.

28. *Koshelek,* St. Petersburg, 1774.

29. *Adskaya pochta,* St. Petersburg, 1769.

30. For a list of the translations, see the bibliography.

31. For a list of translations from these periodicals, see the bibliography.

32. The whole complicated question of the debt of the Russians to the English periodicals of this period would require a detailed analysis of every Russian journal. Such a work was promised by V. Lazurski as a companion volume to his excellent study, *Satiriko-nravouchitelnye zhurnaly Steele i Addison,* Odessa, 1909, but it was never done.

33. "O stikhotvorstve" (*Poleznoe uveselenie,* Moskva, 1762, IV, 195–220, 227–243).

34. *Ibid.,* p. 231.

35. *Ibid.*, p. 232.

36. See Voltaire, *Siècle de Louis XIV* (*Des beaux-arts en Europe*, chapter XXXIV). As a matter of fact, the Russian critic follows Voltaire's opinions on English literature very closely in this work, only occasionally hazarding a judgment of his own.

37. "O stikhotvorstve," *op. cit.*, p. 233.

38. *Opyt trudov, Volnago rossiskago sobraniya*, Moskva, 1775, X, 257–261.

39. References for these, and for all other translations of English authors in the journals, are listed in the bibliography.

40. *Ippokrena, ili utekhi liubosloviya*, Moskva, 1801, IX, No. 25, p. 241.

41. "O epicheskom stikhotvorstve" (*Nevinnoe uprazhnenie*, Moskva, 1763. For his treatment of Milton, see pp. 143–155. The article is not signed, but the author is probably the editor of the journal, I. F. Bogdanovich. He no doubt got his inspiration for the article from Voltaire's *Essai sur la poésie épique*, chapter IX of which is devoted to Milton. Although he may be indebted to some extent to Voltaire, the critic is not afraid to venture his own opinions, and in various matters he questions the French critics of Milton.

42. *Ibid.*, p. 145.

43. He refers to Dryden's *Epigram on Milton*.

44. "O epicheskom stikhotvorstve," *op. cit.*, p. 145.

45. *Ibid.*

46. "Milton" (*Korifei, ili kliuch literatury*, St. Petersburg, 1802, III, 1–220). The author was probably the editor, I. A. Galinkovski. The study includes a translation of Addison's *Spectator* essays on Milton.

47. See *Vestnik Evropy*, Moskva, 1802, IV, 312–313. The unknown author of this anecdote begins by telling us that "love is one of the most powerful of all forces in the growth of genius." He then relates how Milton, when at Cambridge, was playing with some companions on the bank of a river. Becoming tired, he lay down under a tree and fell sound asleep. Two foreign ladies driving by saw the handsome youth. They got out of their carriage and stood for several minutes gazing at him. Finally one of them, "young and beautiful," wrote several lines on a piece of paper and placed it beneath the sleeping Milton. "Farewell Adonis!" they said, and quickly drove off. The companions of Milton, who had observed the whole affair, roused him and told him of the visit. He found the paper and with rapture read certain love verses of the Italian poet, Guarini. From this time on, writes the author, Milton thought ceaselessly of the charming unknown damsel and searched for her in England and Italy. "She influenced his imagination and he began to write verse. Thus to this

young woman of the age of Milton, we and posterity are indebted for one of the best productions of the mind of man, — *Paradise Lost!*"

48. The letter is apropos of Lady Dorothy's marriage.

49. An imitation, *Novy Gulliver*, appeared in 1791.

50. Derzhavin was influenced by this famous tale in his poem, *Videnie Murzy*, 1783.

51. *Istoricheskiya dokazatelstva bozhestvennosti Iisusa Khrista*, St. Petersburg, 1816.

52. *Legkomyslov, poluchivshi zdravy razsudok, otryvki iroid, i stikhotvorenie g. Addison na Rizvikski mir*, St. Petersburg, 1777.

53. Voltaire, *Art dramatique* ("D'Addison").

54. There is also a separate translation, dated 1804.

55. Voltaire, Siècle de Louis XIV (*Des beaux-arts en Europe*, chapter XXXIV).

56. See pp. 114, 116.

57. *Opyt o cheloveke gospodina Pope*, pereveden s frantsusskago yazyka Nikolaem Popovskim, St. Petersburg, 1754 (Predislovie, p. 5).

58. Cf. Veselovski, *op. cit.*, p. 118, n. 2.

59. *Opyt o cheloveke gospodina Pope, op. cit.* (Predislovie, p. 1).

60. There were two editions of this, 1761 and 1790.

61. Cf. *Utrennie chasy*, 1788, II, 25–32.

62. Cf. "Razsuzhdenie o Pope" (*S. Peterburgski merkuri*, 1793, II, 69–76).

CHAPTER VI

1. "Opasnost ot chteniya romanov" (*Pokoiushchisya trudoliubets*, 1784, I, 9).

2. A. T. Bolotov, *Zapiski*, St. Petersburg, 1871, I, 825.

3. Cf. P. Miliukov, *Ocherki po istorii russkoi kultury*, St. Petersburg, 1909–13, Part III, p. 228.

4. *Gespräche mit Goethe von Eckermann* (December 3, 1824).

5. For a discussion of Richardon's influence on Rousseau and Goethe, see J. Texte, *Jean Jacques Rousseau and the Cosmopolitan Spirit in Literature* (translated by J. Matthews), London, 1899; E. Schmidt, *Richardson, Rousseau und Goethe*, Jena, 1875.

6. See N. Belozerskaya, *Vasili Trofimovich Narezhny*, St. Petersburg, 1896, pp. 30–33.

7. The other editions appeared in 1775, 1787, 1792.

8. It is very possible that *Pamela* circulated in a manuscript translation earlier than 1787. Cf. A. Pypin, *Dlya liubitelei knizhnoi stariny*, Moskva, 1888 (see under "Richardson").

9. *Zapiski*, II, 34–35. Cf. also I, 30, 130.

10. "Avtobiograficheskiya zapiski Egora Fedorovicha fon Bradke" (*Russki arkhiv*, 1875, I, 19).

11. *Utra*, 1782, p. 160.

12. "O chtenii romanov voobshche i angliskikh v osobennosti" (*Rossiski muzeum*, 1815, IV, 111–112). For examples of similar criticism of Richardson in the journals, see S. *Peterburgski merkuri*, 1793, IV, 156–172; "Nechto o romanakh" (*Priyatnoe i poleznoe preprovozhdenie vremeni*, 1795, VI); *Patriot*, 1804, II, 205–214; "Roman i komediya" (*Aglaya*, 1809, VI).

13. *Pamela, ili nagrazhdennaya dobrodetel*, St. Petersburg, 1787; see "pismo k izdateliu."

14. *Neonila*, sochinenie A. L., Moskva, 1794, I, 85.

15. V. V. Sipovski, *Ocherki iz istorii russkago romana*, St. Petersburg, 1910, I, 2.

16. A. Pushkin, *Pisma*, red. B. Modzalevskogo, Moskva, 1926, I, 98, No. 106.

17. "Mysli na doroge" (*Pushkin*, red. S. Vengerova, V, 247).

18. Cf. *Evgeni Onegin*, III, ix.

19. *Pisma russkago puteshestvennika*, izd. A. Smirdina, St. Petersburg, 1848, p. 679.

20. *Evgeni Onegin*, II, xxx.

21. P. Lvov, *Rossiskaya Pamela, ili istoriya Marii, dobrodetelnoi poselyanki*, St. Petersburg, 1789.

22. *Ibid.*, predislovie.

23. N. Emin, *Roza, poluspravedlivaya povest*, St. Petersburg, 1786.

24. Cf. *ibid.*, I, 30.

25. *Igra sudby*, St. Petersburg, 1798.

26. *Bednaya Liza*, Moskva, 1792.

27. From 1763 through 1800 only thirty-two original Russian novels appeared.

28. The following works were erroneously ascribed to Fielding: *Sposob byt dobrodetelnym, ili dostopamyatnyya pokhozhdeniya kavalera Kilpara*, St. Petersburg, 1776 (no doubt Montagnac's *Mémoires du Chevalier de Kilpar*, Paris, 1768); *Pokhozhdenie Rodrika Randoma*, Moskva, 1788 (Smollett's *Roderick Random*); *Puteshestvie Gumfriya Klingera*, St. Petersburg, 1789 (Smollett's *Humphry Clinker*); *Neshchastiya ot chuvstvitelnosti*, Moskva, 1791 (*Misfortune of Being Sensitive*).

29. There were three editions of *Joseph Andrews*, 1770, 1772, 1787; two of *Tom Jones*, 1770–71, 1787; and three of *Jonathan Wild*, 1772, 1783, 1785–86.

30. *Zerkalo sveta*, St. Petersburg, 1786, No. 30, pp. 230–231.

31. *Prikliucheniya Josifa Andrevsa*, St. Petersburg, 1772 (Predislovie perevodchika).

32. For examples see V. V. Sipovski, *Iz istorii russkago romana i povesti*, St. Petersburg, 1903, pp. 173, 175.

33. The best critical comparison of the two authors is to be found in *Syn otechestva*, 1834, Part CLXVII.

34. It is worth noting that of the many English classics that have become, so to speak, nationalized in Russia, *Tom Jones* has remained well in the van of the list. It was much read throughout the nineteenth century, and even Soviet youths are not impervious to its charm. Indeed, a new translation appeared as recently as 1931.

35. Cf. "Nechto o romanakh" (*Priyatnoe i poleznoe preprovozhdenie vremeni*, 1795, VI, 109).

36. *Vakefildskoi svyashchennik, istoriya*, Moskva, 1786 (see Predislovie ot perevodchika).

37. Cf. N. Belozerskaya, "Vliyanie perevodnago romana i zapadnoi tsivilizatsii na russkoe obshchestvo XVIII v." (*Russkaya starina*, 1895, LXXXIII, 149).

38. M. A. Dmitriev, *Melochi iz zapasa moei pamyati*, Moskva, 1869, p. 47.

39. *Ibid.*, p. 48.

40. "Dubrovski" (*Pushkin*, red. Vengerova, IV, 309).

41. "Elizaveta Petrovna Glebova-Streshneva (1751–1837). Po vospominaniyam vnuchki eya Natalii Petrovny Brevern" (*Russki arkhiv*, 1895, I, 97).

42. F. Vigel, *Zapiski*, Moskva, 1928, I, 111.

43. P. Shalikov, *Plod svobodnykh chuvstvovani*, Moskva, 1798–1801, III, 10–11.

44. "O nekotorykh noveshikh angliskikh romanakh" (*Liubitel slovesnosti*, 1806, II). *Prince Bova* and *Eruslan Lazarevich* are seventeenth-century Russian versions of mediaeval Carolingian and Oriental romances.

45. *Ippokrena, ili utekhi liubosloviya*, 1799, I, 510–511. Cf. *ibid.*, II, 261.

46. P. Shalikov, *op. cit.*, III, 11.

47. Cf. A. Grigorev, *Vospominaniya*, Moskva, 1930, pp. 67, 128, 137–138, 143.

48. *Syn otechestva*, 1826, Parts CV, CVI.

49. *Moskovski merkuri*, 1803, I, 218–225. It must be added in extenuation here that the critic is laboring under the impression that Radcliffe wrote the *Monk*, one of the many books erroneously ascribed to her.

50. *Vestnik Evropy*, 1807, Part XXXIV.

51. "Otryvok iz knigi" (*Sorevnovatel prosveshcheniya*, 1825, No. 7).

52. *Kharkovski demokrit*, 1816, No. 5.

53. Mrs. Sheridan, *History of Nourjahad*, 1780, 1792; Beckford, *Vathek*, 1792; Inchbald, *A Simple Story*, 1794; Burney, *Cecilia*, 1794, *Evelina*, 1798, 1800; Johnson, *Rasselas*, 1795; S. Fielding, *David Simple*, 1796; Aphra Behn, *Oroonoko*, 1796.

54. *Priyatnoe i poleznoe preprovozhdenie vremeni*, 1778, XVIII, 319.

55. *Liubitel slovesnosti*, 1806, II.

56. *Vestnik Evropy*, 1807, XXXIV.

57. *Rossiski muzeum*, 1815, IV.

58. "O knizhnoi torgovle i liubvi ko chteniiu v Rossii" (*Sochineniya*, izd. Smirdina, St. Petersburg, 1848, III, 548–549).

CHAPTER VII

1. Cf. *Spring*, ll. 388–389.

2. I am aware that critics of *The Seasons* consider Thomson's attitude towards nature quite objective. But there are many passages in which the poet expounds his own views, reactions, and emotions, and it was these passages that particularly impressed his foreign admirers.

3. A small fragment from *The Seasons* was translated as early as 1779 in *Novaya selskaya biblioteka*, St. Petersburg, 1779, II, 132, 412. For periodical renderings, see p. 131.

4. It is worth observing in this connection that Karamzin may well have been inspired by English historians in his great work, *The History of the Russian Empire*. In his *Letters of a Russian Traveller* he writes: "It is unfortunate, but it must be said, that up to this time we have had no fine Russian history, that is, nothing adorned with the philosophical cleverness, criticism, and noble eloquence of a Tacitus, Hume, Robertson, or Gibbon — here are models!" (*Pisma russkago puteshestvennika, Sochineniya Karamzina*, izd. A. Smirdina, St. Petersburg, 1848, II, 511).

5. *Pisma russkago puteshestvennika*, *op. cit.*, II, 659.

6. First printed in the *Moskovski zhurnal*, 1792, III, 260–275. A sorry indication of the progress of Russian literature up to this time is the fact that Karamzin did not consider it worth while to mention one native poet in this work.

7. "Poeziya" (*Sochineniya Karamzina*, Izdanie Otdeleniya russkago yazyka i slovesnosti Akademii Nauk, Petrograd, 1917, I, 11).

8. He may have used the Edinburgh 1780 edition of *The Seasons*.

9. Cf. *Pisma russkago puteshestvennika, op. cit.*, II, 684.

10. Cf. *Ibid.*, II, 219. He quotes from *Autumn*, ll. 209–214. See also *ibid.*, II, 403–404.

11. *Ibid.*, II, 746. Incidentally, this whole section on English literature is proof of the statement (see p. 114) that Karamzin was among the first in Russia to have anything like a correct perspective of English literary history. His account is in sharp contrast to the anonymous survey written some thirty years earlier and already commented on (see pp. 113–114).

12. *Detskoe chtenie dlya serdtsa i razuma*, Moskva, 1789, XI.

13. *Pisma russkago puteshestvennika, op. cit.*, II, 71.

14. *Detskoe chtenie*, 1789, XVIII, 162.

15. *Pisma russkago puteshestvennika, op. cit.*, II, 107.

16. "Derevnya" (*Sochineniya Karamzina*, III, 461).

17. "Anakreonticheskie stikhi" (*Detskoe chtenie*, 1789, XVIII, 93–95).

18. *Chetyre vremeni goda*, perev. D. I. Dimitrevski, Moskva, 1798, pp. iv–v. This is a prose translation from the German with the concluding *Hymn on the Seasons* (pp. 503–516) done into Russian Alexandrines.

19. For examples of such compositions, see the following: "Autumn" (*Detskoe chtenie dlya serdtsa i razuma*, 1787, XI, 193–207); "Winter" (*Novyya ezhemesyachnyya sochineniya*, 1796, CXV, 81–82); "Winter" (*Muza*, 1796, I, 128–138, 181–185); "Winter" (*Ippokrena, ili utekhi liubosloviya*, 1799, I, 517–520); "A Picture of Winter" (*ibid.*, II, 29–31); "The Winter Season" (*ibid.*, III, 31); "Winter" (*ibid.*, 1801, VIII, 385–390); "Autumn" (*ibid.*, XI, 13–16); "Winter" (*Novosti russkoi literatury*, 1802, pp. 95–96).

20. Cf. *Ippokrena*, 1801, IX, 66 ff.

21. *Ippokrena, ili utekhi liubosloviya* and *Priyatnoe i poleznoe preprovozhdenie vremeni*.

22. *Ippokrena*, 1800, VII, 15–16.

23. *Ibid.*, VII, 159–160.

24. V. Zhukovski, *Dnevnik*, St. Petersburg, 1901, p. 6.

25. *Chetyre vremeni goda*, St. Petersburg, 1795. I have been unable to obtain a copy of this work, but from a bibliographical description it would seem that it is closely modelled on Thomson's poem.

26. *Vechera*, 1772, No. 16, pp. 105–136.

27. For a list of the periodical renderings, see p. 131.

28. Cf. *Utrenni svet*, 1777–80.

29. Translated directly from the English.

30. "Poeziya," *op. cit.*, p. 11.

31. Cf. V. V. Sipovski, *N. M. Karamzin*, St. Petersburg, 1899, p. 43.

32. *Pisma russkago puteshestvennika, op. cit.*, II, 749.

33. Cf. "Noch" (*Sochineniya Karamzina, izd.* Smirdina, III, 669, 672).

34. "Sila geniya" (*Aonidy*, 1797, II, 125). Cf. *ibid.*, p. 171.

35. *Ippokrena*, 1799, II, 322.

36. "Mysli o smerti i vechnosti" (*Chtenie dlya vkusa, razuma i chuvst-vovani*, 1791, III, 118).

37. "Smert Narcissa" (*Irtysh prevrashchaiushchisya v ippokrenu*, Tobolsk, 1789, I, 2).

38. *Aglaya*, Moskva, 1808, I, 78–79.

39. Young was his "favorite author." Cf. *Pisma i dnevnik Aleksandra Ivanovicha Turgeneva, 1802–1804*, St. Petersburg, 1911, p. 87.

40. His early "Mysli pri grobnitse" shows the influence of Young. Cf. A. N. Veselovski, *V. A. Zhukovski*, Petrograd, 1918, p. 45.

41. *Zapiski Sergeya Nikolaevicha Glinki*, St. Petersburg, 1895, p. 363.

42. N. Emin, *Roza, poluspravedlivaya povest*, St. Petersburg, 1786, I, 15. See also, I, 18, 20, 30–33, 113–114.

43. *Ibid.*, I, 10.

44. "Felita" (*Ippokrena*, 1799, II, 374–375). Cf. also, A. Klushin, "Neshchastny" (*S. Peterburgski merkuri*, 1793, No. 3, pp. 158–159).

45. For examples see the following, A. Stolypin, "Otryvok" (*Priyatnoe i poleznoe preprovozhdenie vremeni*, 1795, VII, 220–221); G. Kamenev, "Sofya' (*Muza*, 1796, I, No. 3, p. 198); Galinkovski, *Chasy zadumchivosti*, Moskva, 1799, p. 19.

46. Cf. "Description of Night" (*Dobroe namerenie*, 1764, pp. 362–372); "Night" (*Moskovskoe ezhemesyachnoe izdanie*, 1781, III, 285–286); "Night Thoughts" (*Pokoiushchisya trudoliubets*, 1785, XX, 138–141); "Night" (*Utrennie chasy*, 1788, III, 152–157); "My Night" (*Ippokrena*, 1799, II, 263–272); "Complaint at Night" (*ibid.*, II, 363–364); "Evening" (*Novosti russkoi literatury*, 1802, I, 85–91).

47. "Poeziya," *op. cit.*, p. 10.

48. *Poemy drevnikh bardov*. No doubt a rendering of the second part of *Choix de contes de poésies erses*, Amsterdam, 1772.

49. Cf. *Ukatzatel k opytu rossiskoi bibliografii*, V. S. Sopikova, St. Petersburg, 1908, Nos. 8742, 11544, 11545.

50. *Ossian, syn Fingalov*.

51. Cf. N. Trubitsyn, *O narodnoi poezii*, St. Petersburg, 1912, p. 372.

52. "K. D." (*Sochineniya Karamzina, izd.* Smirdina, I, 44).

53. *Pisma russkago puteshestvennika, op. cit.*, II, 139.

54. *Ibid.*, II, 433.

55. Afterwards published in the *Moskovski zhurnal*, 1791, II, 115–147.

56. *Pisma russkago puteshestvennika, op. cit.*, II, 786.

57. *Moskovski zhurnal*, 1791, II, 116–119.

58. Especially in *Evgeni i Iuliya* (1789), *Bednaya Liza* (1792), *Liodor* (1792), *Natalya, boyarskaya doch* (1792), *Marfa posadnitsa* (1803).

59. See, for example, *Bednaya Liza*, description of the Semenov Monastery and the farewell between Liza and Erast; *Marfa posadnitsa*, description of the storm at night in the beginning of the second book.

60. Cf. *Sochineniya Karamzina, op. cit.*, pp. 15–16, 19–20, 39–40.

61. Cf. "Ossian" (*Panteon inostrannoi slovesnosti*, Moskva, 1798, I, 200–201).

62. See the MS. of Shishkov, "Shchtenie dvukh russkikh perevodov s italiyanskago iz Ossiana" (under the title of "Raznyya zapiski" in the Manuscript Section of the Government Public Library in Leningrad).

63. "Liubov i druzhestvo" (*Moskovski zhurnal*, 1791, III, 227–238).

64. Cf. *Stikhotvoreniya N. Grammatina*, St. Petersburg, 1829, II, 137.

65. Cf. *Moskovski zhurnal*, 1791, III, 134–149.

66. *Na vzyatie Izmaila, Varshavy, Na perekhod Alpiskikh gor.*

67. *Vodopad* (1791).

68. For a detailed study of the influence of Ossian on Derzhavin, see *Sochineniya Derzhavina*, red. Ya. Grota, St. Petersburg, 1864, I, 344, 457–488; VIII, 755.

69. V. V. Kapnist, "Gimn k solntsu slepago startsa Ossiana" (*Aonidy*, Moskva, 1797, pp. 127–130); P. S. Kaisarov, "K lune. Otryvok iz Ossiana" (*Aonidy*, 1797, pp. 269–270).

70. I. Galinkovski, *op. cit.*, p. 96.

71. P. Lvov, "Aleksandr i Iuliya" (*Novosti*, 1799, No. 7, p. 57).

72. Cf. A. Klushin, *op. cit.*, and A. Stolypin, *op. cit.*

73. *Slavenski vechera*, St. Petersburg, 1809. For a study of the borrowings from Ossian, see N. Belozerskaya, *V. T. Narezhny*, St. Petersburg, 1896, pp. 68–69.

74. *Pisma N. M. Karamzina k I. I. Dmitrievu*, St. Petersburg, 1866, p. 474.

75. There is a translation of a ballad, which I have been unable to see, from the *Reliques* in *Priyatnoe i poleznoe preprovozhdenie vremeni*, Moskva, 1795, VI; "Vilyam i Margarita" (*Ippokrena*, 1800, VI, 426–429). This latter is a version of Percy's *Sweet William's Ghost*.

76. N. Trubitsyn, *O narodnoi poezii*, St. Petersburg, 1912, p. 373.

77. Cf. P. Potapov, *Zhizn i deyatelnost V. A. Ozerova*, Odessa, 1915, pp. 551 ff.

78. For a consideration of the influence of Ossian on these authors and for bibliographical details, see the following: N. K. Piksanov, "Etiud o vliyanii ossianovskoi poezii v russkoi literature" (*Pushkin*, red. S. Vengerova, I, 108); I. I. Zamotin, *Romantizm dvadtsatykh godov XIX stoletiya v russkoi literature*, St. Petersburg, 1911, I, 34–48; D. N. Vvedenski, *Etiudy o vliyanii ossianovskoi poezii v russkoi literature*, Nezhin, 1916; V. I. Maslov, "Ossian v Rossii, bibliografiya" (*Trudy Pushkinskogo Doma Akademii Nauk*, 1928, L, 9–57).

79. A. N. Veselovski, *V. A. Zhukovski*, Petrograd, 1918, p. 3.

80. *Selskoe kladbishche. Elegiya.* Zhukovski produced still another version of the *Elegy.*

81. For a list of the periodical translations of Gray, see p. 132. Karamzin likewise contributed to the vogue with his poem "Kladbishche" (*Sochineniya Karamzina*, op. cit., I, 65–66).

82. A. N. Veselovski, *op. cit.*, p. 440.

83. I. I. Zamotin, *op. cit.*, I, 39.

84. V. I. Maslov, "Interes k Sternu v russkoi literature kontsa XVIII i nachala XIX veka" (*Istoriko-literaturny sbornik, posvyashchenny V. I. Sreznevskomu*, Leningrad, 1924, p. 355).

85. *Ibid.*, p. 342.

86. For a list see p. 132.

87. There was another rendering of this in 1795.

88. 1793, 1803, 1806.

89. V. V. Sipovski, *N. M. Karamzin*, St. Petersburg, 1899, p. 69.

90. *Moskovski zhurnal*, 1791, II, 51.

91. *Ibid.*, V, 223.

92. They were published over a period of four years. Half of them appeared in the *Moskovski zhurnal* (1791–92); the second half was printed in *Aglaya* (1794–95). A separate edition appeared in 1797.

93. As far as the actual form of the *Letters* is concerned, certain German and French imitators of the *Sentimental Journal* may have had more direct influence. Cf. V. V. Sipovski, *op. cit.*, pp. 243 ff.

94. *Pisma russkago puteshestvennika*, op. cit., II, 207.

95. *Ibid.*, II, 162.

96. See, for example, the following instances: *ibid.*, II, 22–27, 34, 40–41, 53, 84, 91, 113, 115, 162, 233, 329, 421–423, 543, 552, 653, 737.

97. "Filon" (*Muza*, 1796, II, 59).

98. *Puteshestvie iz Peterburga v Moskvu.*

99. Cf. V. P. Semennikov, *Radishchev; ocherki i issledovaniya*, Moskva, 1923, p. 361.

100. See p. 97, where it is noted that Vorontsov sent him *The Wealth of Nations* in English. His poem "Freedom," included in *A Journey from Petersburg to Moscow* (*Polnoe sobranie sochineni*, Moskva, 1907, pp. 446-452), may well have been inspired by his reading of Milton, especially the stanzas on the killing of the king. Cf. Semennikov, *op. cit.*, p. 218.

101. In a letter to A. R. Vorontsov. Cf. *Arkhiv Vorontsova*, V, 320.

102. Cf. *Polnoe sobranie sochineni*, pp. 351 ff.

103. For example, compare the traveller's visit to a peasant's hut (*ibid.*, pp. 356 ff.) with a similar visit of Sterne in his chapter, "The Supper"; also compare the opening chapters of each work. For a detailed study of the borrowings, see Semennikov, *op. cit.*, pp. 443 ff.

104. For bibliography and details see V. V. Sipovski, *op. cit.*, pp. 457 ff.

105. "Voyazh moego druga" (*Priyatnoe i poleznoe preprovozhdenie vremeni*, 1798, XVII, 97).

106. G. Kamenev, "Sofya" (*Muza*, 1796, I, 208–209).

107. See, for example, "Filon" (*Muza*, 1796, II, 58–59); Galinkovski, *Chasy zadumchivosti*, Moskva, 1799, pp. 11–12, 19; *Milyya, nezhnyya serdtsa*, Moskva, 1800.

108. Cf. A. N. Veselovski, *op. cit.*, p. 51.

109. Cf. B. L. Modzalevski, *Biblioteka Pushkina*, St. Petersburg, 1910, pp. 147, 343.

110. *Pisma*, red. B. L. Modzalevskogo, Moskva, 1926, I, 25, No. 3.

111. Cf. B. L. Modzalevski, "Pushkin i Sterne" (*Russki sovremennik*, 1924, No. 2, p. 193).

112. *Ibid.*, p. 193.

113. *Ibid.*

114. For the possible influence of Sterne on Gogol's tales, see V. Vinogradov, "Siuzhet i kompozitsiya povesti Gogolya" (*Nachala*, 1921, No. 1, p. 83).

115. Cf. V. I. Maslov, *op. cit.*

116. Cf. M. K. Azadovski, "Sterne v vospriyatiyakh dekabristov" (*Bunt Dekabristov*, Leningrad, 1926, pp. 382–392).

117. *Ibid.*, p. 384.

118. *Novy Sterne*, St. Petersburg, 1805. (I have used the second edition, 1822.)

119. For contemporary reaction to the play, see *Severny vestnik*, St. Petersburg, 1805, VIII, 105–123.

CHAPTER VIII

1. See pp. 40–42.

2. Cf. P. Morozov, *Ocherki iz istorii russkoi dramy XVII–XVIII stoleti*, St. Petersburg, 1888, p. 266.

3. *Polnoe sobranie sochineni*, Moskva, 1787, X, 103.

4. Cf. G. Shchebalski, "Dramaticheskiya proizvedeniya Ekateriny II" (*Russki vestnik*, 1871, No. 6, p. 780).

5. See pp. 114–115.

6. Cf. *Dramaticheski slovar*, Moskva, 1787, p. 57.

7. See pp. 107–109.

8. J. J. Eschenburg, *William Shakespeare's Schauspiele*, 13 vols., Zürick, 1775–82.

9. A reference to her historical plays.

10. *Pisma imperatritsy Ekateriny II k Grimmu*, izd. Ya. Grota, St. Petersburg, 1878, p. 383.

11. *Dnevnik A. V. Khrapovitskago*, izd. N. Barsukova, Moskva, 1901, p. 6.

12. *Vot kakovo imet korzinu i bele*, volnoe, no slaboe perelozhenie iz Shakespira. (See *Sochineniya imperatritsy Ekateriny II*, red. A. Pypina, St. Petersburg, 1901, II, 354.) Catherine's title is a free rendering of Ford's exclamation: "This 't is to have linen and buck-baskets!" (III, 5).

13. For a detailed comparison of the two plays and a full consideration of Catherine's other "Shaksperean" plays, see the author's article, "Catherine the Great and Shakespeare" (*P.M.L.A.*, XLVII, 1932, No. 3, pp. 790–806).

14. *Rastochitel*, volnoe perelozhenie iz Shakespira. Cf. *Sochineniya*, III, 301–344.

15. Unlike her other plays connected with Shakspere, the *Spendthrift* was not printed or acted in Catherine's lifetime.

16. Cf. *Sochineniya*, II, 219–304.

17. V. Lebedev, "Shekspir v Anglii, Frantsii i Rossii" (*Filologicheskiya zapiski*, Moskva, 1878, III, 65).

18. *Pisma k Grimmu, op. cit.*, pp. 383–384.

19. Cf. *Dnevnik Khrapovitskago, op. cit.*, p. 9.

20. For a list and discussion of the borrowings, see the author's article, "Catherine the Great and Shakespeare," pp. 803–805.

21. Catherine's name did not appear on the title page of her plays, but it was generally known that she was the author.

22. Cf. "Pisma Aleksandra Andrevicha Petrova k Karamzinu" (*Russki arkhiv*, 1863, p. 885).

23. *Sochineniya Karamzina, op. cit.*, pp. 10–11.

24. *Iulii Tsesar*, perevod s Angliskago, prozoiu, St. Petersburg, 1787.

25. *Ibid.*, predislovie.

26. *Ibid.*

27. G. Pogodin, "Detstvo, vospitanie i pervye literaturnye opyty Karamzina" (*Utro, literaturny i politicheski sbornik*, Moskva, 1866, p. 49).

28. *Pisma russkago puteshestvennika, op. cit.*, pp. 472–473.

29. A. Gruzintsov, "Razsuzhdenie o dramaticheskikh tvoreniyakh" (*Novosti russkoi literatury*, Moskva, 1802, V, 161).

30. Apparently in July, 1790.

31. Karamzin gives her name in a note as Billington.

32. *Pisma russkago puteshestvennika*, pp. 732–733.

33. *Ibid.*, p. 733.

34. *Ibid.*, p. 748.

35. *Ibid.*, p. 749.

36. *Ibid.*

37. *Ibid.*, p. 748.

38. *Ibid.*

39. For examples see the following: "Strannost liubvi," "Poslanie k Dmitrievu," and "K Shekspirovu podrazhateliu" (*Sochineniya*, Izdanie Otdeleniya russkago yazyka i slovesnosti Akademii Nauk, Petrograd, 1917, I, 89, 98, 234); "Bednaya Liza," "Prekrasnaya tsarevna i shchastlivoi karla," "Tsvetok na grobe moego Agatona" and "Razgovor o shchastii" (Sochineniya, izd. Smirdina, *op. cit.*, III, 35, 359, 361, 476).

40. *Pisma russkago puteshestvennika*, p. 480.

41. *Sochineniya*, p. 11, note.

42. *Pisma russkago puteshestvennika*, p. 3.

43. *Ibid.*, p. 11.

44. Cf. *Liubitel slovesnosti*, St. Petersburg, 1806, No. 2 (Anthony's funeral oration from *Julius Caesar*); *Minerva*, Moskva, 1806, I and II (fragments from *Richard III*).

45. *Nachertanie glavnoe izyashchnykh nauk*, per. P. Sakhatski, Moskva, 1803. Cf. also, *Dramaticheski vestnik*, St. Petersburg, 1808, I, 21.

46. Cf. *Severny nabliudatel*, St. Petersburg, 1817, No. 6. In the same periodical (1817, No. 22) appeared a fragment of *Julius Caesar*.

47. Not printed, but an analysis of the MS. may be found in A. Lirondelle, *Shakespeare en Russie, 1748–1840*, Paris, 1912, pp. 111–116. This excellent study has been of great assistance in preparing this chapter.

48. Cf. *Arkhiv bratev Turgenevykh*, izd. V. Istrina, St. Petersburg, 1911, pp. 87–88.

49. Cf. A. N. Veselovski, *V. A. Zhukovski,* St. Petersburg, 1918, pp. 54–55.

50. *Literaturnaya gazeta,* 1830, No. 4.

51. *Shekspirovy dukhi.*

52. Unpublished. See Lirondelle for an analysis of the MS., pp. 134–135.

53. "Literaturnyya i teatralnyya vospominaniya" (*Sobranie sochineni S. T. Aksakova,* Moskva, 1895–96, III, 106).

54. Cf. *Sochineniya,* izd. Shlyapkina, St. Petersburg, 1889, I, 187.

55. *Ibid.,* p. xli.

56. *Gruzinskaya noch.*

57. *Pisma, op. cit.,* I, 74, No. 77.

58. *Pushkin,* red. S. Vengerova, St. Petersburg, 1911, II, 382.

59. *Graf Nulin,* 1825.

60. *Pisma,* I, 148, No. 162.

61. *Ibid.,* II, 63, No. 289.

62. *Ibid.,* II, 61, No. 289.

63. *Ibid.,* I, 148, No. 160.

64. For detailed studies of the relations, see N. H. Dole, "Shakespeare and the Russian Drama" (*Poet Lore,* 1889, I, No. 11; 1890, II, No. 3); M. Pokrovski, "Puschkin und Shakespeare" (*Jahrbuch der deutschen Shakespeare Gesellschaft,* Berlin 1907, XLIII, 169–209); Pokrovski, "Shekspirizm Pushkina" (*Pushkin,* Vengerova, IV, 1 ff.); C. N. Herford, *A Russian Shakespearean,* Oxford, 1925.

65. *Kamenny gost* and *Skupoi rytsar.* Both were published in 1836.

66. *Richard III* (I, 2). Cf. Pokrovski, "Shekspirizm Pushkina," p. 16.

67. On the title page Pushkin described the play as "Scenes from Shenstone's tragi-comedy, *The Covetous Knight.*" For a discussion of this misrepresentation, see the author's note, "Pushkin and Shenstone" (*Modern Language Notes,* November, 1930, pp. 454–457).

68. *Polnoe sobranie sochineni V. G. Belinskago,* red. S. Vengerova i V. Spiridonova, St. Petersburg, 1900–26, XII, 203.

69. *Pushkin,* Vengerova, V, 246.

70. Cf. *Merchant of Venice* (I, 3).

71. Cf. *The Avaricious Knight* (scene 1).

72. Pushkin had a particular fondness for *Romeo and Juliet,* if we may judge from his critical remarks on the play. Cf. *Pushkin,* Vengerova, IV, 534.

73. For a study and translation of the play, see the author's "A. S. Pushkin, *The Avaricious Knight*" (*Harvard Studies and Notes in Philology and Literature,* Cambridge, 1933, XV, 329–344).

74. Cf. N. O. Lerner, "O *Skupom Rytsare*" (*Rasskazy o Pushkine*, Leningrad, 1920, pp. 218 ff.).

75. *Moskovski telegraf* and *Moskovski vestnik* For an analysis of Shaksperean articles appearing in the former, see N. K. Kozmin, *Ocherki iz istorii russkago romantizma*, St. Petersburg, 1903, pp. 237 ff.

76. Cf. Kozmin, *op. cit.*, p. 517.

77. For a bibliography, see Lirondelle, pp. 229–234.

78. *Syn otechestva*, 1833, XXXVII–XXXIX.

79. "Literaturnyya mechtaniya" (*Polnoe sobranie sochineni*, I, 321).

80. He also acted in I. Panaev's rendering of *Othello* in 1836.

81. "Mochalov v roli Gamleta" (*Polnoe sobranie sochineni*, III, 259).

82. For an appreciation of Karatygin's performance in this rôle, see Belinski, "G. Karatygin v roli Gamleta" (*Polnoe sobranie sochineni*, III, 300–302).

83. A. Slavin, *Zhizn. W. Shekspira*, Moskva, 1844.

84. Cf. *Sovremennik*, 1838, XIII, 123–144.

85. V. Botkin, "Iuliya i Ofelya" (*Otechestvennyya zapiski*, 1841, XIV).

86. Cf. A. Pypin, *Belinski, ego zhizn i perepiska*, St. Petersburg, 1876, II, 109–110.

CHAPTER IX

1. Cf. F. F. Vigel, *Zapiski*, red. S. Shtraikha, Moskva, 1928, II, 314–316.

2. See Pushkin, *Evgeni Onegin*, I, iv, xvi, xxiii.

3. *Ibid.*, I, xxxviii.

4. See A. Veselovski, *Zapadnoe vliyanie v novoi russkoi literature*, p. 156.

5. Cf. *Evgeni Onegin*, I, lvii.

6. See pp. 97–98.

7. See p. 94–95.

8. "Otryvki iz romana v pismakh," 1830 (*Pushkin*, Vengerova, IV, 139).

9. *Evgeni Onegin*, I, vii.

10. Cf. Veselovski, *op. cit.*, p. 154.

11. Cf. B. L. Modzalevski, "Biblioteka Pushkina, bibliograficheskoe opisanie" (*Pushkin i ego sovremenniki*, St. Petersburg, 1909, IX–X).

12. *Kratkoe nachertanie teorii izyashchnoi slovesnosti*, Moskva, 1822.

13. *Istoriya poezii*, Moskva, 1835.

14. *Moskovski telegraf, Moskovski vestnik, Vestnik Evropy, Otechestvenniyya zapiski, Syn otechestva, Severny arkhiv.*

15. For a study and analysis of these relations, see S. Vesin, *Ocherki russkoi zhurnalistiki dvadtsatykh i tridtsatykh godov*, St. Petersburg, 1881.

16. *Moskovski telegraf*, 1828, No. 6, pp. 251–254.

17. *Ibid.*, 1827, XIV, 195.

18. Cf. A. M. Skabichevski, *Ocherki istorii russkoi tsenzury*, St. Petersburg, 1892, pp. 162–166.

19. Published under the title of "Zamok Smalgolm."

20. Cf. B. L. Modzalevski, "Biblioteka Pushkina," Nos. 1362, 1363, 1364, 1367.

21. *Pushkin*, Vengerova, V, 531, No. 95.

22. Cf. *Pushkin*, Vengerova, II, 356.

23. Cf. *The Lady of the Lake* (Canto I, ix).

24. *Shumit kustarnik*. For an excellent study of Pushkin's indebtedness to *The Lady of the Lake* in these two instances, see D. Yakubovich, "Iz zametok o Pushkine i Valter-Skotte" (*Pushkin i ego sovremenniki*, Leningrad, 1930, XXXVIII–XXXIX, 122–134). *The Lady of the Lake* was translated into Russian in 1828.

25. *Shotlandskaya pesnya* (1829). See Iu. Oksman, "Siuzhety Pushkina" (*Pushkinski sbornik pamyati professora S. A. Vengerova*, Moskva, 1923, pp. 27–34); P. Struve, "Walter Scott and Russia" (*The Slavonic Review*, London, 1933, XI, No. 32, pp. 399–401). *The Twa Corbies* was translated twice again during this period (*Galatei*, 1830, XII, No. 10, p. 193; *Moskovski telegraf*, 1830, No. 8, p. 441).

26. "On byl ubit" (*Sochineniya*, X, 279–280).

27. *Beverlei*, Shotlandskaya ballada (Iz Valter-Skotta).

28. *K Valter Skottu.*

29. "Vospominaniya A. P. Shan-Gireya" (*Russkoe obozrenie*, 1890, No. 8, p. 728).

30. This, along with selected poems of Scott, was translated in 1827 (*Bitva pri Vaterloo, sochinenie Valter-Skotta; s prisovokupleniem izbrannykh ballad sego pisatelya*, Moskva).

31. Cf. N. P. Dashkevich, "Motivy mirovoi poezii v tvorchestve Lermontova" (*Sbornik otdeleniya russkago yazyka i slovesnosti Imperatorskoi Akademii Nauk*, Petrograd, 1914, XCII, 483–484 and note). It is quite possible that Lermontov's *Kazachya kolybelnaya pesnya* (1840) was influenced by Scott's *Lullaby of an Infant Chief;* and his *Izmail Bei* (1843) by Scott's *The Lady of the Lake*. Cf. E. Duchesne, *Michel Iouriévitch Lermontov*, Paris, 1910, pp. 292–294.

32. Cf. *Rossiski muzeum*, Moskva, 1815, I, 378. This is probably the earliest mention of Scott's novels in Russia and seems to have been overlooked by native investigators of the subject.

33. Cf. D. Yakubovich, "Predislovie k *Povestyam Belkina* i povestvovatelnye priemy Valter Skotta" (*Pushkin v mirovoi literature*, Leningrad,

1926, p. 378, n. 23). For a list of translations see N. K. Kozmin, *Ocherki iz istorii russkago romantizma*, St. Petersburg, 1903, p. 73, n. 2.

34. Cf. Kozmin, *op. cit.*, p. 26.

35. A descriptive bibliography and reprints of such articles may be found in S. Vesin, *Ocherki russkoi zhurnalistiki dvadtsatykh i tridtsatykh godov*, St. Petersburg, 1881, pp. 61–63, 354–358; V. V. Sipovski, *Iz istorii russkago romana i povesti*, St. Petersburg, 1903, prilozhenie.

36. *Pisma N. M. Karamzina k I. I. Dmitrievu*, St. Petersburg, 1866, p. 408.

37. Cf. "Vospominaniya T. P. Passek" (*Russki arkhiv*, 1873, p. 299).

38. A play on the Russian word "skot," meaning "animal," of which the readers never seemed to tire in referring to the novelist.

39. P. A. Karatygin, *Zapiski*, 1805–78, St. Petersburg, 1880, p. 168.

40. *Moskovski telegraf*, 1827, XIV, 195.

41. Cf. *Severnaya pchela*, 1838, No. 99; *Sovremennik*, 1839, XV, 92–115; *Biblioteka dlya chteniya*, 1834, III, 31.

42. A letter to S. P. Rumyantsev (*Russki arkhiv*, 1869, p. 592).

43. Cf. D. Yakubovich, "Reministsentsii iz Valter Skotta v *Povestyakh Belkina*" (*Pushkin i ego sovremenniki*, Leningrad, 1928, XXXVII, 102–103).

44. Cf. *Pushkin*, Vengerova, II, 567.

45. Cf. A. Veselovski, *Zapadnoe vliyanie v novoi russkoi literature*, p. 156, n. 5.

46. Southey's *The Old Woman of Berkeley*.

47. "Pismo iz Edinburgh ot 10 avg., 1828" (*Russki arkhiv*, 1895, III, 208). Three years later Turgenev wrote to Zhukovski on the state of Scott's health. Cf. *Russki arkhiv*, 1881, XXXI, 199.

48. Cf. *Perepiska A. I. Turgeneva s P. A. Vyazemskim*, red. N. K. Kulmana, Petrograd, 1921, I, 272–274.

49. Cf. *ibid.*, I, 432.

50. Cf. I. I. Zamotin, *Romanticheski idealizm*, St. Petersburg, 1907, pp. 89–90. Shakhovskoi also dramatized *The Pirate* and *The Fortunes of Nigel*.

51. *Sochineniya*, St. Petersburg, 1884, IX, 92.

52. *Polnoe sobranie sochineni*, II, 54.

53. For a list of the authors and titles see Kozmin, *op. cit.*, pp. 76–77.

54. Such as *Roman i Olga*, *Duma Svyatoslava*, and *Nuezdy*.

55. Cf. *Polnoe sobranie sochineni*, V, 156.

56. It is an interesting fact that Marlinski claimed that he was influenced by Washington Irving, whose works were well known in Russia at

this time, more than by any other writer. Cf. I. I. Zamotin, *Romantizm dvadtsatykh godov XIX stoletiya v russkoi literature*, St. Petersburg, 1911–13, II, 215, 218–219.

57. Cf. "Biografiya M. N. Zagoskin" (*Polnoe sobranie sochineni S. T. Aksakova*, Moskva, 1895–96, III, 273).

58. Translated into Russian in 1824.

59. For such a comparison see I. I. Zamotin, *op. cit.*, II, 347–350.

60. *Sobranie sochineni, op. cit.*, III, 264.

61. Cf. Zamotin, *op. cit.*, II, 303–313.

62. Weiner's *Zeitschrift*, 1831, No. 49. (Translated in *Teleskop*, 1831, III, 126.)

63. *The Foreign Quarterly Review*, 1833, XI, 390.

64. Cf. *Russki arkhiv*, 1902, I, 78. This translation, it appears, was eventually printed, although considerably mangled by the English editor. See *The Young Muscovite; or the Poles in Russia*, edited by Captain Frederic Chamier, London, 1834.

65. *Sobranie sochineni, op. cit.*, III, 266.

66. *Roslavlev, ili russkie v 1812 godu* (1831); *Askoldova mogila* (1833).

67. For bibliographical details and a discussion of the novels of these writers, see Kozmin, *op. cit.*, pp. 77 ff.

68. See the bibliography to this chapter.

69. Cf. V. V. Sipovski, "Pushkin i romantizm" (*Pushkin i ego sovremenniki*, Petrograd, 1916, XXIII–XXIV, 277). Another critic calls it the "Walter Scott Period." Cf. D. Yakubovich, "Reministsentsii iz Valter Skotta v *Povestyakh Belkina*" (*Pushkin i ego sovremenniki*, Leningrad, 1928, XXXVII, 118).

70. Cf. *Graf Nulin* (*Pushkin*, Vengerova, II, 395).

71. Cf. *Evgeni Onegin*, IV, 43.

72. *Otryvki iz romana v pismakh* (*Pushkin*, Vengerova, IV, 135).

73. Cf. *Nabrosok avtobiograficheskago kharaktera* (*Pushkin*, Vengerova, IV, 141).

74. Cf. B. L. Modzalevski, "Biblioteka Pushkina," *op. cit.*, pp. 285, 332–333.

75. *Atenei*, 1924, I–II, 5–6, 13–14. Quoted by P. Struve, "Walter Scott and Russia" (*The Slavonic Review*, London, 1933, XI, No. 32, pp. 401–402).

76. *Literaturnaya gazeta*, 1830, No. 5 (*Pushkin*, Vengerova, IV, 541.).

77. *Literaturnaya gazeta*, 1830, No. 8 (*Pushkin*, Vengerova, IV, 545).

78. *Povesti Belkina* (1831).

79. D. Yakubovich has fully studied this phase of Pushkin's indebtedness to Scott. Cf. "Predislovie k *Povestyam Belkina* i povestvovatelnye priemy Valter Skotta" (*Pushkin v mirovoi literature*, Leningrad, 1926, pp. 160–187).

80. For example, in his *Istoriya sela Goriukhina*, the foreword of which was influenced by the introduction to *The Chronicles of the Canongate*. Cf. D. Yakubovich, "Predislovie k *Povestyam Belkina* i povestvovatelnye priemy Valter Skotta," pp. 179–183.

81. See Gogol's *Vechera na Khutore bliz Dikanki*.

82. *Baryshnya-krestyanka*.

83. For parallel passage comparisons see D. Yakubovich, "Reministsentsii iz Valter Skotta v *Povestyakh Belkina*," pp. 106–111.

84. *Grobovshchik*.

85. *Pushkin*, Vengerova, IV, 146.

86. D. Yakubovich, "Reministsentsii iz Valter Skotta v *Povestyakh Belkina*," p. 118.

87. *Kapitanskaya dochka*.

88. Cf. M. Hofman, "Kapitanskaya dochka" (*Pushkin*, Vengerova, IV, 355).

89. For a list of the parallels, see Hofman, *op. cit.*, p. 356, n. 2.

90. Cf. *ibid.*, p. 369, n. 1.

91. See p. 198–199.

92. Cf. V. Vinogradov, *Evoliutsiya russkago naturalizma*, Leningrad, 1929, p. 90.

93. For a study of these several influences, see the author's article, "Gogol and English Literature" (*Modern Language Review*, 1931, XXVI, No. 4, pp. 445–450).

94. *Gogol v Rime*, St. Petersburg, 1909 (quoted by J. Lavrin, *Gogol*, London, 1925, p. 161).

95. G. Chudakov, "Otnoshenie tvorchestva Gogolya k zapadnoevropeiskim literaturam" (*Universitetskiya izvestiya*, Kiev, 1908, XLVIII, No. 3, p. 90).

96. *Pisma N. V. Gogolya*, red. V. Shenroka, St. Petersburg, 1901, I, 12.

97. Cf. *Sochineniya N. V. Gogolya*, izd. N. Tikhonravovym, Moskva, 1889, V, 466–485, 637–649.

98. *Pushkin*, Vengerova, IV, 355.

99. Cf. E. Duchesne, *op. cit.*, p. 357.

100. *Geroi nashego vremeni* (1840).

101. E. Duchesne, *op. cit.*, p. 294.

102. *Sobranie sochineni Iv. Iv. Panaeva*, Moskva, 1912, VI, 156.

103. Cf. "Istoricheski roman" (*Biblioteka dlya chteniya*, 1834, I, 1–44). See also *Sobranie sochineni Senkovskago*, St. Petersburg, 1859, VIII, 29–59.

104. "Allan Cunningham, o zhizni Valter Skotta" (*Polnoe sobranie sochineni*, II, 265). For an investigation of this controversy between Senkovski and Belinski, see P. Struve, "Walter Scott and Russia," pp. 405–410.

105. *Pisma*, red. E. A. Lyatskago, St. Petersburg, 1914, II, 137.

106. *Ibid.*, II, 126.

107. *Ibid.*, II, 108.

108. *Polnoe sobranie sochineni*, X, 11.

109. "Pismo k V. P. Botkinu" (*Pisma*, III, 325).

110. *Moskvityanin*, 1841, No. 1, pp. 236–237 (quoted by P. Struve, "Walter Scott and Russia," p. 405).

CHAPTER X

1. *Don Juan*, Canto VI, xcii: "In Catherine's reign, whom glory still adores, As greatest of all sovereigns and w - - s."

2. *Ibid.*, Canto VI, xciii.

3. See bibliography to this chapter.

4. "Morskoi Razboinik, v trekh pesnyakh Lorda Birona" (*Rossiski muzeum*, izd. V. Izmailova, Moskva, 1815, I, 37–42). Russian investigators seem to have overlooked this early date. Cf. V. I. Maslov, *Nachalny period baironizma v Rossii*, Kiev, 1915, p. 4; A. Veselovski," Etiudy o baironizme" (*Etiudy i kharakteristiki*, Moskva, 1907, p. 400, n. 3).

5. Cf. *Vestnik Evropy*, 1818, XCIX, 41–42.

6. Cf. *Ostafevski arkhiv*, St. Petersburg, 1899, I, 281–282.

7. From a letter dated October 11, 1819; quoted by Maslov, *op. cit.*; pp. 4–5.

8. For a review and bibliography of this periodical literature, see Maslov, *op. cit.*, pp. 5–14, 51–63.

9. Cf. Maslov, *op. cit.*, pp. 64–89.

10. *Russkaya starina*, 1881, XXXII, 629.

11. Cf. "Zapiski grafa M. D. Buturlina" (*Russki arkhiv*, 1897, II, 74).

12. Cf. *Evgeni Onegin*, VII, xvii.

13. *Russkaya starina*, 1875, XIII, 369.

14. *Ostafevski arkhiv*, III, 48–49.

15. For a bibliography of these tributes, see Maslov, *op. cit.*, Prilozhenie III.

16. *Literaturnye listy*, 1824, II, 426–429.

17. Cf. Maslov, *op. cit.*, pp. 19–21.

18. A. Veselovski, "Etiudy o baironizme," *op. cit.*, p. 400.

19. Cf. V. A. Zhukovski, *Dnevnik*, St. Petersburg, 1901, pp. 119, 137.

20. Letter to N. I. Gnedich, September, 27, 1822 (*Pisma*, I, 38, No. 43).

21. *Pesnya*, 1820.

22. *Pisma*, I, 25, No. 31.

23. Cf. A. N. Veselovski, *V. A. Zhukovski*, St. Petersburg, 1904, p. 326.

24. *Ibid.*, p. 327.

25. For special studies concerning the influence of Byron on Zhukovski, see the following: M. Zdziechowski, *Byron i jego wiek*, Krakowie, 1897, II, 111–127; Nalimov, "Shilonski uznik Bairona v perevode Zhukovskago" (*Literaturny vestnik*, St. Petersburg, 1902, IV, 27–34); A. N. Veselovski, *op. cit.*, pp. 318–327.

26. For examples of such opposition, see the letter of D. N. Runich, reprinted in *Russkaya starina*, 1896, LXXXIII, 135–138; also *Vestnik Evropy*, 1830, No. 1, pp. 26–27, 32–33.

27. Canto IV, clxxviii–clxxix.

28. Cf. A. Veselovski, "Etiudy o baironizme," *op. cit.*, p. 401, n. 2.

29. See M. Zdziechowski, *op. cit.*, II, 123–143; N. M. Danilov, "I. I. Kozlov" (*Izvestiya otdeleniya russkago yazyka i slovesnosti Imperatorskoi Akademii Nauk*, Petrograd, 1914, XIX, 153–175).

30. *Dnevnik Kozlova*, izd. K. Grota, St. Petersburg, 1906, p. 9.

31. Cf. *ibid.*, pp. 6–7.

32. *Sochineniya V. A. Zhukovskago*, red. A. S. Arkhangelskago, St. Petersburg, 1902, X, 72.

33. *Moskovski telegraf*, 1828, XIX, 550.

34. Cf. Veselovski, "Etiudy o baironizme, *op. cit.*, p. 400; *Dnevnik Kozlova*, *op. cit.*, pp. 6–7.

35. *Dnevnik Kozlova*, *op. cit.*, p. 7.

36. For a complete bibliography of Kozlov's translations, see Maslov, *op. cit.*, Prilozhenie, II.

37. *Chernets*, 1825.

38. For a detailed comparison of *The Monk* and *The Giaour*, see V. Zhirmunski, *Bairon i Pushkin*, Leningrad, 1924, pp. 294–296.

39. *Natalya Borisovna Dolgorukaya*, 1828; *Bezumnaya*, 1830.

40. It is possible that the confession of the mad girl in *Bezumnaya* was influenced by Wordsworth's *The Thorn* and *Ruth*.

41. Cf. Zhirmunski, *op. cit.*, pp. 239–252.

42. *Cherep*, 1820.

43. Cf. *Russkaya starina*, 1875, XIII, 357, 375, 490; 1883, XXXIX, 257; 1884, XLI, 76–77.

44. *Smert Bairona*, 1824.

45. *Izhorski*, Misteriya, 1835.

46. *Polnoe sobranie sochineni*, red. Vengerova, II, 151.

47. *Sochineniya i perepiska K. F. Ryleeva*, St. Petersburg, 1872, p. 242.

48. Cf. V. I. Maslov, *Literaturnaya deyatelnost K. F. Ryleeva*, Kiev, 1912, pp. 271–292.

49. Marlinski is a pen name for A. A. Bestuzhev.

50. See pp. 199, 251.

51. Cf. Veselovski, "Etiudy o baironizme," *op. cit.*, p. 522.

52. Cf. I. I. Zamotin, *op. cit.*, II, 222.

53. *Krasnoe pokryvalo.*

54. For a detailed consideration of the borrowings, see Zamotin, *op. cit.*, II, 223–226.

55. It is worth noting that Marlinski's brothers were also much interested in Byron. N. A. Bestuzhev made the first translation of *Parisina* into Russian, directly from the original; and M. A. Bestuzhev wrote many poems in imitation of Byron. Cf. *Russkaya starina*, 1881, XXXII, 629; Maslov, *op. cit.*, p. 33.

56. For a bibliography of such works, see Zhirmunski, *op. cit.*, pp. 317–324.

57. *Venok na grob Pushkina*, 1837.

58. *Demon vdokhnoveniya.*

59. *Pisma*, I, 31, No. 37.

60. Cf. M. Tsyavlovski, "Pushkin i angliski yazyk" (*Pushkin i ego sovremenniki*, St. Petersburg, 1913, XVII, p. 73). Even in the Byron period he apparently made rapid progress. M. V. Iuzefovich, who met Pushkin in the Caucasus, tested the poet's knowledge by requesting him to read from Shakspere while a friend, who knew English perfectly, acted as judge. After the first few lines the friend laughed and demanded: "Say first in what language you are reading!" Laughing in turn, Pushkin explained that he had studied English mostly by himself and hence pronounced it literally, like Latin. Nevertheless, the friend found Pushkin's "translations from the English perfectly correct and his knowledge of the language irreproachable." Cf. "Vospominaniya M. V. Iuzefovich o Pushkine" (*Russki arkhiv*, 1880, III, 444–445). P. Chaadaev reports that Pushkin studied English in the St. Petersburg period (1817–20), and that it was then that he first became acquainted with Byron's poetry. See P. I. Bartenev, *Pushkin v iuzhnoi Rossii*, Moskva, 1914, p. 70.

61. Cf. N. K. Kozmin, "Pushkin o Bairone" (*Pushkin v mirovoi literature*, Moskva, 1926, p. 102).

62. *Pisma*, I, 48, No. 54.

63. *Grechanke*, 1822.

64. For a study of the possible relationship between Calypso Poly-chrone and Byron, see the author's article, "Byron and a Greek Maid" (*Modern Language Review*, 1932, XXVII, No. 3, pp. 318–323).

65. *Pogaslo dnevnoe svetilo*, 1820.

66. Cf. *Childe Harold*, Canto I, xiii.

67. *Kavkazski plennik* (1820–21), *Bratya razboiniki* (1821), *Bakhchi-saraiski fontan* (1822), *Tsygany* (1824). The fragment *Vadim* also belongs to this group. For an exhaustive study of the relations between Pushkin's Southern poems and Byron's Eastern poems, see Zhirmunski, *op. cit.*

68. For parallel passage comparisons, see Zhirmunski, *op. cit.*, pp. 155–157.

69. Pushkin objected to the charge that *Poltava* was an imitation of *Mazeppa*. Cf. *Pisma*, II, 65–66, No. 296.

70. Cf. Zhirmunski, *op. cit.*, pp. 213 ff.

71. Cf. *Docheri Karageoriya* (1820), *Voina* (1821), *Vozstan, O Gretsiya!* (1823).

72. Belonging to this early period is Pushkin's famous ballad, *The Black Shawl* (*Chernaya shal*, 1820), which contains distinct echoes of Byron. Cf. "Baironizm y Pushkina" (*Sochineniya V. D. Spasovicha*, St. Peters-burg, 1889, II, pp. 315 ff.).

73. *Pisma*, I, 85, No. 88.

74. See Modzalevski's note to letter, No. 88 (*Pisma*, I, 333).

75. *K moriu*, 1824.

76. *Pisma*, I, 127, No. 138.

77. *Ibid.*, I, 58, No. 65.

78. *Ibid.*, I, 160, No. 177.

79. *Ibid.*, I, 123, No. 133.

80. *Evgeni Onegin*, IV, xliv.

81. *Ibid.*, I, xxxviii.

82. *Ibid.*, I, xlv–xlvi.

83. *Perepiska Pushkina*, red. V. I. Saitova, St. Petersburg, 1906, I, 216.

84. *Pisma*, I, 148, No. 162.

85. *Pushkin*, Vengerova, IV, 500.

86. "Lord Bairon" (*ibid.*, V, 298).

87. A reference to Byron's memoirs which were burned.

88. *Pisma*, I, 160, No. 177.

89. See pp. 226–228, 258–260.

90. *Pisma*, I, 129, No. 140.

91. *Ibid.*, I, 160, No. 177.

92. *Neizdanny Pushkin*, sobranie A. Onegina, Petersburg, 1922, p. 180.

93. "There is a pleasure in poetic pain" and "Scorn not the sonnet."

94. For a study of the relations between Pushkin and Wordsworth, see N. V. Yakovlev, "Iz razyskani o literaturnykh istochnikakh v tvorchestve Pushkina" (*Pushkin v mirovoi literature*, Leningrad, 1926, p. 222).

95. "I went about my own affairs, rereading Coleridge," "Zametka o kolere" (*Pushkin*, Vengerova, V, 434).

96. *Egipetskiya nochi*, 1835. Cf. Yakovlev, *op. cit.*, pp. 140–145.

97. *Pisma*, I, 32, No. 37.

98. *Literaturnaya gazeta*, 1830, p. 24. Quoted by Yakovlev, *op. cit.*, p. 150.

99. Pushkin also translated Southey's *Hymn to the Penates* and a fragment from *Madoc*. Cf. Yakovlev, *op. cit.*, pp. 145–149.

100. M. de Vogüé, *Le Roman russe*, Paris, 1886, p. 54.

101. Cf. P. Viskovatov, "Biografiya Lermontova" (*Sochineniya Lermontova*, Moskva, 1891, VI, 46).

102. *K . . .* , 1830.

103. Viskovatov, *op. cit.*, I, 117.

104. See p. 262.

105. Cf. Clul Ouudunu, 1830.

106. *Net, Ya ne Bairon*, 1831. Translated by Martha G. D. Bianchi, *Russian Lyrics*, New York, 1910, p. 48.

107. For a study of the poem's sources, which may have included *Paradise Lost* and Moore's *Loves of the Angels*, see N. P. Dashkevich, "Motivy mirovoi poezii v tvorchestve Lermontova," *op. cit.*, pp. 435–514.

108. *Noch I*, 1830.

109. *Noch II*, 1830.

110. *Podrazhanie Baironu*, 1830.

111. Another of Byron's lyrics on the same theme, *Well! Thou Art Happy*, inspired the excellent poem of Lermontov, *To a Child* (*Rebenku*, 1840). Byron's sentiments on seeing the child of Mary Chaworth are closely paralleled by Lermontov, who writes of the child of Varvara Lopukhin, whom he still loves.

112. *U nog drugikh ne zabyval*, 1831; *Evreiskaya melodiya*, 1836.

113. Canto IV, cxl–cxli.

114. *Menschen und Leidenschaften*, 1830; *Stranny chelovek*, 1831.

115. *Kavkazski plennik*, 1828.

116. *Korsar*, 1828.

117. *Kally*, 1831–32.

118. *Ispoved*, 1829–30; *Boyarin Orsha*, 1835–36; *Mtsiri*, 1839–40.

119. *Geroi nashego vremeni* (written in 1839, published in 1840).

120. *Lara*, canto I, xvii.

INDICES

INDEX OF NON–RUSSIAN NAMES AND TITLES

[English translations of Russian titles are also listed here. The author's name follows each title.]

INDEX OF RUSSIAN NAMES AND TITLES